Go Design Patterns

Learn idiomatic, efficient, clean, and extensible Go design and concurrency patterns by using TDD

Mario Castro Contreras

BIRMINGHAM - MUMBAI

Go Design Patterns

First published: February 2017

Production reference: 1170217

Published by Packt Publishing Ltd.
Livery Place
35 Livery Street
Birmingham
B3 2PB, UK.
ISBN 978-1-78646-620-4

www.packtpub.com

Credits

Author

Mario Castro Contreras

Reviewer

Shiju Varghese

Commissioning Editor

Kunal Parikh

Acquisition Editor

Chaitanya Nair

Content Development Editor

Zeeyan Pinheiro

Technical Editor

Pavan Ramchandani

Copy Editor

Safis Editing

Project Coordinator

Izzat Contractor

Proofreader

Safis Editing

Indexer

Mariammal Chettiyar

Graphics

Abhinash Sahu

Production Coordinator

Deepika Naik

About the Author

Mario Castro Contreras is a software engineer who has specialized in distributed systems and big data solutions. He works as a site reliability engineer, and now he is focused on containerized solutions and apps using most of Google Cloud suite; especially, Kubernetes. He has a wide experience in systems and solutions integration, and he has written many scalable and reliable 12 factor apps using Go and Docker. He has designed Big Data architectures for financial services and media, and he has written data processing pipelines using event-driven architectures written purely in Go. He is also very active in the open source community, and you can find him on his GitHub account with the username *sayden*. In the past, he has also written mobile applications and backends in Java.

Mario is passionate about programming languages, and he found the best balance between fun and productivity in Go; however, recently, he enjoys writing in Rust and embedded systems in C. He is also passionate about road cycling and winter sports.

I'd like to express my deep gratitude to my parents for supporting me in my journey through computers since I was 8. To Urszula, Tyrion and Tesla for their daily support and for being with me in the long nights writing this book.

I'd like to thank Chaitanya, for her guidance at the beginning of the book, Zeeyan, for his patience and help on every chapter, and Pavan, for the help and explanations. But also to all the reviewers, especially to Shiju, and the entire team at Packt that made this book possible.

About the Reviewer

Shiju Varghese is a solutions architect focused on building highly scalable cloud native applications with a special interest in APIs, microservices, containerized architectures, and distributed systems. He currently specializes in Go, Google Cloud, and container technologies. He is an early adopter of the Go programming language and provides consultation and training for building backend systems and microservices with Go ecosystem. He has been a mentor to various start-ups and enterprises for the technology transformation to Go. He has been a speaker at numerous technology conferences, including GopherCon India.

Shiju has authored two books on Go, titled *Web Development with Go* and Go *Recipes*, both published by Apress.

www.PacktPub.com

For support files and downloads related to your book, please visit www.PacktPub.com.

Did you know that Packt offers eBook versions of every book published, with PDF and ePub files available? You can upgrade to the eBook version at www.PacktPub.com and as a print book customer, you are entitled to a discount on the eBook copy. Get in touch with us at service@packtpub.com for more details.

At www.PacktPub.com, you can also read a collection of free technical articles, sign up for a range of free newsletters and receive exclusive discounts and offers on Packt books and eBooks.

https://www.packtpub.com/mapt

Get the most in-demand software skills with Mapt. Mapt gives you full access to all Packt books and video courses, as well as industry-leading tools to help you plan your personal development and advance your career.

Why subscribe?

- Fully searchable across every book published by Packt
- Copy and paste, print, and bookmark content
- On demand and accessible via a web browser

Customer Feedback

Thanks for purchasing this Packt book. At Packt, quality is at the heart of our editorial process. To help us improve, please leave us an honest review on this book's Amazon page at `https://www.amazon.com/dp/1786466201`.

If you'd like to join our team of regular reviewers, you can email us at `customerreviews@packtpub.com`. We award our regular reviewers with free eBooks and videos in exchange for their valuable feedback. Help us be relentless in improving our products!

Table of Contents

Preface

Welcome to the book *Go Design Patterns*! With this book, you'll learn basic and advanced techniques and patterns with the Go language. Don't worry if you have never written Go code before; this book will gradually introduce you to the various concepts in Go programming. At the same time, experts will find many tips and tricks on the language, so I encourage you to not miss any chapter. If you already know the classic design patterns, you'll find this book very handy, not only as a reference book but also as a way to learn idiomatic Go approaches to solve common problems that you may already know.

The book is divided in three sections:

- Introduction to the Go language: This is the first part of the book, where you'll learn the basic syntax, the tools that comes with the binary distributions, basic testing, JSON parsing, and more. We leave concurrency for a later chapter to focus on the way that the syntax and the compiler work in a typical Go app.
- Classic design patterns in idiomatic Go: The second section presents the classic design patterns but as we will see, they are quite different, partly because of the lack of inheritance in Go, but also because we have different and more optimal ways to solve the same problems. A newcomer to the language will find the examples in this section very useful as a way to understand the roots of Go and the idiomatic ways in which you can solve problems using Go in the same manner as you would solve in languages such as Java or C++. Most examples are presented by using TDD and some of them even show examples within Go standard library that uses these patterns.
- Concurrency patterns: The focus in this section is learning about concurrent structures and parallel execution. You will learn most of the primitives in Go to write concurrent apps, and we will develop some of the classical design patterns with concurrent structures to maximize parallelism. Also, we will learn some of the typical structures to develop concurrent apps in Go. You learn how a classical pattern can become more complex if we need it to work in a concurrent way but the idea is to understand Go concurrent primitives so that the reader finishes the book knowing how to write their own concurrent design patterns by using the knowledge taken from the book.

The book will slowly raise the difficulty of some tasks. We have explained tips and tricks in every chapter.

What this book covers

Chapter 1, *Ready… Steady…Go!,* attempts to help newcomers to the Go programming language who have some background in any other programming language. It will begin by showing how to install the Go environment in a Linux machine, moving to syntax, type and flow control.

Chapter 2, *Creational Patterns - Singleton, Builder, Factory, Prototype, and Abstract Factory Design Patterns*, introduces the problems that can arise when an object creation or management is particularly complex or expensive using the Singleton, Builder, Factory, and Abstract Factory design patterns.

Chapter 3, *Structural Patterns - Composite, Adapter, and Bridge Design Patterns*, deals with the first set of Structural patterns about object composition to get some new functionality. Such as creating an intermediate object and using of various objects as if there is only one.

Chapter 4, *Structural Patterns - Proxy, Facade, Decorator, and Flyweight Design Patterns,* is less oriented to multi-object composition but focuses more on obtaining new functionality in existing objects. The Decorator pattern is commonly used to follow the open-closed principle. Facade is extensively used in API's where you want a single source for many sources of information and actions. Flyweight is not so common but it's a very useful pattern when the memory is becoming a problem caused by a large collection of similar objects. Finally, the Proxy pattern wraps on an object to provide the same functionality, but at the same time, adding something to the proxy's functionality.

Chapter 5, *Behavioral patterns - Strategy, Chain of Responsibility, Command, and Mediator Design Patterns*, deals with the first behavioral pattern to make objects react in an expected or bounded way. We'll start with the Strategy pattern, perhaps the most important design pattern in object-oriented programming, as many design patterns have something in common with it. Then we'll move to the Chain of Responsibility to build *chains* of objects that can decide which between them must deal with a particular case. Finally, Command pattern to encapsulate actions that don't necessarily need to be executed immediately or must be stored.

Chapter 6, *Behavioral Patterns - Template, Memento, and Interpreter Design Patterns*, continues with Behavioral patterns introducing the Interpreter pattern, a quite complex pattern to create small languages and Interpreters for them. It can be very useful when a problem can be solved by inventing a small language for it. The Memento pattern is in front of our eyes every day with the **Undo** button in apps. The Template pattern helps developers by defining an initial structure of an operation so that the final users of the code can finish it.

Chapter 7, *Behavioral Patterns - Visitor, State, Mediator, and Observer Design Patterns*, depicts the Observer pattern, an important pattern that is becoming tremendously popular in distributed systems and reactive programming. The Visitor pattern deals with complex hierarchies of objects where you need to apply a particular action depending on the object. Finally, the State pattern is commonly used in video games and finite state machines and allows an object to change its behavior depending on its own state.

Chapter 8, *Introduction to Go's Concurrency*, explains with more detail the CSP concurrency model used in Go by going through some examples using Goroutines and channels, as well as mutexes and syncs.

Chapter 9, *Concurrency Patterns - Barrier, Future, and Pipeline Design Patterns*, will introduce some of the CSP concurrency patterns that are idiomatic to the Go language by walking through some examples and explanations. These are small but really powerful patterns so we will provides a few examples of the use of each of them, as well as some schemas (if possible) that will make the understanding of each of them easier.

Chapter 10, *Concurrency Patterns - Workers Pool, and Publish or Subscriber Design Patterns*, talks about a couple of patterns with concurrent structures. We will explain every step in detail so you can follow the examples carefully. The idea is to learn patterns to design concurrent applications in idiomatic Go. We are using channels and Goroutines heavily, instead of locks or sharing variables.

What you need for this book

Most of the chapters in this book are written following a simple TDD approach, here the requirements are written first, followed by some unit tests and finally the code that satisfies those requirements. We will use only tools that comes with the standard library of Go as a way to better understand the language and its possibilities. This idea is key to follow the book and understanding the way that Go solves problems, especially in distributed systems and concurrent applications.

Who this book is for

This book is for both beginners and advanced-level developers in the Go programming language. No knowledge of design patterns is expected.

Conventions

In this book, you will find a number of text styles that distinguish between different kinds of information. Here are some examples of these styles and an explanation of their meaning.

Code words in text, database table names, folder names, filenames, file extensions, pathnames, dummy URLs, user input, and Twitter handles are shown as follows: "we need a `main` function to use it as libraries cannot be converted to executable files directly."

A block of code is set as follows:

```
package main

func main() {
  ten := 10
  if ten == 20 {
    println("This shouldn't be printed as 10 isn't equal to 20")
  } else {
    println("Ten is not equals to 20")
  }
}
```

When we wish to draw your attention to a particular part of a code block, the relevant lines or items are set in bold:

```
if "a" == "b" || 10 == 10 || true == false {
  println("10 is equal to 10")
} else if 11 == 11 && "go" == "go" {
    println("This won't because previous condition was satisfied")
  }
}
```

Any command-line input or output is written as follows:

```
$ go run main.go
```

New terms and **important words** are shown in bold. Words that you see on the screen, for example, in menus or dialog boxes, appear in the text like this: "In order to download new modules, we will go to **Files** | **Settings** | **Project Name** | **Project Interpreter**."

Warnings or important notes appear in a box like this.

 Tips and tricks appear like this.

Reader feedback

Feedback from our readers is always welcome. Let us know what you think about this book-what you liked or disliked. Reader feedback is important for us as it helps us develop titles that you will really get the most out of. To send us general feedback, simply e-mail feedback@packtpub.com, and mention the book's title in the subject of your message. If there is a topic that you have expertise in and you are interested in either writing or contributing to a book, see our author guide at www.packtpub.com/authors.

Customer support

Now that you are the proud owner of a Packt book, we have a number of things to help you to get the most from your purchase.

Downloading the example code

You can download the example code files for this book from your account at http://www.packtpub.com. If you purchased this book elsewhere, you can visit http://www.packtpub.com/support and register to have the files e-mailed directly to you.

You can download the code files by following these steps:

1. Log in or register to our website using your e-mail address and password.
2. Hover the mouse pointer on the **SUPPORT** tab at the top.
3. Click on **Code Downloads & Errata**.
4. Enter the name of the book in the **Search** box.
5. Select the book for which you're looking to download the code files.
6. Choose from the drop-down menu where you purchased this book from.
7. Click on **Code Download**.

Once the file is downloaded, please make sure that you unzip or extract the folder using the latest version of:

- WinRAR / 7-Zip for Windows
- Zipeg / iZip / UnRarX for Mac
- 7-Zip / PeaZip for Linux

The code bundle for the book is also hosted on GitHub at `https://github.com/PacktPublishing/Go-Design-Patterns`. We also have other code bundles from our rich catalog of books and videos available at `https://github.com/PacktPublishing/`. Check them out!

Errata

Although we have taken every care to ensure the accuracy of our content, mistakes do happen. If you find a mistake in one of our books-maybe a mistake in the text or the code- we would be grateful if you could report this to us. By doing so, you can save other readers from frustration and help us improve subsequent versions of this book. If you find any errata, please report them by visiting `http://www.packtpub.com/submit-errata`, selecting your book, clicking on the **Errata Submission Form** link, and entering the details of your errata. Once your errata are verified, your submission will be accepted and the errata will be uploaded to our website or added to any list of existing errata under the Errata section of that title.

To view the previously submitted errata, go to `https://www.packtpub.com/books/content/support`and enter the name of the book in the search field. The required information will appear under the **Errata** section.

Piracy

Piracy of copyrighted material on the Internet is an ongoing problem across all media. At Packt, we take the protection of our copyright and licenses very seriously. If you come across any illegal copies of our works in any form on the Internet, please provide us with the location address or website name immediately so that we can pursue a remedy.

Please contact us at `copyright@packtpub.com` with a link to the suspected pirated material.

We appreciate your help in protecting our authors and our ability to bring you valuable content.

Questions

If you have a problem with any aspect of this book, you can contact us
at questions@packtpub.com, and we will do our best to address the problem.

1
Ready... Steady... Go!

Design Patterns have been the foundation for hundreds of thousands of pieces of software. Since the *Gang Of Four* (Erich Gamma, Richard Helm, Ralph Johnson and John Vlissides) wrote the book *Design Patterns: Elements of Reusable Object-Oriented Software* in 1994 with examples in C++ and Smalltalk, the twenty-three classic patterns have been re-implemented in most of major languages of today and they have been used in almost every project you know about.

The *Gang of Four* detected that many small architectures were present in many of their projects, they started to rewrite them in a more abstract way and they released the famous book.

This book is a comprehensive explanation and implementation of the most common design patterns from the *Gang of Four* and today's patterns plus some of the most idiomatic concurrency patterns in Go.

But what is Go…?

A little bit of history

On the last 20 years, we have lived an incredible growth in computer science. Storage spaces have been increased dramatically, RAM has suffered a substantial growth, and CPU's are... well... simply faster. Have they grown as much as storage and RAM memory? Not really, CPU industry has reached a limit in the speed that their CPU's can deliver, mainly because they have become so fast that they cannot get enough power to work while they dissipate enough heat. The CPU manufacturers are now shipping more cores on each computer. This situation crashes against the background of many systems programming languages that weren't designed for multi-processor CPUs or large distributed systems that act as a unique machine. In Google, they realized that this was becoming more than an issue while they were struggling to develop distributed applications in languages like Java or C++ that weren't designed with concurrency in mind.

At the same time, our programs were bigger, more complex, more difficult to maintain and with a lot of room for bad practices. While our computers had more cores and were faster, we were not faster when developing our code neither our distributed applications. This was Go's target.

Go design started in 2007 by three Googlers in the research of a programming language that could solve common issues in large scale distributed systems like the ones you can find at Google. The creators were:

- Rob Pike: Plan 9 and Inferno OS.
- Robert Griesemer: Worked at Google's V8 JavaScript engine that powers Google Chrome.
- Ken Thompson: Worked at Bell labs and the Unix team. It has been involved in designing of the Plan 9 operating system as well as the definition of the UTF-8 encoding.

In 2008, the compiler was done and the team got the help of Russ Cox and Ian Lance Taylor. The team started their journey to open source the project in 2009 and in March 2012 they reached a version 1.0 after more than fifty releases.

Installing Go

Any Go Installation needs two basic things: the binaries of the language somewhere on your disk and a **GOPATH** path in your system where your projects and the projects that you download from other people will be stored.

In the following lines, we will explore how to install Go binaries in Linux, Windows and OS X. For a detailed explanation of how to install the latest version of Go, you can refer to the official documentation at `https://golang.org/doc/install`.

Linux

To install Go in Linux you have two options:

- **Easy option**: Use your distribution package manager:
  - RHEL/Fedora/Centos users with YUM/DNF:
    ```
    sudo yum install -y golang
    ```
  - Ubuntu/Debian users using APT with:
    ```
    sudo apt-get install -y golang
    ```
- **Advanced**: Downloading the latest distribution from `https://golang.org`.

I recommend using the second and downloading a distribution. Go's updates maintains backward compatility and you usually should not be worried about updating your Go binaries frequently.

Go Linux advanced installation

The advanced installation of Go in Linux requires you to download the binaries from **golang** webpage. After entering `https://golang.org`, click the **Download Go** button (usually at the right) some **Featured Downloads** option is available for each distribution. Select **Linux** distribution to download the latest stable version.

 At `https://golang.org` you can also download beta versions of the language.

Let's say we have saved the `tar.gz` file in Downloads folder so let's extract it and move it to a different path. By convention, Go binaries are usually placed in `/usr/local/go` directory:

```
tar -zxvf go*.*.*.linux-amd64.tar.gz
sudo mv go /usr/local/go
```

On extraction remember to replace asterisks (*) with the version you have downloaded.

Now we have our Go installation in `/usr/local/go` path so now we have to add the `bin` subfolder to our `PATH` and the `bin` folder within our GOPATH.

```
mkdir -p $HOME/go/bin
```

With -p we are telling bash to create all directories that are necessary. Now we need to append bin folder paths to our PATH, append the following lines at the end of your `~/.bashrc`:

```
export PATH=$PATH:/usr/local/go/bin
```

Check that our `go/bin` directory is available:

```
$ go version
Go version go1.6.2 linux/amd64
```

Windows

To install Go in Windows, you will need administrator privileges. Open your favorite browser and navigate to `https://golang.org`. Once there click the **Download Go** button and select **Microsoft Windows** distribution. A `*.msi` file will start downloading.

Execute the MSI installer by double clicking it. An installer will appear asking you to accept the **End User License Agreement** (**EULA**) and select a target folder for your installation. We will continue with the default path that in my case was `C:\Go`.

Once the installation is finished you will have to add the **binary Go** folder, located in `C:\Go\bin` to your Path. For this, you must go to Control Panel and select **System** option. Once in System, select the **Advanced** tab and click the **Environment variables** button. Here you'll find a window with variables for your current user and system variables. In system variables, you'll find the **Path** variable. Click it and click the **Edit** button to open a text box. You can add your path by adding `;C:\Go/bin` at the end of the current line (note the semicolon at the beginning of the path). In recent Windows versions (Windows 10) you will have a manager to add variables easily.

Mac OS X

In Mac OS X the installation process is very similar to Linux. Open your favorite browser and navigate to `https://golang.org` and click the **Download Go**. From the list of possible distributions that appear, select **Apple OS X**. This will download a `*.pkg` file to your download folder.

A window will guide you through the installation process where you have to type your administrator password so that it can put Go binary files in `/usr/local/go/bin` folder with the proper permissions. Now, open **Terminal** to test the installation by typing this on it:

```
$ go version
Go version go1.6.2 darwin/amd64
```

If you see the installed version, everything was fine. If it doesn't work check that you have followed correctly every step or refer to the documentation at `https://golang.org`.

Setting the workspace – Linux and Apple OS X

Go will always work under the same workspace. This helps the compiler to find packages and libraries that you could be using. This workspace is commonly called **GOPATH**.

GOPATH has a very important role in your working environment while developing Go software. When you import a library in your code it will search for this library in your `$GOPATH/src`. The same when you install some Go apps, binaries will be stored in `$GOPATH/bin`.

At the same, all your source code must be stored in a valid route within `$GOPATH/src` folder. For example, I store my projects in GitHub and my username is *Sayden* so, for a project called **minimal-mesos-go-framework** I will have this folder structure like `$GOPATH/src/github.com/sayden/minimal-mesos-go-framework` which reflects the URI where this repo is stored at GitHub:

```
mkdir -p $HOME/go
```

The `$HOME/go` path is going to be the destination of our `$GOPATH`. We have to set an environment variable with our `$GOPATH` pointing to this folder. To set the environment variable, open again the file `$HOME/.bashrc` with your favorite text editor and add the following line at the end of it:

```
export GOPATH=${HOME}/go
```

Save the file and open a new terminal. To check that everything is working, just write an echo to the `$GOPATH` variable like this:

```
echo $GOPATH/home/mcastro/go
```

If the output of the preceding command points to your chosen Go path, everything is correct and you can continue to write your first program.

Starting with Hello World

This wouldn't be a good book without a Hello World example. Our Hello World example can't be simpler, open your favorite text editor and create a file called `main.go` within our `$GOPATH/src/[your_name]/hello_world` with the following content:

```
package main

func main(){
println("Hello World!")
}
```

Save the file. To run our program, open the Terminal window of your operating system:

- In Linux, go to programs and find a program called **Terminal**.
- In Windows, hit Windows + *R*, type `cmd` without quotes on the new window and hit *Enter*.
- In Mac OS X, hit Command + Space to open a spotlight search, type `terminal` without quotes. The terminal app must be highlighted so hit Enter.

Once we are in our terminal, navigate to the folder where we have created our `main.go` file. This should be under your `$GOPATH/src/[your_name]/hello_world` and execute it:

```
go run main.go
Hello World!
```

That's all. The `go run [file]` command will compile and execute our application but it won't generate an executable file. If you want just to build it and get an executable file, you must build the app using the following command:

```
go build -o hello_world
```

Nothing happens. But if you search in the current directory (`ls` command in Linux and Mac OS X; and `dir` in Windows), you'll find an executable file with the name `hello_world`. We have given this name to the executable file when we wrote `-o hello_world` command while building. You can now execute this file:

```
/hello_world
Hello World!
```

And our message appeared! In Windows, you just need to type the name of the `.exe` file to get the same result.

The `go run [my_main_file.go]` command will build and execute the app without intermediate files.
The `go build -o [filename]` command will create an executable file that I can take anywhere and has no dependencies.

Integrated Development Environment – IDE

An **IDE (Integrated Development Environment)** is basically a user interface to help developers, code their programs by providing a set of tools to speed up common tasks during development process like compiling, building, or managing dependencies. The IDEs are powerful tools that take some time to master and the purpose of this book is not to explain them (an IDE like Eclipse has its own books).

In Go, you have many options but there are only two that are fully oriented to Go development **LiteIDE** and **Intellij Gogland**. LiteIDE is not the most powerful though but Intellij has put lots of efforts to make Gogland a very nice editor with completion, debugging, refactoring, testing, visual coverage, inspections, etc. Common IDEs or text editors that have a Go plugin/integration are as following:

- IntelliJ Idea
- Sublime Text 2/3
- Atom
- Eclipse

But you can also find Go plugins for:

- Vim
- Visual Studio and Visual Code

The IntelliJ Idea and Atom IDEs, for the time of this writing, has the support for debugging using a plugin called **Delve**. The IntelliJ Idea is bundled with the official Go plugin. In Atom you'll have to download a plugin called **Go-plus** and a debugger that you can find searching the word `Delve`.

Types

Types give the user the ability to store values in mnemonic names. All programming languages have types related with numbers (to store integers, negative numbers, or floating point for example) with characters (to store a single character) with strings (to store complete words) and so on. Go language has the common types found in most programming languages:

- The `bool` keyword is for Boolean type which represents a `True` or `False` state.
- Many numeric types being the most common:
    - The `int` type represents a number from 0 to 4294967295 in 32 bits machines and from 0 to 18446744073709551615 in 64 bits.
    - The `byte` type represents a number from 0 to 255.
    - The `float32` and `float64` types are the set of all IEEE-754 64/-bit floating-point numbers respectively.
    - You also have `signed int` type like `rune` which is an alias of `int32` type, a number that goes from -2147483648 to 2147483647 and `complex64` and `complex128` which are the set of all complex numbers with `float32`/ `float64` real and imaginary parts like *2.0i*.
- The `string` keyword for string type represents an array of characters enclosed in quotes like `"golang"` or `"computer"`.
- An `array` that is a numbered sequence of elements of a single type and a fixed size (more about arrays later in this chapter). A list of numbers or lists of words with a fixed size is considered arrays.
- The `slice` type is a segment of an underlying array (more about this later in this chapter). This type is a bit confusing at the beginning because it seems like an array but we will see that actually, they are more powerful.
- The structures that are the objects that are composed of another objects or types.
- The pointers (more about this later in this chapter)are like directions in the memory of our program (yes, like mailboxes that you don't know what's inside).
- The functions are interesting (more about this later in this chapter). You can also define functions as variables and pass them to other functions (yes, a function that uses a function, did you like Inception movie?).
- The `interface` is incredibly important for the language as they provide many encapsulation and abstraction functionalities that we'll need often. We'll use interfaces extensively during the book and they are presented in greater detail later.

- The `map` types are unordered key-value structures. So for a given key, you have an associated value.
- The channels are the communication primitive in Go for concurrency programs. We'll look on channels with more detail on Chapter 8, *Dealing with Go's CSP concurrency*.

Variables and constants

Variables are spaces in computer's memory to store values that can be modified during the execution of the program. Variables and constants have a type like the ones described in preceding text. Although, you don't need to explicitly write the type of them (although you can do it). This property to avoid explicit type declaration is what is called **Inferred types**. For example:

```
//Explicitly declaring a "string" variable
var explicit string = "Hello, I'm a explicitly declared variable"
```

Here we are declaring a variable (with the keyword `var`) called `explicit` of string type. At the same time, we are defining the value to `Hello World!`.

```
//Implicitly declaring a "string". Type inferred
inferred := ", I'm an inferred variable "
```

But here we are doing exactly the same thing. We have avoided the `var` keyword and the `string` type declaration. Internally, Go's compiler will infer (guess) the type of the variable to a string type. This way you have to write much less code for each variable definition.

The following lines use the `reflect` package to gather information about a variable. We are using it to print the type of (the `TypeOf` variable in the code) of both variables:

```
fmt.Println("Variable 'explicit' is of type:",
    reflect.TypeOf(explicit))
fmt.Println("Variable 'inferred' is of type:",
    reflect.TypeOf(inferred))
```

When we run the program, the result is the following:

```
$ go run main.go
Hello, I'm a explicitly declared variable
Hello, I'm an inferred variable
Variable 'explicit' is of type: string
Variable 'inferred' is of type: string
```

As we expected, the compiler has inferred the type of the implicit variable to string too. Both have written the expected output to the console.

Operators

The operators are used to perform arithmetic operations and make comparisons between many things. The following operators are reserved by Go language.

+	&	+=	&=	&&	==	!=	(	)
-	|	-=	|=	||	<	<=	[	]
*	^	*=	^=	<-	>	>=	{	}
/	<<	/=	<<=	++	=	:=	,	;
%	>>	%=	>>=	--	!	...	.	:
	&^		&^=					

Most commonly used operators are the arithmetic operators and comparators. Arithmetic operators are as following:

- The + operator for sums
- The – operator for subtractions
- The * operator for multiplications
- The / operator for divisions
- The % operator for division remainders
- The ++ operator to add 1 to the current variable
- The -- operator to subtract 1 to the current variable

On the other side, comparators are used to check the differences between two statements:

- The == operator to check if two values are equal
- The != operator to check if two values are different
- The > operator to check if left value is higher than right value
- The < operator to check if left value is lower than right value
- The >= operator to check if left value is higher or equal to right value
- The <= operator to check if left value is lower or equal to right value
- The && operator to check if two values are `true`

You also have the shifters to perform a binary shift to left or right of a value and a negated operator to invert some value. We'll use these operators a lot during the following chapters so don't worry too much about them now, just keep in mind that you cannot set the name of any variable, field or function in your code like this operators.

> What's the inverted value of 10? What's the negated value of 10? -10? Incorrect.. 10 in binary code is `1010` so if we negate every number we will have `0101` or `101` which is the number 5.

Flow control

Flow control is referred as the ability to decide which portion of code or how many times you execute some code on a condition. In Go, it is implemented using familiar imperative clauses like if, else, switch and for. The syntax is easy to grasp. Let's review major flow control statements in Go.

The if... else statement

Go language, like most programming languages, has `if...else` conditional statement for flow control. The Syntax is similar to other languages but you don't need to encapsulate the condition between parenthesis:

```
ten := 10
if ten == 20 {
    println("This shouldn't be printed as 10 isn't equal to 20")
} else {
    println("Ten is not equals to 20");
}
```

The `else...if` condition works in a similar fashion, you don't need parentheses either and they are declared as programmer would expect:

```
if "a" == "b" || 10 == 10 || true == false {
    println("10 is equal to 10")
    } else if 11 == 11 &&"go" == "go" {
    println("This isn't print because previous condition was satisfied");
    } else {
        println("In case no condition is satisfied, print this")
    }
}
```

Go does not have ternary conditions like `condition ? true : false`.

The switch statement

The `switch` statement is also similar to most imperative languages. You take a variable and check possible values for it:

```
number := 3
switch(number){
    case 1:
        println("Number is 1")
    case 2:
        println("Number is 2")
    case 3:
        println("Number is 3")
}
```

The for...range statement

The _for_ loop is also similar than in common programming languages but you don't use parentheses either

```
for i := 0; i<=10; i++ {
    println(i)
}
```

As you have probably imagined if you have computer science background, we infer an `int` variable defined as `0` and execute the code between the brackets while the condition (`i<=10`) is satisfied. Finally, for each execution, we added `1` to the value of `i`. This code will print the numbers from 0 to 10. You also have a special syntax to iterate over arrays or slices which is `range`:

```
for index, value := range my_array {
    fmt.Printf("Index is %d and value is %d", index, value)
}
```

First, the `fmt` (format) is a very common Go package that we will use extensively to give shape to the message that we will print in the console.

Regarding for, you can use the `range` keyword to retrieve every item in a collection like `my_array` and assign them to the value temporal variable. It will also give you an `index` variable to know the position of the value you're retrieving. It's equivalent to write the following:

```
for index := 0, index < len(my_array); index++ {
    value := my_array[index]
    fmt.Printf("Index is %d and value is %d", index, value)
}
```

 The `len` method is used to know the length of a collection.

If you execute this code, you'll see that the result is the same.

Functions

A function is a small portion of code that surrounds some action you want to perform and returns one or more values (or nothing). They are the main tool for developer to maintain structure, encapsulation, and code readability but also allow an experienced programmer to develop proper unit tests against his or her functions.

Functions can be very simple or incredibly complex. Usually, you'll find that simpler functions are also easier to maintain, test and debug. There is also a very good advice in computer science world that says: *A function must do just one thing, but it must do it damn well.*

What does a function look like?

A function is a piece of code with its own variables and flow that doesn't affect anything outside of the opening and close brackets but global package or program variables. Functions in Go has the following composition:

```
func [function_name] (param1 type, param2 type...) (returned type1,
returned type2...) {
    //Function body
}
```

Following the previous definition, we could have the following example:

```
func hello(message string) error {
```

```
        fmt.Printf("Hello %s\n", message)
        return nil
}
```

Functions can call other functions. For example, in our previous `hello` function, we are receiving a message argument of type string and we are calling a different function `fmt.Printf("Hello %s\n", message)` with our argument as parameter. Functions can also be used as parameters when calling other functions or be returned.

It is very important to choose a good name for your function so that it is very clear what it is about without writing too many comments over it. This can look a bit trivial but choosing a good name is not so easy. A short name must show what the function does and let the reader imagine what error is it handling or if it's doing any kind of logging. Within your function, you want to do everything that a particular behavior need but also to control expected errors and wrapping them properly.

So, to write a function is more than simply throw a couple of lines that does what you need, that's why it is important to write a unit test, make them small and concise.

What is an anonymous function?

An anonymous function is a function without a name. This is useful when you want to return a function from another function that doesn't need a context or when you want to pass a function to a different function. For example, we will create a function that accepts one number and returns a function that accepts a second number that it adds it to the first one. The second function does not have a declarative name (as we have assigned it to a variable) that is why it is said to be anonymous:

```
func main(){
    add := func(m int){
        return m+1
}

    result := add(6)

    //1 + 6 must print 7
    println(result)
}
```

The `add` variable points to an anonymous function that adds one to the specified parameter. As you can see, it can be used only for the scope its parent function `main` and cannot be called from anywhere else.

Anonymous functions are really powerful tools that we will use extensively on design patterns.

Closures

Closures are something very similar to anonymous functions but even more powerful. The key difference between them is that an anonymous function has no context within itself and a closure has. Let's rewrite the previous example to add an arbitrary number instead of one:

```
func main(){
    addN := func(m int){
        return func(n int){
            return m+n
        }
    }

    addFive := addN(5)
    result := addN(6)
    //5 + 6 must print 7
    println(result)
}
```

The addN variable points to a function that returns another function. But the returned function has the context of the m parameter within it. Every call to addN will create a new function with a fixed m value, so we can have main addN functions, each adding a different value.

This ability of closures is very useful to create libraries or deal with functions with unsupported types.

Creating errors, handling errors and returning errors.

Errors are extensively used in Go, probably thanks to its simplicity. To create an error simply make a call to errors.New(string) with the text you want to create on the error. For example:

```
err := errors.New("Error example")
```

As we have seen before, we can return errors to a function. To handle an error you'll see the following pattern extensively in Go code:

```
func main(){
    err := doesReturnError()
    if err != nil {
        panic(err)
    }
}

func doesReturnError() error {
    err := errors.New("this function simply returns an error")
    return err
}
```

Function with undetermined number of parameters

Functions can be declared as *variadic*. This means that its number of arguments can vary. What this does is to provide an array to the scope of the function that contains the arguments that the function was called with. This is convenient if you don't want to force the user to provide an array when using this function. For example:

```
func main() {
    fmt.Printf("%d\n", sum(1,2,3))
    fmt.Printf("%d\n", sum(4,5,6,7,8))
}

func sum(args ...int) (result int) {
    for _, v := range args {
        result += v
    }
    return
}
```

In this example, we have a sum function that will return the sum of all its arguments but take a closer look at the main function where we call sum. As you can see now, first we call sum with three arguments and then with five arguments. For sum functions, it doesn't matter how many arguments you pass as it treats its arguments as an array all in all. So on our sum definition, we simply iterate over the array to add each number to the result integer.

Naming returned types

Have you realized that we have given a name to the returned type? Usually, our declaration would be written as `func sum(args int) int` but you can also name the variable that you'll use within the function as a return value. Naming the variable in the return type would also zero-value it (in this case, an `int` will be initialized as zero). At the end, you just need to return the function (without value) and it will take the respective variable from the scope as returned value. This also makes easier to follow the mutation that the returning variable is suffering as well as to ensure that you aren't returning a mutated argument.

Arrays, slices, and maps

Arrays are one of the most widely used types of computer programming. They are lists of other types that you can access by using their position on the list. The only downside of an array is that its size cannot be modified. Slices allow the use of arrays with variable size. The `maps` type will let us have a dictionary like structures in Go. Let's see how each work.

Arrays

An array is a numbered sequence of elements of a single type. You can store 100 different unsigned integers in a unique variable, three strings or 400 `bool` values. Their size cannot be changed.

You must declare the length of the array on its creation as well as the type. You can also assign some value on creation. For example here you have 100 `int` values all with 0 as value:

```
var arr [100]int
```

Or an array of size 3 with `strings` already assigned:

```
arr := [3]string{"go", "is", "awesome"}
```

Here you have an array of 2 `bool` values that we initialize later:

```
var arr [2]bool
arr[0] = true
arr[1] = false
```

Zero-initialization

In our previous example, we have initialized an `array` of `bool` values of size 2. We wouldn't need to assign `arr[1]` to `false` because of the nature of zero-initialization in the language. Go will initialize every value in a `bool` array to `false`. We will look deeper to zero-initialization later in this chapter.

Slices

Slices are similar to arrays, but their size can be altered on runtime. This is achieved, thanks to the underlying structure of a slice that is an array. So, like arrays, you have to specify the type of the slice and its size. So, use the following line to create a slice:

```
mySlice := make([]int, 10)
```

This command has created an underlying array of ten elements. If we need to change the size of the slice by, for example, adding a new number, we would append the number to the slice:

```
mySlice := append(mySlice, 5)
```

The syntax of append is of the form ([array to append an item to], [item to append]) and returns the new slice, it does not modify the actual slice. This is also true to delete an item. For example, let's delete the first item of the array as following:

```
mySlice := mySlice[1:]
```

Yes, like in arrays. But what about deleting the second item? We use the same syntax:

```
mySlice = append(mySlice[:1], mySlice[2:]...)
```

We take all elements from zero index (included) to the first index (not included) and each element from the second index (included) to the end of the array, effectively deleting the value at the second position in the slice (index 1 as we start counting with 0). As you can see, we use the undetermined arguments syntax as the second parameter.

Maps

Maps are like dictionaries–for each word, we have a definition but we can use any type as word or definition and they'll never be ordered alphabetically. We can create maps of string that point to numbers, a string that points to `interfaces` and `structs` that point to `int` and `int` to `function`. You cannot use as key: slices, the functions, and maps. Finally, you create maps by using the keyword make and specifying the key type and the value type:

```
myMap := make(map[string]int)
myMap["one"] = 1
myMap["two"] = 2
fmt.Println(myMap["one"])
```

When parsing JSON content, you can also use them to get a `string[interface]` map:

```
myJsonMap := make(map[string]interface{})
jsonData := []byte(`{"hello":"world"}`)
err := json.Unmarshal(jsonData, &myJsonMap)
if err != nil {
panic(err)
}
fmt.Printf("%s\n", myJsonMap["hello"])
```

The `myJsonMap` variable is a map that will store the contents of JSON and that we will need to pass its pointer to the `Unmarshal` function. The `jsonData` variable declares an array of bytes with the typical content of a JSON object; we are using this as the mock object. Then, we unmarshal the contents of the JSON storing the result of the memory location of `myJsonMap` variable. After checking that the conversion was ok and the JSON byte array didn't have syntax mistakes, we can access the contents of the map in a JSON-like syntax.

Visibility

Visibility is the attribute of a function or a variable to be visible to different parts of the program. So a variable can be used only in the function that is declared, in the entire package or in the entire program.

How can I set the visibility of a variable or function? Well, it can be confusing at the beginning but it cannot be simpler:

- Uppercase definitions are public (visible in the entire program).
- Lowercase are private (not seen at the package level) and function definitions (variables within functions) are visible just in the scope of the function.

Here you can see an example of a `public` function:

```
package hello

func Hello_world(){
    println("Hello World!")
}
```

Here, `Hello_world` is a global function (a function that is visible across the entire source code and to third party users of your code). So, if our package is called `hello`, we could call this function from outside of this package by using `hello.Hello_world()` method.

```
package different_package

import "github.com/sayden/go-design-patters/first_chapter/hello"

func myLibraryFunc() {
hello.Hello_world()
}
```

As you can see, we are in the `different_package` package. We have to import the package we want to use with the keyword import. The route then is the path within your `$GOPATH/src` that contains the package we are looking for. This path conveniently matches the URL of a GitHub account or any other **Concurrent Versions System(CVS)** repository.

Zero-initialization

Zero-initialization is a source of confusion sometimes. They are default values for many types that are assigned even if you don't provide a value for the definition. Following are the zero-initialization for various types:

- The `false` initialization for `bool` type.
- Using `0` values for `int` type.
- Using `0.0` for `float` type.
- Using `""` (empty strings) for `string` type.
- Using `nil` keyword for pointers, functions, interfaces, slices, channels and maps.
- Empty `struct` for structures without fields.
- Zero-initialized `struct` for structures with fields. The zero value of a structure is defined as the structure that has its fields initialized as zero value too.

Zero-initialization is important when programming in Go because you won't be able to return a `nil` value if you have to return an `int` type or a `struct`. Keep this in mind, for example, in functions where you have to return a `bool` value. Imagine that you want to know if a number is divisible by a different number but you pass 0 (zero) as the divisor.

```
func main() {
    res := divisibleBy(10,0)
    fmt.Printf("%v\n", res)
}

func divisibleBy(n, divisor int) bool {
    if divisor == 0 {
        //You cannot divide by zero
        return false
    }

    return (n % divisor == 0)
}
```

The output of this program is `false` but this is incorrect. A number divided by zero is an error, it's not that 10 isn't divisible by zero but that a number cannot be divided by zero by definition. Zero-initialization is making things awkward in this situation. So, how can we solve this error? Consider the following code:

```
func main() {
    res, err := divisibleBy(10,0)
    if err != nil {
log.Fatal(err)
    }

    log.Printf("%v\n", res)
}

func divisibleBy(n, divisor int) (bool, error) {
    if divisor == 0 {
        //You cannot divide by zero
        return false, errors.New("A number cannot be divided by zero")
    }

    return (n % divisor == 0), nil
}
```

We're dividing 10 by 0 again but now the output of this function is `A number cannot be divided by zero`. Error captured, the program finished gracefully.

Pointers and structures

Pointers are the number one source of a headache of every C or C++ programmer. But they are one of the main tools to achieve high-performance code in non-garbage-collected languages. Fortunately for us, Go's pointers have achieved the best of both worlds by providing high-performance pointers with garbage-collector capabilities and easiness.

On the other side for its detractors, Go lacks inheritance in favor of composition. Instead of talking about the objects that *are* in Go, your objects *have other* . So, instead of having a `car` structure that inherits the class `vehicle` (a car is a vehicle), you could have a `vehicle` structure that contains a `car` structure within.

What is a pointer? Why are they good?

Pointers are hated, loved, and very useful at the same time. To understand what a pointer is can be difficult so let's try with a real world explanation. As we mentioned earlier in this chapter, a pointer is a like a mailbox. Imagine a bunch of mailboxes in a building; all of them have the same size and shape but each refers to a different house within the building. Just because all mailboxes are the same size does not mean that each house will have the same size. We could even have a couple of houses joined, a house that was there but now has a license of commerce, or a house that is completely empty. So the pointers are the mailboxes, all of them of the same size and that refer to a house. The building is our memory and the houses are the types our pointers refer to and the memory they allocate. If you want to receive something in your house, it's far easier to simply send the address of your house (to send the pointer) instead of sending the entire house so that your package is deposited inside. But they have some drawbacks as if you send your address and your house (variable it refers to) disappears after sending, or its type owner change–you'll be in trouble.

How is this useful? Imagine that somehow you have 4 GB of data in a variable and you need to pass it to a different function. Without a pointer, the entire variable is cloned to the scope of the function that is going to use it. So, you'll have 8 GB of memory occupied by using this variable twice that, hopefully, the second function isn't going to use in a different function again to raise this number even more.

You could use a pointer to pass a very small reference to this chunk to the first function so that just the small reference is cloned and you can keep your memory usage low.

While this isn't the most academic nor exact explanation, it gives a good view of what a pointer is without explaining what a stack or a heap is or how they work in x86 architectures.

Pointers in Go are very limited compared with C or C++ pointers. You can't use pointer arithmetic nor can you create a pointer to reference an exact position in the stack.

Pointers in Go can be declared like this:

```
number := 5
```

Here `number := 5` code represents our 4 GB variable and `pointer_to_number` contains the reference (represented by an ampersand) to this variable. It's the direction to the variable (the one that you put in the mailbox of this `house/type/variable`). Let's print the variable `pointer_to_number` , which is a simple variable:

```
println(pointer_to_number)
0x005651FA
```

What's that number? Well, the direction to our variable in memory. And how can I print the actual value of the house? Well, with an asterisk (`*`) we tell the compiler to take the value that the pointer is referencing, which is our 4 GB variable.

```
println(*pointer_to_number)
5
```

Structs

A struct is an object in Go. It has some similarities with classes in OOP as they have fields. Structs can implement interfaces and declare methods. But, for example, in Go, there's not inheritance. Lack of inheritance looks limiting but in fact, *composition over inheritance* was a requirement of the language.

To declare a structure, you have to prefix its name with the keyword `type` and suffix with the keyword `struct` and then you declare any field or method between brackets, for example:

```
type Person struct {
    Name string
    Surname string
    Hobbies []string
    id string
}
```

In this piece of code, we have declared a `Person` structure with three public fields (`Name`, `Age`, and `Hobbies`) and one private field (`id`, if you recall the *Visibility* section in this chapter, lowercase fields in Go refers to private fields are just visible within the same package). With this `struct`, we can now create as many instances of `Person` as we want. Now we will write a function called `GetFullName` that will give the composition of the name and the surname of the `struct` it belongs to:

```
func (person *Person) GetFullName() string {
    return fmt.Sprintf("%s %s", person.Name, person.Surname)
}

func main() {
    p := Person{
        Name: "Mario",
        Surname: "Castro",
        Hobbies: []string{"cycling", "electronics", "planes"},
        id: "sa3-223-asd",
    }

    fmt.Printf("%s likes %s, %s and %s\n", p.GetFullName(), p.Hobbies[0],
p.Hobbies[1], p.Hobbies[2])
}
```

Methods are defined similarly to functions but in a slightly different way. There is a `(p *Person)` that refers to a pointer to the created instance of the `struct` (recall the *Pointers* section in this chapter). It's like using the keyword `this` in Java or `self` in Python when referring to the pointing object.

Maybe you are thinking why does `(p *Person)` have the pointer operator to reflect that `p` is actually a pointer and not a value? This is because you can also pass Person by value by removing the pointer signature, in which case a copy of the value of Person is passed to the function. This has some implications, for example, any change that you make in `p` if you pass it by value won't be reflected in source `p`. But what about our `GetFullName()` method?

```
func (person Person) GetFullName() string {
    return fmt.Sprintf("%s %s", person.Name, person.Surname)
}
```

Its console output has no effect in appearance but a full copy was passed before evaluating the function. But if we modify `person` here, the source `p` won't be affected and the new `person` value will be available only on the scope of this function.

On the `main` function, we create an instance of our structure called p. As you can see, we have used implicit notation to create the variable (the : = symbol). To set the fields, you have to refer to the name of the field, colon, the value, and the comma (don't forget the comma at the end!). To access the fields of the instantiated structure, we just refer to them by their name like p.Name or p.Surname. You use the same syntax to access the methods of the structure like p.GetFullName().

The output of this program is:

```
$ go run main.go
Mario Castro likes cycling, electronics and planes
```

Structures can also contain another structure (composition) and implement interface methods apart from their own but, what's an interface method?

Interfaces

Interfaces are essential in object-oriented programming, in functional programming (`traits`) and, especially, in design patterns. Go's source code is full of interfaces everywhere because they provide the abstraction needed to deliver uncoupled code with the help of functions. As a programmer, you also need this type of abstraction when you write libraries but also when you write code that is going to be maintained in the future with new functionality.

Interfaces are something difficult to grasp at the beginning but very easy once you have understood their behavior and provide very elegant solutions for common problems. We will use them extensively during this book so put special focus on this section.

Interfaces – signing a contract

An interface is something really simple but powerful. It's usually defined as a contract between the objects that implement it but this explanation isn't clear enough in my honest opinion for newcomers to the interface world.

A water-pipe is a contract too; whatever you pass through it must be a liquid. Anyone can use the pipe, and the pipe will transport whatever liquid you put in it (without knowing the content). The water-pipe is the interface that enforces that the users must pass liquids (and not something else).

Let's think about another example: a train. The railroads of a train are like an interface. A train must construct (implement) its width with a specified value so that it can enter the railroad but the railroad never knows exactly what it's carrying (passengers or cargo). So for example, an interface of the railroad will have the following aspect:

```
type RailroadWideChecker interface {
    CheckRailsWidth() int
}
```

The `RailroadWideChecker` is the type our trains must implement to provide information about their width. The trains will verify that the train isn't too wide or too narrow to use its railroads:

```
type Railroad struct {
    Width int
}

func (r *Railroad) IsCorrectSizeTrain(r RailRoadWideChecker) bool {
    return r.CheckRailsWidth() != r.Width
}
```

The `Railroad` is implemented by an imaginary station object that contains the information about the width of the railroads in this station and that has a method to check whether a train fits the needs of the railroad with the `IsCorrectSizeTrain` method. The `IsCorrectSizeTrain` method receives an interface object which is a pointer to a train that implements this interface and returns a validation between the width of the train and the railroad:

```
Type Train struct {
    TrainWidth int
}

func (p *Train) CheckRailsWidth() int {
    return p.TrainWidth
}
```

Now we have created a passenger's train. It has a field to contain its width and implements our `CheckRailsWidth` interface method. This structure is considered to fulfill the needs of a `RailRoadWideChecker` interface (because it has an implementation of the methods that the interfaces ask for).

So now, we'll create a railroad of 10 units wide and two trains–one of 10 units wide that fit the railroad size and another of 15 units that cannot use the railroad.

```
func main(){
    railroad := Railroad{Width:10}
```

```
    passengerTrain := Train{TrainWidth: 10}
    cargoTrain := Train {TrainWidth: 15}

    canPassengerTrainPass := railroad.IsCorrectSizeTrain(passengerTrain)
    canCargoTrainPass := railroad.IsCorrectSizeTrain(cargoTrain)

    fmt.Printf("Can passenger train pass? %b\n", canPassengerTrainPass)
    fmt.Printf("Can cargo train pass? %b\n", canCargoTrainPass)
}
```

Let's dissect this `main` function. First, we created a railroad object of 10 units called `railroad`. Then two trains, of 10 and 15 units' width for passengers and cargo respectively. Then, we pass both objects to the railroad method that accepts interfaces of the `RailroadWideChecker` interface. The railroad itself does not know the width of each train separately (we'll have a huge list of trains) but it has an interface that trains must implement so that it can ask for each width and returns a value telling you if a train can or cannot use of the railroads. Finally, the output of the call to `printf` function is the following:

```
Can passenger train pass? true
Can cargo train pass? false
```

As I mentioned earlier, interfaces are so widely used during this book that it doesn't matter if it still looks confusing for the reader as they'll be plenty of examples during the book.

Testing and TDD

When you write the first lines of some library, it's difficult to introduce many bugs. But once the source code gets bigger and bigger, it becomes easier to break things. The team grows and now many people are writing the same source code, new functionality is added on top of the code that you wrote at the beginning. And code stopped working by some modification in some function that now nobody can track down.

This is a common scenario in enterprises that testing tries to reduce (it doesn't completely solve it, it's not a holy grail). When you write unit tests during your development process, you can check whether some new feature is breaking something older or whether your current new feature is achieving everything expected in the requirements.

Go has a powerful testing package that allows you also to work in a TDD environment quite easily. It is also very convenient to check the portions of your code without the need to write an entire main application that uses it.

The testing package

Testing is very important in every programming language. Go creators knew it and decided to provide all libraries and packages needed for the test in the core package. You don't need any third-party library for testing or code coverage.

The package that allows for testing Go apps is called, conveniently, testing. We will create a small app that sums two numbers that we provide through the command line:

```go
func main() {
    //Atoi converts a string to an int
    a, _ := strconv.Atoi(os.Args[1])
    b, _ := strconv.Atoi(os.Args[2])

    result := sum(a,b)
    fmt.Printf("The sum of %d and %d is %d\n", a, b, result)
}

func sum(a, b int) int {
    return a + b
}
```

Let's execute our program in the terminal to get the sum:

```
$ go run main.go 3 4
The sum of 3 and 4 is 7
```

By the way, we're using the strconv package to convert strings to other types, in this case, to int. The method Atoi receives a string and returns an int and an error that, for simplicity, we are ignoring here (by using the underscore).

> You can ignore variable returns by using the underscores if necessary, but usually, you don't want to ignore errors.

Ok, so let's write a test that checks the correct result of the sum. We're creating a new file called main_test.go. By convention, test files are named like the files they're testing plus the _test suffix:

```go
func TestSum(t *testing.T) {
    a := 5
    b := 6
    expected := 11

    res := sum(a, b)
```

```
    if res != expected {
        t.Errorf("Our sum function doens't work, %d+%d isn't %d\n", a, b,
res)
    }
}
```

Testing in Go is used by writing methods started with the prefix `Test`, a test name, and the injection of the `testing.T` pointer called `t`. Contrary to other languages, there are no asserts nor special syntax for testing in Go. You can use Go syntax to check for errors and you call `t` with information about the error in case it fails. If the code reaches the end of the `Test` function without arising errors, the function has passed the tests.

To run a test in Go, you must use the `go test -v` command (`-v` is to receive verbose output from the test) keyword, as following:

```
$ go test -v
=== RUN   TestSum
--- PASS: TestSum (0.00s)
PASS
ok    github.com/go-design-patterns/introduction/ex_xx_testing 0.001s
```

Our tests were correct. Let's see what happens if we break things on purpose and we change the expected value of the test from `11` to `10`:

```
$ go test
--- FAIL: TestSum (0.00s)
    main_test.go:12: Our sum function doens't work, 5+6 isn't 10
FAIL
exit status 1
FAIL  github.com/sayden/go-design-patterns/introduction/ex_xx_testing
0.002s
```

The test has failed (as we expected). The testing package provides the information you set on the test. Let's make it work again and check test coverage. Change the value of the variable `expected` from `10` to `11` again and run the command `go test -cover` to see code coverage:

```
$ go test -cover
PASS
coverage: 20.0% of statements
ok    github.com/sayden/go-design-patterns/introduction/ex_xx_testing
0.001s
```

The `-cover` options give us information about the code coverage for a given package. Unfortunately, it doesn't provide information about overall application coverage.

What is TDD?

TDD is the acronym for **Test Driven Development**. It consists of writing the tests first before writing the function (instead of what we did just before when we wrote the sum function first and then we wrote the test function).

TDD changes the way to write code and structure code so that it can be tested (a lot of code you can find in GitHub, even code that you have probably written in the past is probably very difficult, if not impossible, to test).

So, how does it work? Let's explain this with a real life example–imagine that you are in summer and you want to be refreshed somehow. You can build a pool, fill it with cold water, and jump into it. But in TDD terms, the steps will be:

1. You jump into a place where the pool will be built (you write a test that you know it will fail).
2. It hurts… and you aren't cool either (yes… the test failed, as we predicted).
3. You build a pool and fill it with cold water (you code the functionality).
4. You jump into the pool (you repeat the point 1 test again).
5. You're cold now. Awesome! Object completed (test passed).
6. Go to the fridge and take a beer to the pool. Drink. Double awesomeness (refactor the code).

So let's repeat the previous example but with a multiplication. First, we will write the declaration of the function that we're going to test:

```
func multiply(a, b int) int {
    return 0
}
```

Now let's write the test that will check the correctness of the previous function:

```
import "testing"

func TestMultiply(t *testing.T) {
    a := 5
    b := 6
    expected := 30

    res := multiply(a, b)
    if res != expected {
        t.Errorf("Our multiply function doens't work, %d*%d isn't %d\n", a,
b, res)
    }
```

```
}
```

And we test it through the command line:

```
$ go test
--- FAIL: TestMultiply (0.00s)
main_test.go:12: Our multiply function doens't work, 5+6 isn't 0
FAIL
exit status 1
FAIL    github.com/sayden/go-
designpatterns/introduction/ex_xx_testing/multiply
0.002s
```

Nice. Like in our pool example where the water wasn't there yet, our function returns an incorrect value too. So now we have a function declaration (but isn't defined yet) and the test that fails. Now we have to make the test pass by writing the function and executing the test to check:

```
func multiply(a, b int) int {
    return a*b
}
```

And we execute again our testing suite. After writing our code correctly, the test should pass so we can continue to the refractoring process:

```
$ go test
PASS
ok      github.com/sayden/go-design-
patterns/introduction/ex_xx_testing/multiply
0.001s
```

Great! We have developed the `multiply` function following TDD. Now we must refactor our code but we cannot make it more simple or readable so the loop can be considered closed.

During this book, we will write many tests that define the functionality that we want to achieve in our patterns. TDD promotes encapsulation and abstraction (just like design patterns do).

Libraries

Until now, most of our examples were applications. An application is defined by its `main` function and package. But with Go, you can also create pure libraries. In libraries, the package need not be called main nor do you need the `main` function.

As libraries aren't applications, you cannot build a binary file with them and you need the `main` package that is going to use them.

For example, let's create an arithmetic library to perform common operations on integers: sums, subtractions, multiplications, and divisions. We'll not get into many details about the implementation to focus on the particularities of Go's libraries:

```
package arithmetic

func Sum(args ...int) (res int) {
    for _, v := range args {
        res += v
    }
    return
}
```

First, we need a name for our library; we set this name by giving a name to the entire package. This means that every file in this folder must have this package name too and the entire group of files composes the library called **arithmetic** too in this case (because it only contains one package). This way, we won't need to refer to the filenames for this library and to provide the library name and path will be enough to import and use it. We have defined a `Sum` function that takes as many arguments as you need and that will return an integer that, during the scope of the function, is going to be called `res`. This allows us to initialize to 0 the value we're returning. We defined a package (not the `main` package but a library one) and called it `arithmetic`. As this is a library package, we can't run it from the command line directly so we'll have to create the `main` function for it or a unit test file. For simplicity , we'll create a `main` function that runs some of the operations now but let's finish the library first:

```
func Subtract(args ...int) int {
    if len(args) < 2 {
        return 0
    }

    res := args[0]
    for i := 1; i < len(args); i++ {
        res -= args[i]
    }
    return res
}
```

The `Subtraction` code will return 0 if the number of arguments is less than zero and the subtraction of all its arguments if it has two arguments or more:

```
func Multiply(args ...int) int {
```

```
    if len(args) < 2 {
        return 0
    }

    res := 1
    for i := 0; i < len(args); i++ {
        res *= args[i]
    }
    return res
}
```

The `Multiply` function works in a similar fashion. It returns 0 when arguments are less than two and the multiplication of all its arguments when it has two or more. Finally, the `Division` code changes a bit because it will return an error if you ask it to divided by zero:

```
func Divide(a, b int) (float64, error) {
    if b == 0 {
        return 0, errors.New("You cannot divide by zero")
    }
    return float64(a) / float64(b), nil
}
```

So now we have our library finished, but we need a `main` function to use it as libraries cannot be converted to executable files directly. Our main function looks like the following:

```
package main

import (
"fmt"

"bitbucket.org/mariocastro/go-design-
patterns/introduction/libraries/arithmetic"
)

func main() {
    sumRes := arithmetic.Sum(5, 6)
    subRes := arithmetic.Subtract(10, 5)
    multiplyRes := arithmetic.Multiply(8, 7)
    divideRes, _ := arithmetic.Divide(10, 2)

    fmt.Printf("5+6 is %d. 10-5 is %d, 8*7 is %d and 10/2 is %f\n", sumRes,
subRes, multiplyRes, divideRes)
}
```

We are performing an operation over every function that we have defined. Take a closer look at the `import` clause. It is taking the library we have written from its folder within `$GOPATH` that matches its URL in `https://bitbucket.org/`. Then, to use every one of the functions that are defined within a library, you have to name the package name that the library has before each method.

 Have you realized that we called our functions with uppercase names? Because of the visibility rules we have seen before, exported functions in a package must have uppercase names or they won't be visible outside of the scope of the package. So, with this rule in mind, you cannot call a lowercase function or variable within a package and package calls will always be followed by uppercase names.

Let's recall, some naming conventions about libraries:

- Each file in the same folder must contain the same package name. Files don't need to be named in any special way.
- A folder represents a package name within a library. The folder name will be used on import paths and it doesn't need to reflect the package name (although it's recommended for the parent package).
- A library is one or many packages representing a tree that you import by the parent of all packages folder.
- You call things within a library by their package name.

The Go get tool

Go get is a tool to get third party projects from CVS repositories. Instead of using the `git clone` command, you can use Go get to receive a series of added benefits. Let's write an example using CoreOS's **ETCD** project which is a famous distributed key-value store.

CoreOS's ETCD is hosted on GitHub at `https://github.com/coreos/etcd.git`. To download this project source code using the Go get tool, we must type in the Terminal it's resulting import path that it will have in our GOPATH:

```
$ go get github.com/coreos/etcd
```

Note that we have just typed the most relevant information so that Go get figures out the rest. You'll get some output, depending on the state of the project, but after, while, it will disappear. But what did happen?

- Go get has created a folder in $GOPATH/src/github.com/coreos.
- It has cloned the project in that location, so now the source code of ETCD is available at $GOPATH/src/github.com/coreos/etcd.
- Go get has cloned any repository that ETCD could need.
- It has tried to install the project if it is not a library. This means, it has generated a binary file of ETCD and has put it in $GOPATH/bin folder.

By simply typing the `go get [project]` command, you'll get all that material from a project in your system. Then in your Go apps, you can just use any library by importing the path within the source. So for the ETCD project, it will be:

```
import "github.com/coreos/etcd"
```

It's very important that you get familiar with the use of the Go get tool and stop using `git clone` when you want a project from a Git repository. This will save you some headaches when trying to import a project that isn't contained within your GOPATH.

Managing JSON data

JSON is the acronym for **JavaScript Object Notation** and, like the name implies, it's natively JavaScript. It has become very popular and it's the most used format for communication today. Go has very good support for JSON serialization/deserialization with the `JSON` package that does most of the dirty work for you. First of all, there are two concepts to learn when working with JSON:

- **Marshal**: When you marshal an instance of a structure or object, you are converting it to its JSON counterpart.
- **Unmarshal**: When you are unmarshaling some data, in the form of an array of bytes, you are trying to convert some JSON-expected-data to a known struct or object. You can also *unmarshal* to a `map[string]interface{}` in a fast but not very safe way to interpret the data as we'll see now.

Let's see an example of marshaling a string:

```
import (
"encoding/json"
"fmt"
)

func main(){
    packt := "packt"
```

```
        jsonPackt, ok := json.Marshal(packt)
        if !ok {
            panic("Could not marshal object")
        }
        fmt.Println(string(jsonPackt))
    }
$ "pack"
```

First, we have defined a variable called `packt` to hold the contents of the `packt` string. Then, we have used the `json` library to use the `Marshal` command with our new variable. This will return a new `bytearray` with the JSON and a flag to provide and `boolOK` result for the operation. When we print the contents of the bytes array (previous casting to string) the expected value appears. Note that `packt` appeared actually between quotes as the JSON representation would be.

The encoding package

Have you realized that we have imported the package `encoding/json`? Why is it prefixed with the word `encoding`? If you take a look at Go's source code to the `src/encoding` folder you'll find many interesting packages for encoding/decoding such as, XML, HEX, binary, or even CSV.

Now something a bit more complicated:

```
type MyObject struct {
    Number int
    `json:"number"`
    Word string
}

func main(){
    object := MyObject{5, "Packt"}
    oJson, _ := json.Marshal(object)
    fmt.Printf("%s\n", oJson)
}
$ {"Number":5,"Word":"Packt"}
```

Conveniently, it also works pretty well with structures but what if I want to not use uppercase in the JSON data? You can define the output/input name of the JSON in the structure declaration:

```
type MyObject struct {
    Number int
    Word string
}
```

```
func main(){
    object := MyObject{5, "Packt"}
    oJson, _ := json.Marshal(object)
    fmt.Printf("%s\n", oJson)
}
$ {"number":5,"string":"Packt"}
```

We have not only lowercased the names of the keys, but we have even changed the name of the `Word` key to string.

Enough of marshalling, we will receive JSON data as an array of bytes, but the process is very similar with some changes:

```
type MyObject struct {
Number int`json:"number"`
Word string`json:"string"`
}

func main(){
    jsonBytes := []byte(`{"number":5, "string":"Packt"}`)
    var object MyObject
    err := json.Unmarshal(jsonBytes, &object)
    if err != nil {
        panic(err)
    }
    fmt.Printf("Number is %d, Word is %s\n", object.Number, object.Word)
}
```

The big difference here is that you have to allocate the space for the structure first (with a zero value) and the pass the reference to the method `Unmarshal` so that it tries to fill it. When you use `Unmarshal`, the first parameter is the array of bytes that contains the JSON information while the second parameter is the reference (that's why we are using an ampersand) to the structure we want to fill. Finally, let's use a generic `map[string]interface{}` method to hold the content of a JSON:

```
type MyObject struct {
    Number int      `json:"number"`
    Word string     `json:"string"`
}

func main(){
    jsonBytes := []byte(`{"number":5, "string":"Packt"}`)
    var dangerousObject map[string]interface{}
    err := json.Unmarshal(jsonBytes, &dangerousObject)
    if err != nil {
        panic(err)
    }
```

```
    fmt.Printf("Number is %d, ", dangerousObject["number"])
    fmt.Printf("Word is %s\n", dangerousObject["string"])
    fmt.Printf("Error reference is %v\n",
dangerousObject["nothing"])
}
$ Number is %!d(float64=5), Word is Packt
Error reference is <nil>
```

What happened in the result? This is why we described the object as dangerous. You can point to a `nil` location when using this mode if you call a non-existing key in the JSON. Not only this, like in the example, it could also interpret a value as a `float64` when it is simply a `byte`, wasting a lot of memory.

So remember to just use `map[string]interface{}` when you need dirty quick access to JSON data that is fairly simple and you have under control the type of scenarios described previously.

Go tools

Go comes with a series of useful tools to ease the development process every day. Also in the golang page of GitHub, there are some tools that are supported by the Go team but they are not part of the compiler.

Most of the projects use tools such as `gofmt` so that all the code base looks similar. Godoc helps us to find useful information in Go's documentation and the `goimport` command to auto-import the packages we are using. Let's see them.

The golint tool

A linter analyzes source code to detect errors or improvements. The `golint` linter is available on `https://github.com/golang/lint` for installation (it doesn't come bundled with the compiler). It is very easy to use and is integrated some IDEs to be run when you save a source code file (Atom or Sublime Text, for example). Do you remember the implicit/explicit code that we run when talking about variables? Let's lint it:

```
//Explicitly declaring a "string" variable
var explicit string = "Hello, I'm a explicitly declared variable"
//Implicitly declaring a "string".
Type inferred inferred := ", I'm an inferred variable "
```

```
$ golint main.go
```

The `main.go:10:21:` command should omit the type string from the declaration of the `explicitString` variable; it will be inferred from the right-hand side.

It is telling us that Go compiler will actually infer this type of a variable from the code and you don't need to declare its type. What about the `Train` type on the interface section?

```
Type Train struct {
    TrainWidth int
}
```

```
$ golint main.go
```

The `main.go:5:6:` type exported `Train` type should have a comment or remain not exported.

In this case, it's pointing us that a public type such as `Train` type must be commented so that users can read the generated documentation to know its behavior.

The gofmt tool

The `gofmt` tool comes bundled with the compiler that already has access to it. Its purpose is to provide a set of indentation, formatting, spacing and few other rules to achieve good-looking Go code. For example, let's take the code of Hello World and make it a bit weirder by inserting spaces everywhere:

```
package main

func  main(){
    println("Hello World!")
}
```

```
$ gofmt main.go
package main

func main() {
        println("Hello World!")
}
```

The `gofmt` command prints it correctly again. What is more, we can use the `-w` flag to overwrite the original file:

```
$ gofmt -w main.go
```

And now we'll have our file properly corrected.

The godoc tool

Go documentation is pretty extended and verbose. You can find detailed information about any topic you want to achieve. The `godoc` tool also helps you access this documentation directly from the command line. For example, we can query the package `encoding/json`:

```
$godoc cmd/encoding/json
[...]
FUNCTIONS
func Compact(dst *bytes.Buffer, src []byte) error
Compact appends to dst the JSON-encoded src with insignificant space
characters elided.
func HTMLEscape(dst *bytes.Buffer, src []byte)
[...]
```

You can also use **grep**, a bash utility for Linux and Mac, to find specific information about some functionality. For example, we'll use grep to look for text that mentions anything about parsing JSON files:

```
$ godoc cmd/encoding/json | grep parse
```

The `Unmarshal` command parses the JSON encoded data and stores the result in the object being parsed.

One of the things that the `golint` command warns about is to use the beginning of a comment with the same name of the function it describes. This way, if you don't remember the name of the function that parses JSON, you can use `godoc` with `grep` and search for `parse` so the beginning of the line will always be the function name like in the example preceding the `Unmarshal` command.

The goimport tool

The `goimport` tool is a must have in Go. Sometimes you remember your packages so well that you don't need to search much to remember their API but it's more difficult to remember the project they belong to when doing the import. The `goimport` command helps you by searching your `$GOPATH` for occurrences of a package that you could be using to provide you with the project `import` line automatically. This is very useful if you configure your IDE to run `goimport` on save so that all used packages in the source file are imported automatically if you used them. It also works the other way around–if you delete the function you were using from a package and the package isn't being used anymore, it will remove the `import` line.

Contributing to Go open source projects in GitHub

One important thing to mention about Go packaging system is that it needs to have a proper folder structure within the GOPATH. This introduces a small problem when working with GitHub projects. We are used to forking a project, cloning our fork and start working before committing the pull-request to the original project. Wrong!

When you fork a project, you create a new repository on GitHub within your username. If you clone this repository and start working with it, all new import references in the project will point to your repository instead of the original! Imagine the following case in the original repository:

```
package main
import "github.com/original/a_library"
[some code]
```

Then, you make a fork and add a subfolder with a library called `a_library/my_library` that you want to use from the main package. The result is going to be the following:

```
package main
import (
    "github.com/original/a_library"
    "github.com/myaccount/a_library/my_library"
)
```

Now if you commit this line, the original repository that contains the code you have pushed will download this code anyways from your account again and it will use the references downloaded! Not the ones contained in the project!

So, the solution to this is simply to replace the `git clone` command with a `go get` pointing to the original library:

```
$ go get github.com/original/a_library
$ cd $GOPATH/src/github.com/original/a_library
$ git remote add my_origin https://github.com/myaccount/a_libbrary
```

With this modification, you can work normally in the original code without fear as the references will stay correct. Once you are done you just have to commit and push to your remote.

```
$ git push my_origin my_brach
```

This way, you can now access the GitHub web user interface and open the pull request without polluting the actual original code with references to your account.

Summary

After this first chapter, you must be familiar with the syntax of Go and some of the command-line tools that come bundled with the compiler. We have left apart concurrency capabilities for a later chapter as they are large and pretty complex to grasp at the beginning so that the reader learns the syntax of the language first, becomes familiar and confident with it, and then they can jump to understanding **Communicating Sequential Processes** (**CSP**) concurrency patterns and distributed applications. The next steps are to start with the creational design patterns.

2
Creational Patterns - Singleton, Builder, Factory, Prototype, and Abstract Factory Design Patterns

We have defined two types of cars-luxury and family. The car Factory will have to return The first groups of design patterns that we are going to cover are the Creational patterns. As the name implies, it groups common practices for creating objects, so object creation is more encapsulated from the users that need those objects. Mainly, creational patterns try to give ready-to-use objects to users instead of asking for their creation, which, in some cases, could be complex, or which would couple your code with the concrete implementations of the functionality that should be defined in an interface.

Singleton design pattern – having a unique instance of a type in the entire program

Have you ever done interviews for software engineers? It's interesting that when you ask them about design patterns, more than 80% will mention **Singleton** design pattern. Why is that? Maybe it's because it is one of the most used design patterns out there or one of the easiest to grasp. We will start our journey on creational design patterns because of the latter reason.

Description

The Singleton pattern is easy to remember. As the name implies, it will provide you with a single instance of an object, and guarantee that there are no duplicates.

At the first call to use the instance, it is created and then reused between all the parts in the application that need to use that particular behavior.

You'll use the Singleton pattern in many different situations. For example:

- When you want to use the same connection to a database to make every query
- When you open a **Secure Shell** (**SSH**) connection to a server to do a few tasks, and don't want to reopen the connection for each task
- If you need to limit the access to some variable or space, you use a Singleton as the door to this variable (we'll see in the following chapters that this is more achievable in Go using channels anyway)
- If you need to limit the number of calls to some places, you create a Singleton instance to make the calls in the accepted window

The possibilities are endless, and we have just mentioned some of them.

Objectives

As a general guide, we consider using the Singleton pattern when the following rule applies:

- We need a single, shared value, of some particular type.
- We need to restrict object creation of some type to a single unit along the entire program.

Example – a unique counter

As an example of an object of which we must ensure that there is only one instance, we will write a counter that holds the number of times it has been called during program execution. It shouldn't matter how many instances we have of the counter, all of them must *count* the same value and it must be consistent between the instances.

Requirements and acceptance criteria

There are some requirements and acceptance criteria to write the described single counter.. They are as follows:

- When no counter has been created before, a new one is created with the value 0
- If a counter has already been created, return this instance that holds the actual count
- If we call the method AddOne, the count must be incremented by 1

We have a scenario with three tests to check in our unit tests.

Writing unit tests first

Go's implementation of this pattern is slightly different from what you'll find in pure object-oriented languages such as Java or C++, where you have static members. In Go, there's nothing like static members, but we have package scope to deliver a similar result.

To set up our project, we must create a new folder within our $GOPATH/src directory. The general rule as we mentioned in the Chapter 1, *Ready... Steady... Go!*, is to create a subfolder with the VCS provider (such as GitHub), the username, and the name of the project.

For example, in my case, I use GitHub as my VCS and my username is *sayden*, so I will create the path $GOPATH/src/github.com/sayden/go-design-patterns/creational/singleton. The go-design-patterns instance in the path is the project name, the creational subfolder will also be our library name, and singleton the name of this particular package and subfolder:

```
mkdir -p $GOPATH/src/github.com/sayden/go-design-patterns/creational/singleton

cd $GOPATH/src/github.com/sayden/go-design-patterns/creational/singleton
```

Create a new file inside the singleton folder called singleton.go to also reflect the name of the package and write the following package declarations for the singleton type:

```
package singleton

type Singleton interface {
    AddOne() int
}

type singleton struct {
```

```
        count int
}

var instance *singleton

func GetInstance() Singleton {
    return nil
}
func (s *singleton) AddOne() int {
    return 0
}
```

As we are following a TDD approach while writing the code, let's code the tests that use the functions we have just declared. The tests are going to be defined by following the acceptance criteria that we have written earlier. By convention in test files, we must create a file with the same name as the file to test, suffixed with _test.go. Both must reside in the same folder:

```
package singleton

import "testing"

func TestGetInstance(t *testing.T) {
    counter1 := GetInstance()

    if counter1 == nil {
        //Test of acceptance criteria 1 failed
        t.Error("expected pointer to Singleton after calling
GetInstance(), not nil")
    }

    expectedCounter := counter1
}
```

The first test checks something obvious, but no less important, in complex applications. We actually receive something when we ask for an instance of the counter. We have to think of it as a Creational pattern–we delegate the creation of the object to an unknown package that could fail in the creation or retrieval of the object. We also store the current counter in the expectedCounter variable to make a comparison later:

```
currentCount := counter1.AddOne()
if currentCount != 1 {
    t.Errorf("After calling for the first time to count, the count must be
1 but it is %d\n", currentCount)
}
```

Now we take advantage of the zero-initialization feature of Go. Remember that integer types in Go cannot be nil and as we know, that this is the first call to the counter, and it is an integer type of variable, and we also know that it is zero-initialized. So after the first call to the `AddOne()` function, the value of the count must be 1.

The test that checks the second condition proves that the `expectedConnection` variable is not different to the returned connection that we requested later. If they were different, the message `Singleton instances must be different` will cause the test to fail:

```
counter2 := GetInstance()
if counter2 != expectedCounter {
    //Test 2 failed
    t.Error("Expected same instance in counter2 but it got a different
instance")
}
```

The last test is simply counting 1 again with the second instance. The previous result was 1, so now it must give us 2:

```
currentCount = counter2.AddOne()
if currentCount != 2 {
    t.Errorf("After calling 'AddOne' using the second counter, the current
count must be 2 but was %d\n", currentCount)
}
```

The last thing we have to do to finish our test part is to execute the tests to make sure that they are failing before implementation. If one of them doesn't fail, it implies that we have done something wrong, and we have to reconsider that particular test. We must open the terminal and navigate to the path of the singleton package to execute:

```
$ go test -v .
=== RUN   TestGetInstance
--- FAIL: TestGetInstance (0.00s)
        singleton_test.go:9: expected pointer to Singleton after
calling GetInstance(), not nil
        singleton_test.go:15: After calling for the first time to
count, the count must be 1 but it is 0
        singleton_test.go:27: After calling 'AddOne' using the second
counter, the current count must be 2 but was 0
    FAIL
    exit status 1
    FAIL
```

Implementation

Finally, we have to implement the Singleton pattern. As we mentioned earlier, we'll usually write a `static` method and instance to retrieve the Singleton instance in languages such as Java or C++. In Go, we don't have the keyword `static`, but we can achieve the same result by using the scope of the package. First, we create a `struct` that contains the object which we want to guarantee to be a Singleton during the execution of the program:

```go
package creational

type singleton struct{
    count int
}

var instance *singleton

func GetInstance() *singleton {
    if instance == nil {
        instance = new(singleton)
    }
    return instance
}

func (s *singleton) AddOne() int {
    s.count++
    return s.count
}
```

We must pay close attention to this piece of code. In languages such as Java or C++, the variable instance would be initialized to NULL at the beginning of the program. In Go, you can initialize a pointer to a struct as `nil`, but you cannot initialize a structure to `nil` (the equivalent of NULL). So the `var instance *singleton` line defines a pointer to a struct of type Singleton as nil, and the variable called `instance`.

We created a `GetInstance` method that checks if the instance has not been initialized already (`instance == nil`), and creates an instance in the space already allocated in the line `instance = new(singleton)`. Remember, when we use the keyword `new`, we are creating a pointer to an instance of the type between the parentheses.

The `AddOne` method will take the count of the variable instance, raise it by 1, and return the current value of the counter.

Let's run now our unit tests again:

```
$ go test -v -run=GetInstance
```

```
=== RUN    TestGetInstance
--- PASS: TestGetInstance (0.00s)
PASS
ok
```

A few words about the Singleton design pattern

We have seen a very simple example of the Singleton pattern, partially applied to some situation, that is, a simple counter. Just keep in mind that the Singleton pattern will give you the power to have a unique instance of some struct in your application and that no package can create any clone of this struct.

With Singleton, you are also hiding the complexity of creating the object, in case it requires some computation, and the pitfall of creating it every time you need an instance of it if all of them are similar. All this code writing, checking if the variable already exists, and storage, are encapsulated in the singleton and you won't need to repeat it everywhere if you use a global variable.

Here we are learning the classic singleton implementation for single threaded context. We will see a concurrent singleton implementation when we reach the chapters about concurrency because this implementation is not thread safe!

Builder design pattern – reusing an algorithm to create many implementations of an interface

Talking about **Creational** design patterns, it looks pretty semantic to have a **Builder** design pattern. The Builder pattern helps us construct complex objects without directly instantiating their struct, or writing the logic they require. Imagine an object that could have dozens of fields that are more complex structs themselves. Now imagine that you have many objects with these characteristics, and you could have more. We don't want to write the logic to create all these objects in the package that just needs to use the objects.

Description

Instance creation can be as simple as providing the opening and closing braces { } and leaving the instance with zero values, or as complex as an object that needs to make some API calls, check states, and create objects for its fields. You could also have an object that is composed of many objects, something that's really idiomatic in Go, as it doesn't support inheritance.

At the same time, you could be using the same technique to create many types of objects. For example, you'll use almost the same technique to build a car as you would build a bus, except that they'll be of different sizes and number of seats, so why don't we reuse the construction process? This is where the Builder pattern comes to the rescue.

Objectives

A Builder design pattern tries to:

- Abstract complex creations so that object creation is separated from the object user
- Create an object step by step by filling its fields and creating the embedded objects
- Reuse the object creation algorithm between many objects

Example – vehicle manufacturing

The Builder design pattern has been commonly described as the relationship between a director, a few Builders, and the product they build. Continuing with our example of the car, we'll create a vehicle Builder. The process (widely described as the algorithm) of creating a vehicle (the product) is more or less the same for every kind of vehicle–choose vehicle type, assemble the structure, place the wheels, and place the seats. If you think about it, you could build a car and a motorbike (two Builders) with this description, so we are reusing the description to create cars in manufacturing. The director is represented by the ManufacturingDirector type in our example.

Requirements and acceptance criteria

As far as we have described, we must dispose of a Builder of type `Car` and `Motorbike` and a unique director called `ManufacturingDirector` to take builders and construct products. So the requirements for a `Vehicle` builder example would be the following:

- I must have a manufacturing type that constructs everything that a vehicle needs
- When using a car builder, the `VehicleProduct` with four wheels, five seats, and a structure defined as `Car` must be returned
- When using a motorbike builder, the `VehicleProduct` with two wheels, two seats, and a structure defined as `Motorbike` must be returned
- A `VehicleProduct` built by any `BuildProcess` builder must be open to modifications

Unit test for the vehicle builder

With the previous acceptance criteria, we will create a director variable, the `ManufacturingDirector` type, to use the build processes represented by the product builder variables for a car and motorbike. The director is the one in charge of construction of the objects, but the builders are the ones that return the actual vehicle. So our builder declaration will look as follows:

```
package creational

type BuildProcess interface {
    SetWheels() BuildProcess
    SetSeats() BuildProcess
    SetStructure() BuildProcess
    GetVehicle() VehicleProduct
}
```

This preceding interface defines the steps that are necessary to build a vehicle. Every builder must implement this `interface` if they are to be used by the manufacturing. On every `Set` step, we return the same build process, so we can chain various steps together in the same statement, as we'll see later. Finally, we'll need a `GetVehicle` method to retrieve the `Vehicle` instance from the builder:

```
type ManufacturingDirector struct {}

func (f *ManufacturingDirector) Construct() {
    //Implementation goes here
}
```

```
func (f *ManufacturingDirector) SetBuilder(b BuildProcess) {
    //Implementation goes here
}
```

The `ManufacturingDirector` director variable is the one in charge of accepting the builders. It has a `Construct` method that will use the builder that is stored in `Manufacturing`, and will reproduce the required steps. The `SetBuilder` method will allow us to change the builder that is being used in the `Manufacturing` director:

```
type VehicleProduct struct {
    Wheels    int
    Seats     int
    Structure string
}
```

The product is the final object that we want to retrieve while using the manufacturing. In this case, a vehicle is composed of wheels, seats, and a structure:

```
type CarBuilder struct {}

func (c *CarBuilder) SetWheels() BuildProcess {
    return nil
}

func (c *CarBuilder) SetSeats() BuildProcess {
    return nil
}

func (c *CarBuilder) SetStructure() BuildProcess {
    return nil
}

func (c *CarBuilder) Build() VehicleProduct {
    return VehicleProduct{}
}
```

The first Builder is the `Car` builder. It must implement every method defined in the `BuildProcess` interface. This is where we'll set the information for this particular builder:

```
type BikeBuilder struct {}

func (b *BikeBuilder) SetWheels() BuildProcess {
    return nil
}

func (b *BikeBuilder) SetSeats() BuildProcess {
    return nil
```

```
}

func (b *BikeBuilder) SetStructure() BuildProcess {
    return nil
}

func (b *BikeBuilder) Build() VehicleProduct {
    return VehicleProduct{}
}
```

The `Motorbike` structure must be the same as the `Car` structure, as they are all Builder implementations, but keep in mind that the process of building each can be very different. With this declaration of objects, we can create the following tests:

```
package creational

import "testing"

func TestBuilderPattern(t *testing.T) {
    manufacturingComplex := ManufacturingDirector{}

    carBuilder := &CarBuilder{}
    manufacturingComplex.SetBuilder(carBuilder)
    manufacturingComplex.Construct()

    car := carBuilder.Build()

    //code continues here...
```

We will start with the `Manufacturing` director and the `Car` Builder to fulfill the first two acceptance criteria. In the preceding code, we are creating our `Manufacturing` director that will be in charge of the creation of every vehicle during the test. After creating the `Manufacturing` director, we created a `CarBuilder` that we then passed to manufacturing by using the `SetBuilder` method. Once the `Manufacturing` director knows what it has to construct now, we can call the `Construct` method to create the `VehicleProduct` using `CarBuilder`. Finally, once we have all the pieces for our car, we call the `GetVehicle` method on `CarBuilder` to retrieve a `Car` instance:

```
if car.Wheels != 4 {
    t.Errorf("Wheels on a car must be 4 and they were %d\n", car.Wheels)
}

if car.Structure != "Car" {
    t.Errorf("Structure on a car must be 'Car' and was %s\n",
car.Structure)
}
```

```
if car.Seats != 5 {
    t.Errorf("Seats on a car must be 5 and they were %d\n", car.Seats)
}
```

We have written three small tests to check if the outcome is a car. We checked that the car has four wheels, the structure has the description `Car`, and the number of seats is five. We have enough data to execute the tests and make sure that they are failing so that we can consider them reliable:

```
$ go test -v -run=TestBuilder .
=== RUN    TestBuilderPattern
--- FAIL: TestBuilderPattern (0.00s)
        builder_test.go:15: Wheels on a car must be 4 and they were 0
        builder_test.go:19: Structure on a car must be 'Car' and was
        builder_test.go:23: Seats on a car must be 5 and they were 0
FAIL
```

Perfect! Now we will create tests for a `Motorbike` builder that covers the third and fourth acceptance criteria:

```
bikeBuilder := &BikeBuilder{}

manufacturingComplex.SetBuilder(bikeBuilder)
manufacturingComplex.Construct()

motorbike := bikeBuilder.GetVehicle()
motorbike.Seats = 1

if motorbike.Wheels != 2 {
    t.Errorf("Wheels on a motorbike must be 2 and they were %d\n",
motorbike.Wheels)
}

if motorbike.Structure != "Motorbike" {
    t.Errorf("Structure on a motorbike must be 'Motorbike' and was %s\n",
motorbike.Structure)
}
```

The preceding code is a continuation of the car tests. As you can see, we reuse the previously created manufacturing to create the bike now by passing the `Motorbike` builder to it. Then we hit the `construct` button again to create the necessary parts, and call the builder `GetVehicle` method to retrieve the motorbike instance.

Take a quick look, because we have changed the default number of seats for this particular motorbike to 1. What we want to show here is that even while having a builder, you must also be able to change the default information in the returned instance to fit some specific needs. As we set the wheels manually, we won't test this feature.

Re-running the tests triggers the expected behavior:

```
$ go test -v -run=Builder .
=== RUN    TestBuilderPattern
--- FAIL: TestBuilderPattern (0.00s)
        builder_test.go:15: Wheels on a car must be 4 and they were 0
        builder_test.go:19: Structure on a car must be 'Car' and was
        builder_test.go:23: Seats on a car must be 5 and they were 0
        builder_test.go:35: Wheels on a motorbike must be 2 and they
were 0
        builder_test.go:39: Structure on a motorbike must be
'Motorbike' and was
    FAIL
```

Implementation

We will start implementing the manufacturing. As we said earlier (and as we set in our unit tests), the Manufacturing director must accept a builder and construct a vehicle using the provided builder. To recall, the BuildProcess interface will define the common steps needed to construct any vehicle and the Manufacturing director must accept builders and construct vehicles together with them:

```
package creational

type ManufacturingDirector struct {
    builder BuildProcess
}

func (f *ManufacturingDirector) SetBuilder(b BuildProcess) {
    f.builder = b
}

func (f *ManufacturingDirector) Construct() {
    f.builder.SetSeats().SetStructure().SetWheels()
}
```

Our `ManufacturingDirector` needs a field to store the builder in use; this field will be called `builder`. The `SetBuilder` method will replace the stored builder with the one provided in the arguments. Finally, take a closer look at the `Construct` method. It takes the builder that has been stored and reproduces the `BuildProcess` method that will create a full vehicle of some unknown type. As you can see, we have used all the setting calls in the same line thanks to returning the `BuildProcess` interface on each of the calls. This way the code is more compact:

Have you realized that the director entity in the Builder pattern is a clear candidate for a Singleton pattern too? In some scenarios, it could be critical that just an instance of the Director is available, and that is where you'll create a Singleton pattern for the Director of the Builder only. Design patterns composition is a very common technique and a very powerful one!

```go
type CarBuilder struct {
    v VehicleProduct
}

func (c *CarBuilder) SetWheels() BuildProcess {
    c.v.Wheels = 4
    return c
}

func (c *CarBuilder) SetSeats() BuildProcess {
    c.v.Seats = 5
    return c
}

func (c *CarBuilder) SetStructure() BuildProcess {
    c.v.Structure = "Car"
    return c
}

func (c *CarBuilder) GetVehicle() VehicleProduct {
    return c.v
}
```

Here is our first builder, the `car` builder. A builder will need to store a `VehicleProduct` object, which here we have named `v`. Then we set the specific needs that a car has in our business–four wheels, five seats, and a structure defined as `Car`. In the `GetVehicle` method, we just return the `VehicleProduct` stored within the Builder that must be already constructed by the `ManufacturingDirector` type.

```go
type BikeBuilder struct {
```

```
    v VehicleProduct
}

func (b *BikeBuilder) SetWheels() BuildProcess {
    b.v.Wheels = 2
    return b
}

func (b *BikeBuilder) SetSeats() BuildProcess {
    b.v.Seats = 2
    return b
}

func (b *BikeBuilder) SetStructure() BuildProcess {
    b.v.Structure = "Motorbike"
    return b
}

func (b *BikeBuilder) GetVehicle() VehicleProduct {
    return b.v
}
```

The `Motorbike` Builder is the same as the `car` builder. We defined a motorbike to have two wheels, two seats, and a structure called `Motorbike`. It's very similar to the `car` object, but imagine that you want to differentiate between a sports motorbike (with only one seat) and a cruise motorbike (with two seats). You could simply create a new structure for sports motorbikes that implements the build process.

You can see that it's a repetitive pattern, but within the scope of every method of the `BuildProcess` interface, you could encapsulate as much complexity as you want such that the user need not know the details about the object creation.

With the definition of all the objects, let's run the tests again:

```
=== RUN   TestBuilderPattern
--- PASS: TestBuilderPattern (0.00s)
PASS
ok   _/home/mcastro/pers/go-design-patterns/creational 0.001s
```

Well done! Think how easy it could be to add new vehicles to the `ManufacturingDirector` director just create a new class encapsulating the data for the new vehicle. For example, let's add a `BusBuilder` struct:

```
type BusBuilder struct {
    v VehicleProduct
}
```

```
func (b *BusBuilder) SetWheels() BuildProcess {
    b.v.Wheels = 4*2
    return b
}

func (b *BusBuilder) SetSeats() BuildProcess {
    b.v.Seats = 30
    return b
}

func (b *BusBuilder) SetStructure() BuildProcess {
    b.v.Structure = "Bus"
    return b
}

func (b *BusBuilder) GetVehicle() VehicleProduct {
    return b.v
}
```

That's all; your `ManufacturingDirector` would be ready to use the new product by following the Builder design pattern.

Wrapping up the Builder design pattern

The Builder design pattern helps us maintain an unpredictable number of products by using a common construction algorithm that is used by the director. The construction process is always abstracted from the user of the product.

At the same time, having a defined construction pattern helps when a newcomer to our source code needs to add a new product to the *pipeline*. The `BuildProcess` interface specifies what he must comply to be part of the possible builders.

However, try to avoid the Builder pattern when you are not completely sure that the algorithm is going to be more or less stable because any small change in this interface will affect all your builders and it could be awkward if you add a new method that some of your builders need and others Builders do not.

Factory method – delegating the creation of different types of payments

The Factory method pattern (or simply, Factory) is probably the second-best known and used design pattern in the industry. Its purpose is to abstract the user from the knowledge of the struct he needs to achieve for a specific purpose, such as retrieving some value, maybe from a web service or a database. The user only needs an interface that provides him this value. By delegating this decision to a Factory, this Factory can provide an interface that fits the user needs. It also eases the process of downgrading or upgrading of the implementation of the underlying type if needed.

Description

When using the Factory method design pattern, we gain an extra layer of encapsulation so that our program can grow in a controlled environment. With the Factory method, we delegate the creation of families of objects to a different package or object to abstract us from the knowledge of the pool of possible objects we could use. Imagine that you want to organize your holidays using a trip agency. You don't deal with hotels and traveling and you just tell the agency the destination you are interested in so that they provide you with everything you need. The trip agency represents a Factory of trips.

Objectives

After the previous description, the following objectives of the Factory Method design pattern must be clear to you:

- Delegating the creation of new instances of structures to a different part of the program
- Working at the interface level instead of with concrete implementations
- Grouping families of objects to obtain a family object creator

The example – a factory of payment methods for a shop

For our example, we are going to implement a payments method Factory, which is going to provide us with different ways of paying at a shop. In the beginning, we will have two methods of paying–cash and credit card. We'll also have an interface with the method, `Pay`, which every struct that wants to be used as a payment method must implement.

Acceptance criteria

Using the previous description, the requirements for the acceptance criteria are the following:

- To have a common method for every payment method called `Pay`
- To be able to delegate the creation of payments methods to the Factory
- To be able to add more payment methods to the library by just adding it to the factory method

First unit test

A Factory method has a very simple structure; we just need to identify how many implementations of our interface we are storing, and then provide a method, `GetPaymentMethod`, where you can pass a type of payment as an argument:

```
type PaymentMethod interface {
    Pay(amount float32) string
}
```

The preceding lines define the interface of the payment method. They define a way of making a payment at the shop. The Factory method will return instances of types that implement this interface:

```
const (
    Cash      = 1
    DebitCard = 2
)
```

We have to define the identified payment methods of the Factory as constants so that we can call and check the possible payment methods from outside of the package.

```
func GetPaymentMethod(m int) (PaymentMethod, error) {
```

```
        return nil, errors.New("Not implemented yet")
}
```

The preceding code is the function that will create the objects for us. It returns a pointer, which must have an object that implements the PaymentMethod interface, and an error if asked for a method which is not registered.

```
type CashPM struct{}
type DebitCardPM struct{}

func (c *CashPM) Pay(amount float32) string {
    return ""
}

func (c *DebitCardPM) Pay(amount float32) string {
    return ""
}
```

To finish the declaration of the Factory, we create the two payment methods. As you can see, the CashPM and DebitCardPM structs implement the PaymentMethod interface by declaring a method, Pay(amount float32) string. The returned string will contain information about the payment.

With this declaration, we will start by writing the tests for the first acceptance criteria: to have a common method to retrieve objects that implement the PaymentMethod interface:

```
package creational

import (
    "strings"
    "testing"
)

func TestCreatePaymentMethodCash(t *testing.T) {
    payment, err := GetPaymentMethod(Cash)
    if err != nil {
        t.Fatal("A payment method of type 'Cash' must exist")
    }

    msg := payment.Pay(10.30)
    if !strings.Contains(msg, "paid using cash") {
        t.Error("The cash payment method message wasn't correct")
    }
    t.Log("LOG:", msg)
}
```

Now we'll have to separate the tests among a few of the test functions. `GetPaymentMethod`
is a common method to retrieve methods of payment. We use the constant `Cash`, which we
have defined in the implementation file (if we were using this constant outside for the scope
of the package, we would call it using the name of the package as the prefix, so the syntax
would be `creational.Cash`). We also check that we have not received an error when
asking for a payment method. Observe that if we receive the error when asking for a
payment method, we call `t.Fatal` to stop the execution of the tests; if we called just
`t.Error` like in the previous tests, we would have a problem in the next lines when trying
to access the `Pay` method of a nil object, and our tests would crash execution. We continue
by using the `Pay` method of the interface by passing 10.30 as the amount. The returned
message will have to contain the text `paid using cash`. The `t.Log(string)` method is a
special method in testing. This struct allows us to write some logs when we run the tests if
we pass the `-v` flag.

```
func TestGetPaymentMethodDebitCard(t *testing.T) {
    payment, err = GetPaymentMethod(Debit9Card)

    if err != nil {
        t.Error("A payment method of type 'DebitCard' must exist")
    }

    msg = payment.Pay(22.30)

    if !strings.Contains(msg, "paid using debit card") {
        t.Error("The debit card payment method message wasn't correct")
    }

    t.Log("LOG:", msg)
}
```

We repeat the same operation with the debit card method. We ask for the payment method
defined with the constant `DebitCard`, and the returned message, when paying with debit
card, must contain the `paid using debit card` string.

```
func TestGetPaymentMethodNonExistent(t *testing.T) {
    payment, err = GetPaymentMethod(20)

    if err == nil {
        t.Error("A payment method with ID 20 must return an error")
    }
    t.Log("LOG:", err)
}
```

Finally, we are going to test the situation when we request a payment method that doesn't exist (represented by the number 20, which doesn't match any recognized constant in the Factory). We will check if an error message (any) is returned when asking for an unknown payment method.

Let's check whether all tests are failing:

```
$ go test -v -run=GetPaymentMethod .
=== RUN    TestGetPaymentMethodCash
--- FAIL: TestGetPaymentMethodCash (0.00s)
        factory_test.go:11: A payment method of type 'Cash' must exist
=== RUN    TestGetPaymentMethodDebitCard
--- FAIL: TestGetPaymentMethodDebitCard (0.00s)
        factory_test.go:24: A payment method of type 'DebitCard' must
exist
=== RUN    TestGetPaymentMethodNonExistent
--- PASS: TestGetPaymentMethodNonExistent (0.00s)
        factory_test.go:38: LOG: Not implemented yet
FAIL
exit status 1
FAIL
```

As you can see in this example, we can only see tests that return the `PaymentMethod` interfaces failing. In this case, we'll have to implement just a part of the code, and then test again before continuing.

Implementation

We will start with the `GetPaymentMethod` method. It must receive an integer that matches with one of the defined constants of the same file to know which implementation it should return.

```
package creational

import (
    "errors"
    "fmt"
)

type PaymentMethod interface {
    Pay(amount float32) string
}

const (
    Cash       = 1
```

```
        DebitCard = 2
)

type CashPM struct{}
type DebitCardPM struct{}

func GetPaymentMethod(m int) (PaymentMethod, error) {
    switch m {
        case Cash:
        return new(CashPM), nil
        case DebitCard:
        return new(DebitCardPM), nil
        default:
        return nil, errors.New(fmt.Sprintf("Payment method %d not
recognized\n", m))
    }
}
```

We use a plain switch to check the contents of the argument m (method). If it matches any of the known methods–cash or debit card, it returns a new instance of them. Otherwise, it will return a nil and an error indicating that the payment method has not been recognized. Now we can run our tests again to check the second part of the unit tests:

```
$go test -v -run=GetPaymentMethod .
=== RUN    TestGetPaymentMethodCash
--- FAIL: TestGetPaymentMethodCash (0.00s)
        factory_test.go:16: The cash payment method message wasn't
correct
        factory_test.go:18: LOG:
=== RUN    TestGetPaymentMethodDebitCard
--- FAIL: TestGetPaymentMethodDebitCard (0.00s)
        factory_test.go:28: The debit card payment method message
wasn't correct
        factory_test.go:30: LOG:
=== RUN    TestGetPaymentMethodNonExistent
--- PASS: TestGetPaymentMethodNonExistent (0.00s)
        factory_test.go:38: LOG: Payment method 20 not recognized
FAIL
exit status 1
FAIL
```

Now we do not get the errors saying it couldn't find the type of payment methods. Instead, we receive a message not correct error when it tries to use any of the methods that it covers. We also got rid of the Not implemented message that was being returned when we asked for an unknown payment method. Let's implement the structs now:

```
type CashPM struct{}
```

```
type DebitCardPM struct{}

func (c *CashPM) Pay(amount float32) string {
    return fmt.Sprintf("%0.2f paid using cash\n", amount)
}

func (c *DebitCardPM) Pay(amount float32) string {
    return fmt.Sprintf("%#0.2f paid using debit card\n", amount)
}
```

We just get the amount, printing it in a nicely formatted message. With this implementation, the tests will all be passing now:

```
$ go test -v -run=GetPaymentMethod .
=== RUN   TestGetPaymentMethodCash
--- PASS: TestGetPaymentMethodCash (0.00s)
        factory_test.go:18: LOG: 10.30 paid using cash
=== RUN   TestGetPaymentMethodDebitCard
--- PASS: TestGetPaymentMethodDebitCard (0.00s)
        factory_test.go:30: LOG: 22.30 paid using debit card
=== RUN   TestGetPaymentMethodNonExistent
--- PASS: TestGetPaymentMethodNonExistent (0.00s)
        factory_test.go:38: LOG: Payment method 20 not recognized
PASS
ok
```

Do you see the LOG: messages? They aren't errors, we just print some information that we receive when using the package under test. These messages can be omitted unless you pass the -v flag to the test command:

```
$ go test -run=GetPaymentMethod .
ok
```

Upgrading the Debitcard method to a new platform

Now imagine that your DebitCard payment method has changed for some reason, and you need a new struct for it. To achieve this scenario, you will only need to create the new struct and replace the old one when the user asks for the DebitCard payment method:

```
type CreditCardPM struct {}
  func (d *CreditCardPM) Pay(amount float32) string {
    return fmt.Sprintf("%#0.2f paid using new credit card implementation\n",
amount)
  }
```

This is our new type that will replace the `DebitCardPM` structure. The `CreditCardPM` implements the same `PaymentMethod` interface as the debit card. We haven't deleted the previous one in case we need it in the future. The only difference lies in the returned message that now contains the information about the new type. We also have to modify the method to retrieve the payment methods:

```
func GetPaymentMethod(m int) (PaymentMethod, error) {
    switch m {
        case Cash:
        return new(CashPM), nil
        case DebitCard:
        return new(CreditCardPM), nil
        default:
        return nil, errors.New(fmt.Sprintf("Payment method %d not
recognized\n", m))
    }
}
```

The only modification is in the line where we create the new debit card that now points to the newly created struct. Let's run the tests to see if everything is still correct:

```
$ go test -v -run=GetPaymentMethod .
=== RUN    TestGetPaymentMethodCash
--- PASS: TestGetPaymentMethodCash (0.00s)
        factory_test.go:18: LOG: 10.30 paid using cash
=== RUN    TestGetPaymentMethodDebitCard
--- FAIL: TestGetPaymentMethodDebitCard (0.00s)
        factory_test.go:28: The debit card payment method message
wasn't correct
        factory_test.go:30: LOG: 22.30 paid using new debit card
implementation
=== RUN    TestGetPaymentMethodNonExistent
--- PASS: TestGetPaymentMethodNonExistent (0.00s)
        factory_test.go:38: LOG: Payment method 20 not recognized
FAIL
exit status 1
FAIL
```

Uh, oh! Something has gone wrong. The expected message when paying with a credit card does not match the returned message. Does it mean that our code isn't correct? Generally speaking, yes, you shouldn't modify your tests to make your program work. When defining tests, you should be also aware of not defining them too much because you could achieve some coupling in the tests that you didn't have in your code. With the message restriction, we have a few grammatically correct possibilities for the message, so we'll change it to the following:

```
return fmt.Sprintf("%#0.2f paid using debit card (new)\n", amount)
```

We run the tests again now:

```
$ go test -v -run=GetPaymentMethod .
=== RUN    TestGetPaymentMethodCash
--- PASS: TestGetPaymentMethodCash (0.00s)
        factory_test.go:18: LOG: 10.30 paid using cash
=== RUN    TestGetPaymentMethodDebitCard
--- PASS: TestGetPaymentMethodDebitCard (0.00s)
        factory_test.go:30: LOG: 22.30 paid using debit card (new)
=== RUN    TestGetPaymentMethodNonExistent
--- PASS: TestGetPaymentMethodNonExistent (0.00s)
        factory_test.go:38: LOG: Payment method 20 not recognized
PASS
ok
```

Everything is okay again. This was just a small example of how to write good unit tests, too. When we wanted to check that a debit card payment method returns a message that contains `paid using debit card` string, we were probably being a bit restrictive, and it would be better to check for those words separately or define a better formatting for the returned messages.

What we learned about the Factory method

With the Factory method pattern, we have learned how to group families of objects so that their implementation is outside of our scope. We have also learned what to do when we need to upgrade an implementation of a used structs. Finally, we have seen that tests must be written with care if you don't want to tie yourself to certain implementations that don't have anything to do with the tests directly.

Abstract Factory – a factory of factories

After learning about the factory design pattern, where we grouped a family of related objects in our case payment methods, one can be quick to think–what if I group families of objects in a more structured hierarchy of families?

Description

The Abstract Factory design pattern is a new layer of grouping to achieve a bigger (and more complex) composite object, which is used through its interfaces. The idea behind grouping objects in families and grouping families is to have big factories that can be interchangeable and can grow more easily. In the early stages of development, it is also easier to work with factories and abstract factories than to wait until all concrete implementations are done to start your code. Also, you won't write an Abstract Factory from the beginning unless you know that your object's inventory for a particular field is going to be very large and it could be easily grouped into families.

The objectives

Grouping related families of objects is very convenient when your object number is growing so much that creating a unique point to get them all seems the only way to gain the flexibility of the runtime object creation. The following objectives of the Abstract Factory method must be clear to you:

- Provide a new layer of encapsulation for Factory methods that return a common interface for all factories
- Group common factories into a *super Factory* (also called a factory of factories)

The vehicle factory example, again?

For our example, we are going to reuse the Factory we created in the Builder design pattern. We want to show the similarities to solve the same problem using a different approach so that you can see the strengths and weaknesses of each approach. This is going to show you the power of implicit interfaces in Go, as we won't have to touch almost anything. Finally, we are going to create a new Factory to create shipment orders.

Acceptance criteria

The following are the acceptance criteria for using the `Vehicle` object's Factory method:

- We must retrieve a `Vehicle` object using a factory returned by the abstract factory.
- The vehicle must be a concrete implementation of a `Motorbike` or a `Car` that implements both interfaces (`Vehicle` and `Car` or `Vehicle` and `Motorbike`).

Unit test

This is going to be a long example, so pay attention, please. We will have the following entities:

- **Vehicle**: The interface that all objects in our factories must implement:
    - **Motorbike**: An interface for motorbikes of the types sport (one seat) and cruise (two seats).
    - **Car**: An interface for cars of types luxury (with four doors) and family (with five doors).
- **VehicleFactory**: An interface (the Abstract Factory) to retrieve factories that implement the `VehicleFactory` method:
    - **Motorbike** Factory: A factory that implements the `VehicleFactory` interface to return vehicle that implements the `Vehicle` and `Motorbike` interfaces.
    - **Car** Factory: Another factory that implements the `VehicleFactory` interface to return vehicles that implement the `Vehicle` and `Car` interfaces.

For clarity, we are going to separate each entity into a different file. We will start with the `Vehicle` interface, which will be in the `vehicle.go` file:

```
package abstract_factory

type Vehicle interface {
    NumWheels() int
    NumSeats() int
}
```

The Car and Motorbike interfaces will be in the car.go and motorbike.go files, respectively:

```
// Package abstract_factory file: car.go
package abstract_factory

type Car interface {
    NumDoors() int
}
// Package abstract_factory file: motorbike.go
package abstract_factory

type Motorbike interface {
    GetMotorbikeType() int
}
```

We have one last interface, the one that each factory must implement. This will be in the vehicle_factory.go file:

```
package abstract_factory

type VehicleFactory interface {
    NewVehicle(v int) (Vehicle, error)
}
```

So, now we are going to declare the car factory. It must implement the VehicleFactory interface defined previously to return Vehicles instances:

```
const (
    LuxuryCarType = 1
    FamilyCarType = 2
)

type CarFactory struct{}
func (c *CarFactory) NewVehicle(v int) (Vehicle, error) {
    switch v {
        case LuxuryCarType:
        return new(LuxuryCar), nil
        case FamilyCarType:
        return new(FamilyCar), nil
        default:
        return nil, errors.New(fmt.Sprintf("Vehicle of type %d not
recognized\n", v))
    }
}
```

We have defined two types of cars–luxury and family. The `car` Factory will have to return cars that implement the `Car` and the `Vehicle` interfaces, so we need two concrete implementations:

```go
//luxury_car.go
package abstract_factory

type LuxuryCar struct{}

func (*LuxuryCar) NumDoors() int {
    return 4
}
func (*LuxuryCar) NumWheels() int {
    return 4
}
func (*LuxuryCar) NumSeats() int {
    return 5
}

package abstract_factory

type FamilyCar struct{}

func (*FamilyCar) NumDoors() int {
    return 5
}
func (*FamilyCar) NumWheels() int {
    return 4
}
func (*FamilyCar) NumSeats() int {
    return 5
}
```

That's all for cars. Now we need the motorbike factory, which, like the car factory, must implement the `VehicleFactory` interface:

```go
const (
    SportMotorbikeType = 1
    CruiseMotorbikeType = 2
)

type MotorbikeFactory struct{}

func (m *MotorbikeFactory) Build(v int) (Vehicle, error) {
    switch v {
        case SportMotorbikeType:
        return new(SportMotorbike), nil
        case CruiseMotorbikeType:
```

```
            return new(CruiseMotorbike), nil
        default:
            return nil, errors.New(fmt.Sprintf("Vehicle of type %d not
recognized\n", v))
    }
}
```

For the motorbike Factory, we have also defined two types of motorbikes using the `const` keywords: `SportMotorbikeType` and `CruiseMotorbikeType`. We will switch over the `v` argument in the `Build` method to know which type shall be returned. Let's write the two concrete motorbikes:

```
//sport_motorbike.go
package abstract_factory

type SportMotorbike struct{}

func (s *SportMotorbike) NumWheels() int {
    return 2
}
func (s *SportMotorbike) NumSeats() int {
    return 1
}
func (s *SportMotorbike) GetMotorbikeType() int {
    return SportMotorbikeType
}

//cruise_motorbike.go
package abstract_factory

type CruiseMotorbike struct{}

func (c *CruiseMotorbike) NumWheels() int {
    return 2
}
func (c *CruiseMotorbike) NumSeats() int {
    return 2
}
func (c *CruiseMotorbike) GetMotorbikeType() int {
    return CruiseMotorbikeType
}
```

To finish, we need the abstract factory itself, which we will put in the previously created `vehicle_factory.go` file:

```
package abstract_factory
```

```
import (
    "fmt"
    "errors"
)

type VehicleFactory interface {
    Build(v int) (Vehicle, error)
}

const (
    CarFactoryType = 1
    MotorbikeFactoryType = 2
)

func BuildFactory(f int) (VehicleFactory, error) {
    switch f {
        default:
        return nil, errors.New(fmt.Sprintf("Factory with id %d not
recognized\n", f))
    }
}
```

We are going to write enough tests to make a reliable check as the scope of the book doesn't cover 100% of the statements. It will be a good exercise for the reader to finish these tests. First, a motorbike Factory test:

```
package abstract_factory

import "testing"

func TestMotorbikeFactory(t *testing.T) {
    motorbikeF, err := BuildFactory(MotorbikeFactoryType)
    if err != nil {
        t.Fatal(err)
    }

    motorbikeVehicle, err := motorbikeF.Build(SportMotorbikeType)
    if err != nil {
        t.Fatal(err)
    }

    t.Logf("Motorbike vehicle has %d wheels\n",
motorbikeVehicle.NumWheels())

    sportBike, ok := motorbikeVehicle.(Motorbike)
    if !ok {
        t.Fatal("Struct assertion has failed")
    }
```

```
        t.Logf("Sport motorbike has type %d\n", sportBike.GetMotorbikeType())
    }
```

We use the package method, `BuildFactory`, to retrieve a motorbike Factory (passing the `MotorbikeFactory` ID in the parameters), and check if we get any error. Then, already with the motorbike factory, we ask for a vehicle of the type `SportMotorbikeType` and check for errors again. With the returned vehicle, we can ask for methods of the vehicle interface (`NumWheels` and `NumSeats`). We know that it is a motorbike, but we cannot ask for the type of motorbike without using the type assertion. We use the type assertion on the vehicle to retrieve the motorbike that the `motorbikeVehicle` represents in the code line `sportBike, found := motorbikeVehicle.(Motorbike)`, and we must check that the type we have received is correct.

Finally, now we have a motorbike instance, we can ask for the bike type by using the `GetMotorbikeType` method. Now we are going to write a test that checks the car factory in the same manner:

```
func TestCarFactory(t *testing.T) {
    carF, err := BuildFactory(CarFactoryType)
    if err != nil {
        t.Fatal(err)
    }

    carVehicle, err := carF.Build(LuxuryCarType)
    if err != nil {
        t.Fatal(err)
    }

    t.Logf("Car vehicle has %d seats\n", carVehicle.NumWheels())

    luxuryCar, ok := carVehicle.(Car)
    if !ok {
        t.Fatal("Struct assertion has failed")
    }
    t.Logf("Luxury car has %d doors.\n", luxuryCar.NumDoors())
}
```

Again, we use the `BuildFactory` method to retrieve a `Car` Factory by using the `CarFactoryType` in the parameters. With this factory, we want a car of the `Luxury` type so that it returns a `vehicle` instance. We again do the type assertion to point to a car instance so that we can ask for the number of doors using the `NumDoors` method.

Let's run the unit tests:

```
go test -v -run=Factory .
=== RUN   TestMotorbikeFactory
```

```
--- FAIL: TestMotorbikeFactory (0.00s)
        vehicle_factory_test.go:8: Factory with id 2 not recognized
=== RUN   TestCarFactory
--- FAIL: TestCarFactory (0.00s)
        vehicle_factory_test.go:28: Factory with id 1 not recognized
FAIL
exit status 1
FAIL
```

Done. It can't recognize any factory as their implementation is still not done.

Implementation

The implementation of every factory is already done for the sake of brevity. They are very similar to the Factory method with the only difference being that in the Factory method, we don't use an instance of the Factory method because we use the package functions directly. The implementation of the vehicle Factory is as follows:

```
func BuildFactory(f int) (VehicleFactory, error) {
    switch f {
        case CarFactoryType:
        return new(CarFactory), nil
        case MotorbikeFactoryType:
        return new(MotorbikeFactory), nil
        default:
        return nil, errors.New(fmt.Sprintf("Factory with id %d not
recognized\n", f))
    }
}
```

Like in any factory, we switched between the factory possibilities to return the one that was demanded. As we have already implemented all concrete vehicles, the tests must run too:

```
go test -v -run=Factory -cover .
=== RUN   TestMotorbikeFactory
--- PASS: TestMotorbikeFactory (0.00s)
        vehicle_factory_test.go:16: Motorbike vehicle has 2 wheels
        vehicle_factory_test.go:22: Sport motorbike has type 1
=== RUN   TestCarFactory
--- PASS: TestCarFactory (0.00s)
        vehicle_factory_test.go:36: Car vehicle has 4 seats
        vehicle_factory_test.go:42: Luxury car has 4 doors.
PASS
coverage: 45.8% of statements
ok
```

All of them passed. Take a close look and note that we have used the `-cover` flag when running the tests to return a coverage percentage of the package: 45.8%. What this tells us is that 45.8% of the lines are covered by the tests we have written, but 54.2% are still not under the tests. This is because we haven't covered the cruise motorbike and the family car with the tests. If you write those tests, the result should rise to around 70.8%.

 Type assertion is also known as **casting** in other languages. When you have an interface instance, which is essentially a pointer to a struct, you just have access to the interface methods. With type assertion, you can tell the compiler the type of the pointed struct, so you can access the entire struct fields and methods.

A few lines about the Abstract Factory method

We have learned how to write a factory of factories that provides us with a very generic object of vehicle type. This pattern is commonly used in many applications and libraries, such as cross-platform GUI libraries. Think of a button, a generic object, and button factory that provides you with a factory for Microsoft Windows buttons while you have another factory for Mac OS X buttons. You don't want to deal with the implementation details of each platform, but you just want to implement the actions for some specific behavior raised by a button.

Also, we have seen the differences when approaching the same problem with two different solutions–the Abstract factory and the Builder pattern. As you have seen, with the Builder pattern, we had an unstructured list of objects (cars with motorbikes in the same factory). Also, we encouraged reusing the building algorithm in the Builder pattern. In the Abstract factory, we have a very structured list of vehicles (the factory for motorbikes and a factory for cars). We also didn't mix the creation of cars with motorbikes, providing more flexibility in the creation process. The Abstract factory and Builder patterns can both resolve the same problem, but your particular needs will help you find the slight differences that should lead you to take one solution or the other.

Prototype design pattern

The last pattern we will see in this chapter is the **Prototype** pattern. Like all creational patterns, this too comes in handy when creating objects, and it is very common to see the Prototype pattern surrounded by more patterns.

While with the Builder pattern, we are dealing with repetitive building algorithms and with the factories we are simplifying the creation of many types of objects; with the Prototype pattern, we will use an already created instance of some type to clone it and complete it with the particular needs of each context. Let's see it in detail.

Description

The aim of the Prototype pattern is to have an object or a set of objects that is already created at compilation time, but which you can clone as many times as you want at runtime. This is useful, for example, as a default template for a user who has just registered with your webpage or a default pricing plan in some service. The key difference between this and a Builder pattern is that objects are cloned for the user instead of building them at runtime. You can also build a cache-like solution, storing information using a prototype.

Objective

The main objective for the Prototype design pattern is to avoid repetitive object creation. Imagine a default object composed of dozens of fields and embedded types. We don't want to write everything needed by this type every time that we use the object, especially if we can mess it up by creating instances with different *foundations*:

- Maintain a set of objects that will be cloned to create new instances
- Provide a default value of some type to start working on top of it
- Free CPU of complex object initialization to take more memory resources

Example

We will build a small component of an imaginary customized shirts shop that will have a few shirts with their default colors and prices. Each shirt will also have a **Stock Keeping Unit (SKU)**, a system to identify items stored at a specific location) that will need an update.

Acceptance criteria

To achieve what is described in the example, we will use a prototype of shirts. Each time we need a new shirt we will take this prototype, clone it and work with it. In particular, those are the acceptance criteria for using the Prototype pattern design method in this example:

- To have a shirt-cloner object and interface to ask for different types of shirts (white, black, and blue at 15.00, 16.00, and 17.00 dollars respectively)
- When you ask for a white shirt, a clone of the white shirt must be made, and the new instance must be different from the original one
- The SKU of the created object shouldn't affect new object creation
- An info method must give me all the information available on the instance fields, including the updated SKU

Unit test

First, we will need a `ShirtCloner` interface and an object that implements it. Also, we need a package-level function called `GetShirtsCloner` to retrieve a new instance of the cloner:

```
type ShirtCloner interface {
    GetClone(s int) (ItemInfoGetter, error)
}

const (
    White = 1
    Black = 2
    Blue  = 3
)

func GetShirtsCloner() ShirtCloner {
    return nil
}

type ShirtsCache struct {}
func (s *ShirtsCache)GetClone(s int) (ItemInfoGetter, error) {
    return nil, errors.New("Not implemented yet")
}
```

Now we need an object struct to clone, which implements an interface to retrieve the information of its fields. We will call the object `Shirt` and the `ItemInfoGetter` interface:

```
type ItemInfoGetter interface {
    GetInfo() string
}

type ShirtColor byte

type Shirt struct {
    Price float32
    SKU   string
```

```
    Color ShirtColor
}
func (s *Shirt) GetInfo() string {
    return ""
}

func GetShirtsCloner() ShirtCloner {
    return nil
}

var whitePrototype *Shirt = &Shirt{
    Price: 15.00,
    SKU:   "empty",
    Color: White,
}

func (i *Shirt) GetPrice() float32 {
    return i.Price
}
```

 Have you realized that the type called ShirtColor that we defined is just a byte type? Maybe you are wondering why we haven't simply used the byte type. We could, but this way we created an easily readable struct, which we can upgrade with some methods in the future if required. For example, we could write a String() method that returns the color in the string format (White for type 1, Black for type 2, and Blue for type 3).

With this code, we can already write our first tests:

```
func TestClone(t *testing.T) {
    shirtCache := GetShirtsCloner()
    if shirtCache == nil {
        t.Fatal("Received cache was nil")
    }

    item1, err := shirtCache.GetClone(White)
    if err != nil {
        t.Error(err)
    }
}

//more code continues here...
```

We will cover the first case of our scenario, where we need a cloner object that we can use to ask for different shirt colors.

For the second case, we will take the original object (which we can access because we are in the scope of the package), and we will compare it with our `shirt1` instance.

```
if item1 == whitePrototype {
    t.Error("item1 cannot be equal to the white prototype");
}
```

Now, for the third case. First, we will type assert `item1` to a shirt so that we can set an SKU. We will create a second shirt, also white, and we will type assert it too to check that the SKUs are different:

```
shirt1, ok := item1.(*Shirt)
if !ok {
    t.Fatal("Type assertion for shirt1 couldn't be done successfully")
}
shirt1.SKU = "abbcc"

item2, err := shirtCache.GetClone(White)
if err != nil {
    t.Fatal(err)
}

shirt2, ok := item2.(*Shirt)
if !ok {
    t.Fatal("Type assertion for shirt1 couldn't be done successfully")
}

if shirt1.SKU == shirt2.SKU {
    t.Error("SKU's of shirt1 and shirt2 must be different")
}

if shirt1 == shirt2 {
    t.Error("Shirt 1 cannot be equal to Shirt 2")
}
```

Finally, for the fourth case, we log the info of the first and second shirts:

```
t.Logf("LOG: %s", shirt1.GetInfo())
t.Logf("LOG: %s", shirt2.GetInfo())
```

We will be printing the memory positions of both shirts, so we make this assertion at a more physical level:

```
t.Logf("LOG: The memory positions of the shirts are different %p != %p
\n\n", &shirt1, &shirt2)
```

Finally, we run the tests so we can check that it fails:

```
go test -run=TestClone .
--- FAIL: TestClone (0.00s)
prototype_test.go:10: Not implemented yet
FAIL
FAIL
```

We have to stop there so that the tests don't panic if we try to use a nil object that is returned by the GetShirtsCloner function.

Implementation

We will start with the GetClone method. This method should return an item of the specified type and we have three type: white, black and blue:

```
var whitePrototype *Shirt = &Shirt{
    Price: 15.00,
    SKU:    "empty",
    Color: White,
}

var blackPrototype *Shirt = &Shirt{
    Price: 16.00,
    SKU:    "empty",
    Color: Black,
}

var bluePrototype *Shirt = &Shirt{
    Price: 17.00,
    SKU:    "empty",
    Color: Blue,
}
```

So now that we have the three prototypes to work over we can implement GetClone(s int) method:

```
type ShirtsCache struct {}
func (s *ShirtsCache)GetClone(s int) (ItemInfoGetter, error) {
    switch m {
        case White:
            newItem := *whitePrototype
            return &newItem, nil
        case Black:
            newItem := *blackPrototype
            return &newItem, nil
        case Blue:
```

```
                newItem := *bluePrototype
                return &newItem, nil
        default:
            return nil, errors.New("Shirt model not recognized")
    }
}
```

The `Shirt` structure also needs a `GetInfo` implementation to print the contents of the instances.

```
type ShirtColor byte

type Shirt struct {
    Price float32
    SKU   string
    Color ShirtColor
}

func (s *Shirt) GetInfo() string {
    return fmt.Sprintf("Shirt with SKU '%s' and Color id %d that costs
%f\n", s.SKU, s.Color, s.Price)
}
```

Finally, let's run the tests to see that everything is now working:

```
go test -run=TestClone -v .
=== RUN   TestClone
--- PASS: TestClone (0.00s)
prototype_test.go:41: LOG: Shirt with SKU 'abbcc' and Color id 1 that costs
15.000000
prototype_test.go:42: LOG: Shirt with SKU 'empty' and Color id 1 that costs
15.000000
prototype_test.go:44: LOG: The memory positions of the shirts are different
0xc42002c038 != 0xc42002c040

PASS
ok
```

In the log, (remember to set the -v flag when running the tests) you can check that `shirt1` and `shirt2` have different SKUs. Also, we can see the memory positions of both objects. Take into account that the positions shown on your computer will probably be different.

What we learned about the Prototype design pattern

The Prototype pattern is a powerful tool to build caches and default objects. You have probably realized too that some patterns can overlap a bit, but they have small differences that make them more appropriate in some cases and not so much in others.

Summary

We have seen the five main creational design patterns commonly used in the software industry. Their purpose is to abstract the user from the creation of objects for complexity or maintainability purposes. They have been the foundation of thousands of applications and libraries since the 1990s, and most of the software we use today has many of these creational patterns under the hood.

It's worth mentioning that these patterns are not thread-free. In a more advanced chapter, we will see concurrent programming in Go, and how to create some of the more critical design patterns using a concurrent approach.

3
Structural Patterns - Composite, Adapter, and Bridge Design Patterns

We are going to start our journey through the world of structural patterns. Structural patterns, as the name implies, help us to shape our applications with commonly used structures and relationships.

The Go language, by nature, encourages use of composition almost exclusively by its lack of inheritance. Because of this, we have been using the **Composite** design pattern extensively until now, so let's start by defining the Composite design pattern.

Composite design pattern

The Composite design pattern favors composition (commonly defined as a *has a* relationship) over inheritance (an *is a* relationship). The *composition over inheritance* approach has been a source of discussions among engineers since the nineties. We will learn how to create object structures by using a *has a* approach. All in all, Go doesn't have inheritance because it doesn't need it!

Description

In the Composite design pattern, you will create hierarchies and trees of objects. Objects have different objects with their own fields and methods inside them. This approach is very powerful and solves many problems of inheritance and multiple inheritances. For example, a typical inheritance problem is when you have an entity that inherits from two completely different classes, which have absolutely no relationship between them. Imagine an athlete who trains, and who is a swimmer who swims:

- The `Athlete` class has a `Train()` method
- The `Swimmer` class has a `Swim()` method

The `Swimmer` class inherits from the `Athlete` class, so it inherits its `Train` method and declares its own `Swim` method. You could also have a cyclist who is also an athlete, and declares a `Ride` method.

But now imagine an animal that eats, like a dog that also barks:

- The `Cyclist` class has a `Ride()` method
- The `Animal` class has `Eat()`, `Dog()`, and `Bark()` methods

Nothing fancy. You could also have a fish that is an animal, and yes, swims! So, how do you solve it? A fish cannot be a swimmer that also trains. Fish don't train (as far as I know!). You could make a `Swimmer` interface with a `Swim` method, and make the swimmer athlete and fish implement it. This would be the best approach, but you still would have to implement `swim` method twice, so code reusability would be affected. What about a triathlete? They are athletes who swim, run, and ride. With multiple inheritances, you could have a sort of solution, but that will become complex and not maintainable very soon.

Objectives

As you have probably imagined already, the objective of the composition is to avoid this type of hierarchy hell where the complexity of an application could grow too much, and the clarity of the code is affected.

The swimmer and the fish

We will solve the described problem of the athlete and the fish that swims in a very idiomatic Go way. With Go, we can use two types of composition–the **direct** composition and the **embedding** composition. We will first solve this problem by using direct composition which is having everything that is needed as fields within the struct.

Requirements and acceptance criteria

Requirements are like the ones described previously. We'll have an athlete and a swimmer. We will also have an animal and a fish. The `Swimmer` and the `Fish` methods must share the code. The athlete must train, and the animal must eat:

- We must have an `Athlete` struct with a `Train` method
- We must have a `Swimmer` with a `Swim` method
- We must have an `Animal` struct with an `Eat` method
- We must have a `Fish` struct with a `Swim` method that is shared with the `Swimmer`, and not have inheritance or hierarchy issues

Creating compositions

The Composite design pattern is a pure structural pattern, and it doesn't have much to test apart from the structure itself. We won't write unit tests in this case, and we'll simply describe the ways to create those compositions in Go.

First, we'll start with the `Athlete` structure and its `Train` method:

```
type Athlete struct{}

func (a *Athlete) Train() {
  fmt.Println("Training")
}
```

The preceding code is pretty straightforward. Its `Train` method prints the word `Training` and a new line. We'll create a composite swimmer that has an `Athlete` struct inside it:

```
type CompositeSwimmerA struct{
  MyAthlete Athlete
  MySwim func()
}
```

The `CompositeSwimmerA` type has a `MyAthlete` field of type `Athlete`. It also stores a `func()` type. Remember that in Go, functions are first-class citizens and they can be used as parameters, fields, or arguments just like any variable. So `CompositeSwimmerA` has a `MySwim` field that stores a **closure**, which takes no arguments and returns nothing. How can I assign a function to it? Well, let's create a function that matches the `func()` signature (no arguments, no return):

```
func Swim(){
    fmt.Println("Swimming!")
}
```

That's all! The `Swim()` function takes no arguments and returns nothing, so it can be used as the `MySwim` field in the `CompositeSwimmerA` struct:

```
swimmer := CompositeSwimmerA{
    MySwim: Swim,
}

swimmer.MyAthlete.Train()
swimmer.MySwim()
```

Because we have a function called `Swim()`, we can assign it to the `MySwim` field. Note that the `Swim` type doesn't have the parenthesis that will execute its contents. This way we take the entire function and copy it to `MySwim` method.

But wait. We haven't passed any athlete to the `MyAthlete` field and we are using it! It's going to fail! Let's see what happens when we execute this snippet:

```
$ go run main.go
Training
Swimming!
```

That's weird, isn't it? Not really because of the nature of zero-initialization in Go. If you don't pass an `Athlete` struct to the `CompositeSwimmerA` type, the compiler will create one with its values zero-initialized, that is, an `Athlete` struct with its fields initialized to zero. Check out `Chapter 1`, *Ready... Steady... Go!* to recall zero-initialization if this seems confusing. Consider the `CompositeSwimmerA` struct code again:

```
type CompositeSwimmerA struct{
    MyAthlete Athlete
    MySwim    func()
}
```

Now we have a pointer to a function stored in the `MySwim` field. We can assign the `Swim` function the same way, but with an extra step:

```
localSwim := Swim

swimmer := CompositeSwimmerA{
    MySwim: localSwim,
}

swimmer.MyAthlete.Train()
swimmer.MySwim ()
```

First, we need a variable that contains the function `Swim`. This is because a function doesn't have an address to pass it to the `CompositeSwimmerA` type. Then, to use this function within the struct, we have to make a two-step call.

What about our fish problem? With our `Swim` function, it is not a problem anymore. First, we create the `Animal` struct:

```
type Animal struct{}

func (r *Animal)Eat() {
    println("Eating")
}
```

Then we'll create a `Shark` object that embeds the `Animal` object:

```
type Shark struct{
    Animal
    Swim func()
}
```

Wait a second! Where is the field name of the `Animal` type? Did you realize that I used the word *embed* in the previous paragraph? This is because, in Go, you can also embed objects within objects to make it look a lot like inheritance. That is, we won't have to explicitly call the field name to have access to its fields and method because they'll be part of us. So the following code will be perfectly okay:

```
fish := Shark{
    Swim: Swim,
}

fish.Eat()
fish.Swim()
```

Now we have an `Animal` type, which is zero-initialized and embedded. This is why I can call the `Eat` method of the `Animal` struct without creating it or using the intermediate field name. The output of this snippet is the following:

```
$ go run main.go
Eating
Swimming!
```

Finally, there is a third method to use the Composite pattern. We could create a `Swimmer` interface with a `Swim` method and a `SwimmerImpl` type to embed it in the athlete swimmer:

```
type Swimmer interface {
  Swim()
}
type Trainer interface {
  Train()
}

type SwimmerImpl struct{}
func (s *SwimmerImpl) Swim(){
  println("Swimming!")
}

type CompositeSwimmerB struct{
  Trainer
  Swimmer
}
```

With this method, you have more explicit control over object creation. The `Swimmer` field is embedded, but won't be zero-initialized as it is a pointer to an interface. The correct use of this approach will be the following:

```
swimmer := CompositeSwimmerB{
  &Athlete{},
  &SwimmerImpl{},
}

swimmer.Train()
swimmer.Swim()
```

And the output for `CompositeSwimmerB` is the following, as expected:

```
$ go run main.go
Training
Swimming!
```

Which approach is better? Well, I have a personal preference, which shouldn't be considered the rule of thumb. In my opinion, the *interfaces* approach is the best for quite a few reasons, but mainly for explicitness. First of all, you are working with interfaces which are preferred instead of structs. Second, you aren't leaving parts of your code to the zero-initialization feature of the compiler. It's a really powerful feature, but one that must be used with care, because it can lead to runtime problems which you'll find at compile time when working with interfaces. In different situations, zero-initialization will save you at runtime, in fact! But I prefer to work with interfaces as much as possible, so this is not actually one of the options.

Binary Tree compositions

Another very common approach to the Composite pattern is when working with Binary Tree structures. In a Binary Tree, you need to store instances of itself in a field:

```
type Tree struct {
   LeafValue int
   Right     *Tree
   Left      *Tree
}
```

This is some kind of recursive compositing, and, because of the nature of recursivity, we must use pointers so that the compiler knows how much memory it must reserve for this struct. Our `Tree` struct stored a `LeafValue` object for each instance and a new `Tree` in its `Right` and `Left` fields.

With this structure, we could create an object like this:

```
root := Tree{
   LeafValue: 0,
   Right:&Tree{
     LeafValue: 5,
     Right: &1Tree{ 6, nil, nil },
     Left: nil,
   },
   Left:&Tree{ 4, nil, nil },
}
```

We can print the contents of its deepest branch like this:

```
fmt.Println(root.Right.Right.LeafValue)

$ go run main.go
6
```

Composite pattern versus inheritance

When using the Composite design pattern in Go, you must be very careful not to confuse it with inheritance. For example, when you embed a `Parent` struct within a `Son` struct, like in the following example:

```
type Parent struct {
  SomeField int
}

type Son struct {
  Parent
}
```

You cannot consider that the `Son` struct is also the `Parent` struct. What this means is that you cannot pass an instance of the `Son` struct to a function that is expecting a `Parent` struct like the following:

```
func GetParentField(p *Parent) int{
  fmt.Println(p.SomeField)
}
```

When you try to pass a `Son` instance to the `GetParentField` method, you will get the following error message:

```
cannot use son (type Son) as type Parent in argument to GetParentField
```

This, in fact, makes a lot of sense. What's the solution for this? Well, you can simply composite the `Son` struct with the parent without embedding so that you can access the `Parent` instance later:

```
type Son struct {
  P Parent
}
```

So now you could use the `P` field to pass it to the `GetParentField` method:

```
son := Son{}
GetParentField(son.P)
```

Final words on the Composite pattern

At this point, you should be really comfortable using the Composite design pattern. It's a very idiomatic Go feature, and the switch from a pure object-oriented language is not very painful. The Composite design pattern makes our structures predictable but also allows us to create most of the design patterns as we will see in later chapters.

Adapter design pattern

One of the most commonly used structural patterns is the **Adapter** pattern. Like in real life, where you have plug adapters and bolt adapters, in Go, an adapter will allow us to use something that wasn't built for a specific task at the beginning.

Description

The Adapter pattern is very useful when, for example, an interface gets outdated and it's not possible to replace it easily or fast. Instead, you create a new interface to deal with the current needs of your application, which, under the hood, uses implementations of the old interface.

Adapter also helps us to maintain the *open/closed principle* in our apps, making them more predictable too. They also allow us to write code which uses some base that we can't modify.

 The open/closed principle was first stated by Bertrand Meyer in his book *Object-Oriented Software Construction*. He stated that code should be open to new functionality, but closed to modifications. What does it mean? Well, it implies a few things. On one hand, we should try to write code that is extensible and not only one that works. At the same time, we should try not to modify the source code (yours or other people's) as much as we can, because we aren't always aware of the implications of this modification. Just keep in mind that extensibility in code is only possible through the use of design patterns and interface-oriented programming.

Objectives

The Adapter design pattern will help you fit the needs of two parts of the code that are incompatible at first. This is the key to being kept in mind when deciding if the Adapter pattern is a good design for your problem–two interfaces that are incompatible, but which must work together, are good candidates for an Adapter pattern (but they could also use the facade pattern, for example).

Using an incompatible interface with an Adapter object

For our example, we will have an old `Printer` interface and a new one. Users of the new interface don't expect the signature that the old one has, and we need an Adapter so that users can still use old implementations if necessary (to work with some legacy code, for example).

Requirements and acceptance criteria

Having an old interface called `LegacyPrinter` and a new one called `ModernPrinter`, create a structure that implements the `ModernPrinter` interface and can use the `LegacyPrinter` interface as described in the following steps:

1. Create an Adapter object that implements the `ModernPrinter` interface.
2. The new Adapter object must contain an instance of the `LegacyPrinter` interface.
3. When using `ModernPrinter`, it must call the `LegacyPrinter` interface under the hood, prefixing it with the text `Adapter`.

Unit testing our Printer adapter

We will write the legacy code first, but we won't test it as we should imagine that it isn't our code:

```
type LegacyPrinter interface {
  Print(s string) string
}
type MyLegacyPrinter struct {}
```

```
func (l *MyLegacyPrinter) Print(s string) (newMsg string) {
  newMsg = fmt.Sprintf("Legacy Printer: %s\n", s)
  println(newMsg)
  return
}
```

The legacy interface called `LegacyPrinter` has a `Print` method that accepts a string and returns a message. Our `MyLegacyPrinter` struct implements the `LegacyPrinter` interface and modifies the passed string by prefixing the text `Legacy Printer:`. After modifying the text, the `MyLegacyPrinter` struct prints the text on the console, and then returns it.

Now we'll declare the new interface that we'll have to adapt:

```
type ModernPrinter interface {
  PrintStored() string
}
```

In this case, the new `PrintStored` method doesn't accept any string as an argument, because it will have to be stored in the implementers in advance. We will call our Adapter pattern's `PrinterAdapter` interface:

```
type PrinterAdapter struct{
  OldPrinter LegacyPrinter
  Msg        string
}
func(p *PrinterAdapter) PrintStored() (newMsg string) {
  return
}
```

As mentioned earlier, the `PrinterAdapter` adapter must have a field to store the string to print. It must also have a field to store an instance of the `LegacyPrinter` adapter. So let's write the unit tests:

```
func TestAdapter(t *testing.T){
  msg := "Hello World!"
```

We will use the message `Hello World!` for our adapter. When using this message with an instance of the `MyLegacyPrinter` struct, it prints the text `Legacy Printer: Hello World!`:

```
adapter := PrinterAdapter{OldPrinter: &MyLegacyPrinter{}, Msg: msg}
```

We created an instance of the `PrinterAdapter` interface called `adapter`. We passed an instance of the `MyLegacyPrinter` struct as the `LegacyPrinter` field called `OldPrinter`. Also, we set the message we want to print in the `Msg` field:

---

[103]

```
returnedMsg := adapter.PrintStored()

if returnedMsg != "Legacy Printer: Adapter: Hello World!\n" {
  t.Errorf("Message didn't match: %s\n", returnedMsg)
}
```

Then we used the `PrintStored` method of the `ModernPrinter` interface; this method doesn't accept any argument and must return the modified string. We know that the `MyLegacyPrinter` struct returns the passed string prefixed with the text `LegacyPrinter:`, and the adapter will prefix it with the text `Adapter:` So, in the end, we must have the text `Legacy Printer: Adapter: Hello World!\n`.

As we are storing an instance of an interface, we must also check that we handle the situation where the pointer is nil. This is done with the following test:

```
adapter = PrinterAdapter{OldPrinter: nil, Msg: msg}
returnedMsg = adapter.PrintStored()

if returnedMsg != "Hello World!" {
  t.Errorf("Message didn't match: %s\n", returnedMsg)
}
```

If we don't pass an instance of the `LegacyPrinter` interface, the Adapter must ignore its adapt nature, and simply print and return the original message. Time to run our tests; consider the following:

```
$ go test -v .
=== RUN   TestAdapter
--- FAIL: TestAdapter (0.00s)
        adapter_test.go:11: Message didn't match:
        adapter_test.go:17: Message didn't match:
FAIL
exit status 1
FAIL
```

Implementation

To make our single test pass, we must reuse the old `MyLegacyPrinter` that is stored in `PrinterAdapter` struct:

```
type PrinterAdapter struct{
  OldPrinter LegacyPrinter
  Msg        string
}
```

```
func(p *PrinterAdapter) PrintStored() (newMsg string) {
  if p.OldPrinter != nil {
    newMsg = fmt.Sprintf("Adapter: %s", p.Msg)
    newMsg = p.OldPrinter.Print(newMsg)
  }
  else {
    newMsg = p.Msg
  }
return
}
```

In the `PrintStored` method, we check whether we actually have an instance of a `LegacyPrinter`. In this case, we compose a new string with the stored message and the `Adapter` prefix to store it in the returning variable (called `newMsg`). Then we use the pointer to the `MyLegacyPrinter` struct to print the composed message using the `LegacyPrinter` interface.

In case there is no `LegacyPrinter` instance stored in the `OldPrinter` field, we simply assign the stored message to the returning variable `newMsg` and return the method. This should be enough to pass our tests:

```
$ go test -v .
=== RUN   TestAdapter
Legacy Printer: Adapter: Hello World!
--- PASS: TestAdapter (0.00s)
PASS
ok
```

Perfect! Now we can still use the old `LegacyPrinter` interface by using this `Adapter` while we use the `ModernPrinter` interface for future implementations. Just keep in mind that the Adapter pattern must ideally just provide the way to use the old `LegacyPrinter` and nothing else. This way, its scope will be more encapsulated and more maintainable in the future.

Examples of the Adapter pattern in Go's source code

You can find Adapter implementations at many places in the Go language's source code. The famous `http.Handler` interface has a very interesting adapter implementation. A very simple, `Hello World` server in Go is usually done like this:

```
package main
```

```
import (
    "fmt"
    "log"
    "net/http"
)
type MyServer struct{
  Msg string
}
func (m *MyServer) ServeHTTP(w http.ResponseWriter,r *http.Request){
    fmt.Fprintf(w, "Hello, World")
}

func main() {
    server := &MyServer{
    Msg:"Hello, World",
}

http.Handle("/", server)
log.Fatal(http.ListenAndServe(":8080", nil))
}
```

The HTTP package has a function called `Handle` (like a `static` method in Java) that accepts two parameters–a string to represent the route and a `Handler` interface. The `Handler` interface is like the following:

```
type Handler interface {
    ServeHTTP(ResponseWriter, *Request)
}
```

We need to implement a `ServeHTTP` method that the server side of an HTTP connection will use to execute its context. But there is also a function `HandlerFunc` that allows you to define some endpoint behavior:

```
func main() {
    http.HandleFunc("/", func(w http.ResponseWriter, r *http.Request) {
        fmt.Fprintf(w, "Hello, World")
    })

    log.Fatal(http.ListenAndServe(":8080", nil))
}
```

The `HandleFunc` function is actually part of an adapter for using functions directly as `ServeHTTP` implementations. Read the last sentence slowly again–can you guess how it is done?

```
type HandlerFunc func(ResponseWriter, *Request)
```

```
func (f HandlerFunc) ServeHTTP(w ResponseWriter, r *Request) {
  f(w, r)
}
```

We can define a type that is a function in the same way that we define a struct. We make this function-type to implement the ServeHTTP method. Finally, from the ServeHTTP function, we call the receiver itself f(w, r).

You have to think about the implicit interface implementation of Go. When we define a function like func(ResponseWriter, *Request), it is implicitly being recognized as HandlerFunc. And because the HandleFunc function implements the Handler interface, our function implements the Handler interface implicitly too. Does this sound familiar to you? If *A* = *B* and *B* = *C*, then *A* = *C*. Implicit implementation gives a lot of flexibility and power to Go, but you must also be careful, because you don't know if a method or function could be implementing some interface that could provoke undesirable behaviors.

We can find more examples in Go's source code. The io package has another powerful example with the use of pipes. A pipe in Linux is a flow mechanism that takes something on the input and outputs something else on the output. The io package has two interfaces, which are used everywhere in Go's source code–the io.Reader and the io.Writer interface:

```
type Reader interface {
  Read(p []byte) (n int, err error)
}

type Writer interface {
  Write(p []byte) (n int, err error)
}
```

We use io.Reader everywhere, for example, when you open a file using os.OpenFile, it returns a file, which, in fact, implements the io.Reader interface. Why is it useful? Imagine that you write a Counter struct that counts from the number you provide to zero:

```
type Counter struct {}
func (f *Counter) Count(n uint64) uint64 {
  if n == 0 {
    println(strconv.Itoa(0))
    return 0
  }

  cur := n
  println(strconv.FormatUint(cur, 10))
  return f.Count(n - 1)
}
```

If you provide the number 3 to this small snippet, it will print the following:

```
3
2
1
```

Well, not really impressive! What if I want to write to a file instead of printing? We can implement this method too. What if I want to print to a file and to the console? Well, we can implement this method too. We must modularize it a bit more by using the io.Writer interface:

```
type Counter struct {
  Writer io.Writer
}
func (f *Counter) Count(n uint64) uint64 {
  if n == 0 {
    f.Writer.Write([]byte(strconv.Itoa(0) + "\n"))
    return 0
  }

  cur := n
  f.Writer.Write([]byte(strconv.FormatUint(cur, 10) + "\n"))
  return f.Count(n - 1)
}
```

Now we provide an io.Writer in the Writer field. This way, we could create the counter like this: c := Counter{os.Stdout}, and we will get a console Writer. But wait a second, we haven't solved the issue where we wanted to take the count to many Writer consoles. But we can write a new Adapter with an io.Writer and, using a Pipe() to connect a reader with a writer, we can read on the opposite extreme. This way, you can solve the issue where these two interfaces, Reader and Writer, which are incompatible, can be used together.

In fact, we don't need to write the Adapter–the Go's io library has one for us in io.Pipe(). The pipe will allow us to convert a Reader to a Writer interface. The io.Pipe() method will provide us a Writer (the entrance of the pipe) and a Reader (the exit) to play with. So let's create a pipe, and assign the provided writer to the Counter of the preceding example:

```
pipeReader, pipeWriter := io.Pipe()
defer pw.Close()
defer pr.Close()

counter := Counter{
  Writer: pipeWriter,
}
```

Now we have a `Reader` interface where we previously had a `Writer`. Where can we use the `Reader`? The `io.TeeReader` function helps us to copy the stream of data from a `Reader` interface to the `Writer` interface and, it returns a new `Reader` that you can still use to stream data again to a second writer. So we will stream the data from the same reader to two writers—the `file` and the `Stdout`.

```
tee := io.TeeReader(pipeReader, file)
```

So now we know that we are writing to a file that we have passed to the `TeeReader` function. We still need to print to the console. The `io.Copy` adapter can be used like `TeeReader`—it takes a reader and writes its contents to a writer:

```
go func(){
    io.Copy(os.Stdout, tee)
}()
```

We have to launch the `Copy` function in a different Go routine so that the writes are performed concurrently, and one read/write doesn't block a different read/write. Let's modify the `counter` variable to make it count till 5 again:

```
counter.Count(5)
```

With this modification to the code, we get the following output:

```
$ go run counter.go
5
4
3
2
1
0
```

Okay, the count has been printed on the console. What about the file?

```
$ cat /tmp/pipe
5
4
3
2
1
0
```

Awesome! By using the `io.Pipe()` adapter provided in the Go native library, we have uncoupled our counter from its output, and we have adapted a `Writer` interface to a `Reader` one.

What the Go source code tells us about the Adapter pattern

With the Adapter design pattern, you have learned a quick way to achieve the open/close principle in your applications. Instead of modifying your old source code (something which could not be possible in some situations), you have created a way to use the old functionality with a new signature.

Bridge design pattern

The **Bridge** pattern is a design with a slightly cryptic definition from the original *Gang of Four* book. It decouples an abstraction from its implementation so that the two can vary independently. This cryptic explanation just means that you could even decouple the most basic form of functionality: decouple an object from what it does.

Description

The Bridge pattern tries to decouple things as usual with design patterns. It decouples abstraction (an object) from its implementation (the thing that the object does). This way, we can change what an object does as much as we want. It also allows us to change the abstracted object while reusing the same implementation.

Objectives

The objective of the Bridge pattern is to bring flexibility to a struct that change often. Knowing the inputs and outputs of a method, it allows us to change code without knowing too much about it and leaving the freedom for both sides to be modified more easily.

Two printers and two ways of printing for each

For our example, we will go to a console printer abstraction to keep it simple. We will have two implementations. The first will write to the console. Having learned about the io.Writer interface in the previous section, we will make the second write to an io.Writer interface to provide more flexibility to the solution. We will also have two abstracted object users of the implementations–a Normal object, which will use each implementation in a straightforward manner, and a Packt implementation, which will append the sentence Message from Packt: to the printing message.

At the end of this section, we will have two abstraction objects, which have two different implementations of their functionality. So, actually, we will have 2^2 possible combinations of object functionality.

Requirements and acceptance criteria

As we mentioned previously, we will have two objects (Packt and Normal printer) and two implementations (PrinterImpl1 and PrinterImpl2) that we will join by using the Bridge design pattern. More or less, we will have the following requirements and acceptance criteria:

- A PrinterAPI that accepts a message to print
- An implementation of the API that simply prints the message to the console
- An implementation of the API that prints to an io.Writer interface
- A Printer abstraction with a Print method to implement in printing types
- A normal printer object, which will implement the Printer and the PrinterAPI interface
- The normal printer will forward the message directly to the implementation
- A Packt printer, which will implement the Printer abstraction and the PrinterAPI interface
- The Packt printer will append the message Message from Packt: to all prints

Unit testing the Bridge pattern

Let's start with *acceptance criteria 1*, the PrinterAPI interface. Implementers of this interface must provide a PrintMessage(string) method that will print the message passed as an argument:

```
type PrinterAPI interface {
  PrintMessage(string) error
}
```

We will pass to *acceptance criteria 2* with an implementation of the previous API:

```
type PrinterImpl1 struct{}

func (p *PrinterImpl1) PrintMessage(msg string) error {
  return errors.New("Not implemented yet")
}
```

Our `PrinterImpl1` is a type that implements the `PrinterAPI` interface by providing an implementation of the `PrintMessage` method. The `PrintMessage` method is not implemented yet, and returns an error. This is enough to write our first unit test to cover `PrinterImpl1`:

```
func TestPrintAPI1(t *testing.T){
  api1 := PrinterImpl1{}

  err := api1.PrintMessage("Hello")
  if err != nil {
    t.Errorf("Error trying to use the API1 implementation: Message: %s\n",
err.Error())
  }
}
```

In our test to cover `PrintAPI1`, we created an instance of `PrinterImpl1` type. Then we used its `PrintMessage` method to print the message `Hello` to the console. As we have no implementation yet, it must return the error srring `Not implemented yet`:

```
$ go test -v -run=TestPrintAPI1 .
=== RUN   TestPrintAPI1
--- FAIL: TestPrintAPI1 (0.00s)
        bridge_test.go:14: Error trying to use the API1 implementation:
Message: Not implemented yet
FAIL
exit status 1
FAIL    _/C_/Users/mario/Desktop/go-design-
patterns/structural/bridge/traditional
```

Okay. Now we have to write the second API test that will work with an `io.Writer` interface:

```
type PrinterImpl2 struct{
  Writer io.Writer
}
```

```
func (d *PrinterImpl2) PrintMessage(msg string) error {
  return errors.New("Not implemented yet")
}
```

As you can see, our `PrinterImpl2` struct stores an `io.Writer` implementer. Also, our `PrintMessage` method follows the `PrinterAPI` interface.

Now that we are familiar with the `io.Writer` interface, we are going to make a test object that implements this interface, and stores whatever is written to it in a local field. This will help us check the contents that are being sent through the writer:

```
type TestWriter struct {
  Msg string
}

func (t *TestWriter) Write(p []byte) (n int, err error) {
  n = len(p)
  if n > 0 {
    t.Msg = string(p)
    return n, nil
  }
  err = errors.New("Content received on Writer was empty")
  return
}
```

In our test object, we checked that the content isn't empty before writing it to the local field. If it's empty, we return the error, and if not, we write the contents of p in the `Msg` field. We will use this small struct in the following tests for the second API:

```
func TestPrintAPI2(t *testing.T){
  api2 := PrinterImpl2{}

  err := api2.PrintMessage("Hello")
  if err != nil {
    expectedErrorMessage := "You need to pass an io.Writer to PrinterImpl2"
    if !strings.Contains(err.Error(), expectedErrorMessage) {
      t.Errorf("Error message was not correct.\n
      Actual: %s\nExpected: %s\n", err.Error(), expectedErrorMessage)
    }
  }
```

Let's stop for a second here. We create an instance of `PrinterImpl2` called `api2` in the first line of the preceding code. We haven't passed any instance of `io.Writer` on purpose, so we also checked that we actually receive an error first. Then we try to use its `PrintMessage` method, but we must get an error because it doesn't have any `io.Writer` instance stored in the `Writer` field. The error must be `You need to pass an io.Writer to PrinterImpl2`, and we implicitly check the contents of the error. Let's continue with the test:

```
testWriter := TestWriter{}
api2 = PrinterImpl2{
  Writer: &testWriter,
}

expectedMessage := "Hello"
err = api2.PrintMessage(expectedMessage)
if err != nil {
  t.Errorf("Error trying to use the API2 implementation: %s\n",
err.Error())
}

if testWriter.Msg !=  expectedMessage {
  t.Fatalf("API2 did not write correctly on the io.Writer. \n  Actual:
%s\nExpected: %s\n", testWriter.Msg, expectedMessage)
  }
}
```

For the second part of this unit test, we use an instance of the `TestWriter` object as an `io.Writer` interface, `testWriter`. We passed the message `Hello` to `api2`, and checked whether we receive any error. Then, we check the contents of the `testWriter.Msg` field–remember that we have written an `io.Writer` interface that stored any bytes passed to its `Write` method in the `Msg` field. If everything is correct, the message should contain the word `Hello`.

Those were our tests for `PrinterImpl2`. As we don't have any implementations yet, we should get a few errors when running this test:

```
$ go test -v -run=TestPrintAPI2 .
=== RUN    TestPrintAPI2
--- FAIL: TestPrintAPI2 (0.00s)
bridge_test.go:39: Error message was not correct.
Actual: Not implemented yet
Expected: You need to pass an io.Writer to PrinterImpl2
bridge_test.go:52: Error trying to use the API2 implementation: Not
implemented yet
bridge_test.go:57: API2 did not write correctly on the io.Writer.
```

```
Actual:
Expected: Hello
FAIL
exit status 1
FAIL
```

At least one test passes–the one that checks that an error message (any) is being returned when using the `PrintMessage` without `io.Writer` being stored. Everything else fails, as expected at this stage.

Now we need a printer abstraction for objects that can use `PrinterAPI` implementers. We will define this as the `PrinterAbstraction` interface with a `Print` method. This covers the *acceptance criteria 4*:

```
type PrinterAbstraction interface {
    Print() error
}
```

For *acceptance criteria 5*, we need a normal printer. A `Printer` abstraction will need a field to store a `PrinterAPI`. So our the `NormalPrinter` could look like the following:

```
type NormalPrinter struct {
    Msg      string
    Printer PrinterAPI
}

func (c *NormalPrinter) Print() error {
    return errors.New("Not implemented yet")
}
```

This is enough to write a unit test for the `Print()` method:

```
func TestNormalPrinter_Print(t *testing.T) {
    expectedMessage := "Hello io.Writer"

    normal := NormalPrinter{
        Msg:expectedMessage,
        Printer: &PrinterImpl1{},
    }

    err := normal.Print()
    if err != nil {
        t.Errorf(err.Error())
    }
}
```

The first part of the test checks that the `Print()` method isn't implemented yet when using `PrinterImpl1 PrinterAPI` interface. The message we'll use along this test is `Hello io.Writer`. With the `PrinterImpl1`, we don't have an easy way to check the contents of the message, as we print directly to the console. Checking, in this case, is visual, so we can check *acceptance criteria 6:*

```
testWriter := TestWriter{}
normal = NormalPrinter{
  Msg: expectedMessage,
  Printer: &PrinterImpl2{
    Writer:&testWriter,
  },
}

err = normal.Print()
if err != nil {
  t.Error(err.Error())
}

if testWriter.Msg != expectedMessage {
  t.Errorf("The expected message on the io.Writer doesn't match actual.\n
Actual: %s\nExpected: %s\n", testWriter.Msg, expectedMessage)
  }
}
```

The second part of `NormalPrinter` tests uses `PrinterImpl2`, the one that needs an `io.Writer` interface implementer. We reuse our `TestWriter` struct here to check the contents of the message. So, in short, we want a `NormalPrinter` struct that accepts a `Msg` of type string and a Printer of type `PrinterAPI`. At this point, if I use the `Print` method, I shouldn't get any error, and the `Msg` field on `TestWriter` must contain the message we passed to `NormalPrinter` on its initialization.

Let's run the tests:

```
$ go test -v -run=TestNormalPrinter_Print .
=== RUN    TestNormalPrinter_Print
--- FAIL: TestNormalPrinter_Print (0.00s)
        bridge_test.go:72: Not implemented yet
        bridge_test.go:85: Not implemented yet
        bridge_test.go:89: The expected message on the io.Writer doesn't
match actual.
                Actual:
                Expected: Hello io.Writer
FAIL
exit status 1
FAIL
```

There is a trick to quickly check the validity of a unit test–the number of times we called `t.Error` or `t.Errorf` must match the number of messages of error on the console and the lines where they were produced. In the preceding test results, there are three errors at *lines 72, 85,* and *89,* which exactly match the checks we wrote.

Our `PacktPrinter` struct will have a very similar definition to `NormalPrinter` at this point:

```
type PacktPrinter struct {
   Msg      string
   Printer PrinterAPI
}

func (c *PacktPrinter) Print() error {
   return errors.New("Not implemented yet")
}
```

This covers *acceptance criteria 7.* And we can almost copy and paste the contents of the previous test with a few changes:

```
func TestPacktPrinter_Print(t *testing.T) {
   passedMessage := "Hello io.Writer"
   expectedMessage := "Message from Packt: Hello io.Writer"

   packt := PacktPrinter{
     Msg:passedMessage,
     Printer: &PrinterImpl1{},
   }

   err := packt.Print()
   if err != nil {
     t.Errorf(err.Error())
   }

   testWriter := TestWriter{}
   packt = PacktPrinter{
     Msg: passedMessage,
     Printer:&PrinterImpl2{
       Writer:&testWriter,
     },
   }

   err = packt.Print()
   if err != nil {
     t.Error(err.Error())
   }
```

```
    if testWriter.Msg != expectedMessage {
       t.Errorf("The expected message on the io.Writer doesn't match actual.\n
Actual: %s\nExpected: %s\n", testWriter.Msg,expectedMessage)
    }
}
```

What have we changed here? Now we have `passedMessage`, which represents the message we are passing to `PackPrinter`. We also have an expected message that contains the prefixed message from `Packt`. If you remember *acceptance criteria 8*, this abstraction must prefix the text `Message from Packt:` to any message that is passed to it, and, at the same time, it must be able to use any implementation of a `PrinterAPI` interface.

The second change is that we actually create `PacktPrinter` structs instead of the `NormalPrinter` structs; everything else is the same:

```
$ go test -v -run=TestPacktPrinter_Print .
=== RUN   TestPacktPrinter_Print
--- FAIL: TestPacktPrinter_Print (0.00s)
        bridge_test.go:104: Not implemented yet
        bridge_test.go:117: Not implemented yet
        bridge_test.go:121: The expected message on the io.Writer doesn't
match actual.
        Actual:
        Expected: Message from Packt: Hello io.Writer
FAIL
exit status 1
FAIL
```

Three checks, three errors. All tests have been covered, and we can finally move on to the implementation.

Implementation

We will start implementing in the same order that we created our tests, first with the `PrinterImpl1` definition:

```
type PrinterImpl1 struct{}
func (d *PrinterImpl1) PrintMessage(msg string) error {
  fmt.Printf("%s\n", msg)
  return nil
}
```

Our first API takes the message `msg` and prints it to the console. In the case of an empty string, nothing will be printed. This is enough to pass the first test:

```
$ go test -v -run=TestPrintAPI1 .
=== RUN   TestPrintAPI1
Hello
--- PASS: TestPrintAPI1 (0.00s)
PASS
ok
```

You can see the `Hello` message in the second line of the output of the test, just after the `RUN` message.

The `PrinterImpl2` struct isn't very complex either. The difference is that instead of printing to the console, we are going to write on an `io.Writer` interface, which must be stored in the struct:

```go
type PrinterImpl2 struct {
  Writer io.Writer
}

func (d *PrinterImpl2) PrintMessage(msg string) error {
  if d.Writer == nil {
    return errors.New("You need to pass an io.Writer to PrinterImpl2")
  }

  fmt.Fprintf(d.Writer, "%s", msg)
  return nil
}
```

As defined in our tests, we checked the contents of the `Writer` field first and returned the expected error message **You need to pass an io.Writer to PrinterImpl2**, if nothing is stored. This is the message we'll check later in the test. Then, the `fmt.Fprintf` method takes an `io.Writer` interface as the first field and a message formatted as the rest, so we simply forward the contents of the `msg` argument to the `io.Writer` provided:

```
$ go test -v -run=TestPrintAPI2 .
=== RUN   TestPrintAPI2
--- PASS: TestPrintAPI2 (0.00s)
PASS
ok
```

Now we'll continue with the normal printer. This printer must simply forward the message to the `PrinterAPI` interface stored without any modification. In our test, we are using two implementations of `PrinterAPI`—one that prints to the console and one that writes to an `io.Writer` interface:

```go
type NormalPrinter struct {
  Msg     string
```

```
    Printer PrinterAPI
}

func (c *NormalPrinter) Print() error {
  c.Printer.PrintMessage(c.Msg)
  return nil
}
```

We returned nil as no error has occurred. This should be enough to pass the unit tests:

```
$ go test -v -run=TestNormalPrinter_Print .
=== RUN   TestNormalPrinter_Print
Hello io.Writer
--- PASS: TestNormalPrinter_Print (0.00s)
PASS
ok
```

In the preceding output, you can see the Hello io.Writer message that the PrinterImpl1 struct writes to stdout. We can consider this check as having passed:

Finally, the PackPrinter method is similar to NormalPrinter, but just prefixes every message with the text Message from Packt::

```
type PacktPrinter struct {
  Msg     string
  Printer PrinterAPI
}

func (c *PacktPrinter) Print() error {
  c.Printer.PrintMessage(fmt.Sprintf("Message from Packt: %s", c.Msg))
  return nil
}
```

Like in the NormalPrinter method, we accepted a Msg string and a PrinterAPI implementation in the Printer field. Then we used the fmt.Sprintf method to compose a new string with the text Message from Packt: and the provided message. We took the composed text and passed it to the PrintMessage method of PrinterAPI stored in the Printer field of the PacktPrinter struct:

```
$ go test -v -run=TestPacktPrinter_Print .
=== RUN   TestPacktPrinter_Print
Message from Packt: Hello io.Writer
--- PASS: TestPacktPrinter_Print (0.00s)
PASS
ok
```

Again, you can see the results of using `PrinterImpl1` for writing to `stdout` with the text `Message from Packt: Hello io.Writer`. This last test should cover all of our code in the Bridge pattern. As you have seen previously, you can check the coverage by using the `–cover` flag:

```
$ go test -cover .
ok
2.622s  coverage: 100.0% of statements
```

Wow! 100% coverage–this looks good. However, this doesn't mean that the code is perfect. We haven't checked that the contents of the messages weren't empty, maybe something that should be avoided, but it isn't a part of our requirements, which is also an important point. Just because some feature isn't in the requirements or the acceptance criteria doesn't mean that it shouldn't be covered.

Reuse everything with the Bridge pattern

With the Bridge pattern, we have learned how to uncouple an object and its implementation for the `PrintMessage` method. This way, we can reuse its abstractions as well as its implementations. We can swap the printer abstractions as well as the printer APIs as much as we want without affecting the user code.

We have also tried to keep things as simple as possible, but I'm sure that you have realized that all implementations of the `PrinterAPI` interface could have been created using a factory. This would be very natural, and you could find many implementations that have followed this approach. However, we shouldn't get into over-engineering, but should analyze each problem to make a precise design of its needs and finds the best way to create a reusable, maintainable, and *readable* source code. Readable code is commonly forgotten, but a robust and uncoupled source code is useless if nobody can understand it to maintain it. It's like a book of the tenth century–it could be a precious story but pretty frustrating if we have difficulty understanding its grammar.

Summary

We have seen the power of composition in this chapter and many of the ways that Go takes advantage of it by its own nature. We have seen that the Adapter pattern can help us make two incompatible interfaces work together by using an `Adapter` object in between. At the same time, we have seen some real-life examples in Go's source code, where the creators of the language used this design pattern to improve the possibilities of some particular piece of the standard library. Finally, we have seen the Bridge pattern and its possibilities, allowing us to create swapping structures with complete reusability between objects and their implementations.

Also, we have used the Composite design pattern throughout the chapter, not only when explaining it. We have mentioned it earlier but design patterns make use of each other very frequently. We have used pure composition instead of embedding to increase readability, but, as you have learned, you can use both interchangeably according to your needs. We will keep using the Composite pattern in the following chapters, as it is the foundation for building relationships in the Go programming language.

4

Structural Patterns - Proxy, Facade, Decorator, and Flyweight Design Patterns

With this chapter, we will finish with the Structural patterns. We have left some of the most complex ones till the end so that you get more used to the mechanics of design patterns, and the features of Go language.

In this chapter, we will work at writing a cache to access a database, a library to gather weather data, a server with runtime middleware, and discuss a way to save memory by saving shareable states between the types values.

Proxy design pattern

We'll start the final chapter on structural patterns with the Proxy pattern. It's a simple pattern that provides interesting features and possibilities with very little effort.

Description

The Proxy pattern usually wraps an object to hide some of its characteristics. These characteristics could be the fact that it is a remote object (remote proxy), a very heavy object such as a very big image or the dump of a terabyte database (virtual proxy), or a restricted access object (protection proxy).

Objectives

The possibilities of the Proxy pattern are many, but in general, they all try to provide the same following functionalities:

- Hide an object behind the proxy so the features can be hidden, restricted, and so on
- Provide a new abstraction layer that is easy to work with, and can be changed easily

Example

For our example, we are going to create a remote proxy, which is going to be a cache of objects before accessing a database. Let's imagine that we have a database with many users, but instead of accessing the database each time we want information about a user, we will have a **First In First Out** (**FIFO**) stack of users in a Proxy pattern (FIFO is a way of saying that when the cache needs to be emptied, it will delete the first object that entered first).

Acceptance criteria

We will wrap an imaginary database, represented by a slice, with our Proxy pattern. Then, the pattern will have to stick to the following acceptance criteria:

1. All accesse to the database of users will be done through the Proxy type.
2. A stack of n number of recent users will be kept in the Proxy.
3. If a user already exists in the stack, it won't query the database, and will return the stored one
4. If the queried user doesn't exist in the stack, it will query the database, remove the oldest user in the stack if it's full, store the new one, and return it.

Unit test

Since version 1.7 of Go, we can embed tests within tests by using closures so we can group them in a more human-readable way, and reduce the number of Test_ functions. Refer to Chapter 1, *Ready... Steady... Go!* to learn how to install the new version of Go if your current version is older than version 1.7.

The types for this pattern will be the proxy user and user list structs as well as a `UserFinder` interface that the database and the Proxy will implement. This is key because the Proxy must implement the same interfaces as the features of the type it tries to wrap:

```
type UserFinder interface {
    FindUser(id int32) (User, error)
}
```

The `UserFinder` is the interface that the database and the Proxy implement. The `User` is a type with a member called `ID`, which is `int32` type:

```
type User struct {
    ID int32
}
```

Finally, the `UserList` is a type of a slice of users. Consider the following syntax for that:

```
type UserList []User
```

If you are asking why we aren't using a slice of users directly, the answer is that by declaring a sequence of users this way, we can implement the `UserFinder` interface but with a slice, we can't.

Finally, the Proxy type, called `UserListProxy` will be composed of a `UserList` slice, which will be our database representation. The `StackCache` members which will also be of `UserList` type for simplicity, `StackCapacity` to give our stack the size we want.

We will cheat a bit for the purpose of this tutorial and declare a Boolean state on a field called `DidDidLastSearchUsedCache` that will hold if the last performed search has used the cache, or has accessed the database:

```
type UserListProxy struct {
    SomeDatabase UserList
    StackCache UserList
    StackCapacity int
    DidDidLastSearchUsedCache bool
}

func (u *UserListProxy) FindUser(id int32) (User, error) {
    return User{}, errors.New("Not implemented yet")
}
```

The `UserListProxy` type will cache a maximum of `StackCapacity` users, and rotate the cache if it reaches this limit. The `StackCache` members will be populated from objects from `SomeDatabase` type.

The first test is called `TestUserListProxy`, and is listed next:

```
import (
   "math/rand"
   "testing"
)

func Test_UserListProxy(t *testing.T) {
  someDatabase := UserList{}

  rand.Seed(2342342)
  for i := 0; i < 1000000; i++ {
    n := rand.Int31()
    someDatabase = append(someDatabase, User{ID: n})
  }
```

The preceding test creates a user list of 1 million users with random names. To do so, we feed the random number generator by calling the `Seed()` function with some constant seed so our randomized results are also constant; and the user IDs are generated from it. It might have some duplicates, but it serves our purpose.

Next, we need a proxy with a reference to `someDatabase`, which we have just created:

```
proxy := UserListProxy{
   SomeDatabase:  &someDatabase,
   StackCapacity:  2,
   StackCache: UserList{},
}
```

At this point, we have a `proxy` object composed of a mock database with 1 million users, and a cache implemented as a FIFO stack with a size of 2. Now we will get three random IDs from `someDatabase` to use in our stack:

```
knownIDs := [3]int32 {someDatabase[3].ID,
someDatabase[4].ID,someDatabase[5].ID}
```

We took the fourth, fifth, and sixth IDs from the slice (remember that arrays and slices start with 0, so the index 3 is actually the fourth position in the slice).

This is going to be our starting point before launching the embedded tests. To create an embedded test, we have to call the `Run` method of the `testing.T` pointer, with a description and a closure with the `func(t *testing.T)` signature:

```
t.Run("FindUser - Empty cache", func(t *testing.T) {
  user, err := proxy.FindUser(knownIDs[0])
  if err != nil {
    t.Fatal(err)
```

```
    }
```

For example, in the preceding code snippet, we give the description `FindUser - Empty cache`. Then we define our closure. First it tries to find a user with a known ID, and checks for errors. As the description implies, the cache is empty at this point, and the user will have to be retrieved from the `someDatabase` array:

```
    if user.ID != knownIDs[0] {
        t.Error("Returned user name doesn't match with expected")
    }

    if len(proxy.StackCache) != 1 {
        t.Error("After one successful search in an empty cache, the size of it
    must be one")
    }

    if proxy.DidLastSearchUsedCache {
        t.Error("No user can be returned from an empty cache")
    }
}
```

Finally, we check whether the returned user has the same ID as that of the expected user at index 0 of the `knownIDs` slice, and that the proxy cache now has a size of 1. The state of the member `DidLastSearchUsedCache` proxy must not be `true`, or we will not pass the test. Remember, this member tells us whether the last search has been retrieved from the slice that represents a database, or from the cache.

The second embedded test for the Proxy pattern is to ask for the same user as before, which must now be returned from the cache. It's very similar to the previous test, but now we have to check if the user is returned from the cache:

```
t.Run("FindUser - One user, ask for the same user", func(t *testing.T) {
    user, err := proxy.FindUser(knownIDs[0])
    if err != nil {
        t.Fatal(err)
    }

    if user.ID != knownIDs[0] {
        t.Error("Returned user name doesn't match with expected")
    }

    if len(proxy.StackCache) != 1 {
        t.Error("Cache must not grow if we asked for an object that is stored
    on it")
    }

    if !proxy.DidLastSearchUsedCache {
```

```
      t.Error("The user should have been returned from the cache")
   }
})
```

So, again we ask for the first known ID. The proxy cache must maintain a size of 1 after this search, and the `DidLastSearchUsedCache` member must be true this time, or the test will fail.

The last test will overflow the `StackCache` array on the `proxy` type. We will search for two new users that our `proxy` type will have to retrieve from the database. Our stack has a size of 2, so it will have to remove the first user to allocate space for the second and third users:

```
user1, err := proxy.FindUser(knownIDs[0])
if err != nil {
  t.Fatal(err)
}

user2, _ := proxy.FindUser(knownIDs[1])
if proxy.DidLastSearchUsedCache {
  t.Error("The user wasn't stored on the proxy cache yet")
}

user3, _ := proxy.FindUser(knownIDs[2])
if proxy.DidLastSearchUsedCache {
  t.Error("The user wasn't stored on the proxy cache yet")
}
```

We have retrieved the first three users. We aren't checking for errors because that was the purpose of the previous tests. This is important to recall that there is no need to over-test your code. If there is any error here, it will arise in the previous tests. Also, we have checked that the `user2` and `user3` queries do not use the cache; they shouldn't be stored there yet.

Now we are going to look for the `user1` query in the Proxy. It shouldn't exist, as the stack has a size of 2, and `user1` was the first to enter, hence, the first to go out:

```
for i := 0; i < len(proxy.StackCache); i++ {
  if proxy.StackCache[i].ID == user1.ID {
    t.Error("User that should be gone was found")
  }
}

if len(proxy.StackCache) != 2 {
  t.Error("After inserting 3 users the cache should not grow" +
" more than to two")
}
```

It doesn't matter if we ask for a thousand users; our cache can't be bigger than our configured size.

Finally, we are going to again range over the users stored in the cache, and compare them with the last two we queried. This way, we will check that just those users are stored in the cache. Both must be found on it:

```
for _, v := range proxy.StackCache {
    if v != user2 && v != user3 {
        t.Error("A non expected user was found on the cache")
    }
}
}
```

Running the tests now should give some errors, as usual. Let's run them now:

```
$ go test -v .
=== RUN    Test_UserListProxy
=== RUN    Test_UserListProxy/FindUser_-_Empty_cache
=== RUN    Test_UserListProxy/FindUser_-_One_user,_ask_for_the_same_user
=== RUN    Test_UserListProxy/FindUser_-_overflowing_the_stack
--- FAIL: Test_UserListProxy (0.06s)
    --- FAIL: Test_UserListProxy/FindUser_-_Empty_cache (0.00s)
        proxy_test.go:28: Not implemented yet
    --- FAIL: Test_UserListProxy/FindUser_-
_One_user,_ask_for_the_same_user (0.00s)
        proxy_test.go:47: Not implemented yet
    --- FAIL: Test_UserListProxy/FindUser_-_overflowing_the_stack
(0.00s)
        proxy_test.go:66: Not implemented yet
FAIL
exit status 1
FAIL
```

So, let's implement the FindUser method to act as our Proxy.

Implementation

In our Proxy, the FindUser method will search for a specified ID in the cache list. If it finds it, it will return the ID. If not, it will search in the database. Finally, if it's not in the database list, it will return an error.

If you remember, our Proxy pattern is composed of two `UserList` types (one of them a pointer), which are actually slices of `User` type. We will implement a `FindUser` method in `User` type too, which, by the way, has the same signature as the `UserFinder` interface:

```
type UserList []User

func (t *UserList) FindUser(id int32) (User, error) {
   for i := 0; i < len(*t); i++ {
     if (*t)[i].ID == id {
       return (*t)[i], nil
     }
   }
   return User{}, fmt.Errorf("User %s could not be found\n", id)
}
```

The `FindUser` method in the `UserList` slice will iterate over the list to try and find a user with the same ID as the `id` argument, or return an error if it can't find it.

You may be wondering why the pointer `t` is between parentheses. This is to dereference the underlying array before accessing its indexes. Without it, you'll have a compilation error, because the compiler tries to search the index before dereferencing the pointer.

So, the first part of the proxy `FindUser` method can be written as follows:

```
func (u *UserListProxy) FindUser(id int32) (User, error) {
   user, err := u.StackCache.FindUser(id)
   if err == nil {
     fmt.Println("Returning user from cache")
     u.DidLastSearchUsedCache = true
     return user, nil
   }
}
```

We use the preceding method to search for a user in the `StackCache` member. The error will be nil if it can find it, so we check this to print a message to the console, change the state of `DidLastSearchUsedCache` to `true` so that the test can check whether the user was retrieved from cache, and finally, return the user.

So, if the error was not nil, it means that it couldn't find the user in the stack. So, the next step is to search in the database:

```
user, err = u.SomeDatabase.FindUser(id)
if err != nil {
   return User{}, err
}
```

We can reuse the `FindUser` method we wrote for `UserList` database in this case, because both have the same type for the purpose of this example. Again, it searches the user in the database represented by the `UserList` slice, but in this case, if the user isn't found, it returns the error generated in `UserList`.

When the user is found (`err` is nil), we have to add the user to the stack. For this purpose, we write a dedicated private method that receives a pointer of type `UserListProxy`:

```
func (u *UserListProxy) addUserToStack(user User) {
  if len(u.StackCache) >= u.StackCapacity {
    u.StackCache = append(u.StackCache[1:], user)
  }
  else {
    u.StackCache.addUser(user)
  }
}

func (t *UserList) addUser(newUser User) {
  *t = append(*t, newUser)
}
```

The `addUserToStack` method takes the user argument, and adds it to the stack in place. If the stack is full, it removes the first element in it before adding. We have also written an `addUser` method to `UserList` to help us in this. So, now in `FindUser` method, we just have to add one line:

```
u.addUserToStack(user)
```

This adds the new user to the stack, removing the last if necessary.

Finally, we just have to return the new user of the stack, and set the appropriate value on `DidLastSearchUsedCache` variable. We also write a message to the console to help in the testing process:

```
    fmt.Println("Returning user from database")
    u.DidLastSearchUsedCache = false
    return user, nil
}
```

With this, we have enough to pass our tests:

```
    $ go test -v .
    === RUN   Test_UserListProxy
    === RUN   Test_UserListProxy/FindUser_-_Empty_cache
    Returning user from database
    === RUN   Test_UserListProxy/FindUser_-_One_user,_ask_for_the_same_user
    Returning user from cache
```

```
=== RUN    Test_UserListProxy/FindUser_-_overflowing_the_stack
Returning user from cache
Returning user from database
Returning user from database
--- PASS: Test_UserListProxy (0.09s)
--- PASS: Test_UserListProxy/FindUser_-_Empty_cache (0.00s)
--- PASS: Test_UserListProxy/FindUser_-_One_user,_ask_for_the_same_user
(0.00s)
--- PASS: Test_UserListProxy/FindUser_-_overflowing_the_stack (0.00s)
PASS
ok
```

You can see in the preceding messages that our Proxy has worked flawlessly. It has returned the first search from the database. Then, when we search for the same user again, it uses the cache. Finally, we made a new test that calls three different users and we can observe, by looking at the console output, that just the first was returned from the cache and that the other two were fetched from the database.

Proxying around actions

Wrap proxies around types that need some intermediate action, like giving authorization to the user or providing access to a database, like in our example.

Our example is a good way to separate application needs from database needs. If our application accesses the database too much, a solution for this is not in your database. Remember that the Proxy uses the same interface as the type it wraps, and, for the user, there shouldn't be any difference between the two.

Decorator design pattern

We'll continue this chapter with the big brother of the Proxy pattern, and maybe, one of the most powerful design patterns of all. The **Decorator** pattern is pretty simple, but, for instance, it provides a lot of benefits when working with legacy code.

Description

The Decorator design pattern allows you to decorate an already existing type with more functional features without actually touching it. How is it possible? Well, it uses an approach similar to *matryoshka dolls*, where you have a small doll that you can put inside a doll of the same shape but bigger, and so on and so forth.

The Decorator type implements the same interface of the type it decorates, and stores an instance of that type in its members. This way, you can stack as many decorators (dolls) as you want by simply storing the old decorator in a field of the new one.

Objectives

When you think about extending legacy code without the risk of breaking something, you should think of the Decorator pattern first. It's a really powerful approach to deal with this particular problem.

A different field where the Decorator is very powerful may not be so obvious though it reveals itself when creating types with lots of features based on user inputs, preferences, or similar inputs. Like in a Swiss knife, you have a base type (the frame of the knife), and from there you unfold its functionalities.

So, precisely when are we going to use the Decorator pattern? Answer to this question:

- When you need to add functionality to some code that you don't have access to, or you don't want to modify to avoid a negative effect on the code, and follow the open/close principle (like legacy code)
- When you want the functionality of an object to be created or altered dynamically, and the number of features is unknown and could grow fast

Example

In our example, we will prepare a `Pizza` type, where the core is the pizza and the ingredients are the decorating types. We will have a couple of ingredients for our pizza–onion and meat.

Acceptance criteria

The acceptance criteria for a Decorator pattern is to have a common interface and a core type, the one that all layers will be built over:

- We must have the main interface that all decorators will implement. This interface will be called `IngredientAdd`, and it will have the `AddIngredient()` `string` method.
- We must have a core `PizzaDecorator` type (the decorator) that we will add ingredients to.

- We must have an ingredient "onion" implementing the same `IngredientAdd` interface that will add the string `onion` to the returned pizza.
- We must have a ingredient "meat" implementing the `IngredientAdd` interface that will add the string `meat` to the returned pizza.
- When calling `AddIngredient` method on the top object, it must return a fully decorated `pizza` with the text `Pizza with the following ingredients: meat, onion`.

Unit test

To launch our unit tests, we must first create the basic structures described in accordance with the acceptance criteria. To begin with, the interface that all decorating types must implement is as follows:

```
type IngredientAdd interface {
  AddIngredient() (string, error)
}
```

The following code defines the `PizzaDecorator` type, which must have `IngredientAdd` inside, and which implements `IngredientAdd` too:

```
type PizzaDecorator struct{
  Ingredient IngredientAdd
}

func (p *PizzaDecorator) AddIngredient() (string, error) {
  return "", errors.New("Not implemented yet")
}
```

The definition of the `Meat` type will be very similar to that of the `PizzaDecorator` structure:

```
type Meat struct {
  Ingredient IngredientAdd
}

func (m *Meat) AddIngredient() (string, error) {
  return "", errors.New("Not implemented yet")
}
```

Now we define the `Onion` struct in a similar fashion:

```
type Onion struct {
  Ingredient IngredientAdd
```

```
}

func (o *Onion) AddIngredient() (string, error) {
  return "", errors.New("Not implemented yet")
}
```

This is enough to implement the first unit test, and to allow the compiler to run them without any compiling errors:

```
func TestPizzaDecorator_AddIngredient(t *testing.T) {
  pizza := &PizzaDecorator{}
  pizzaResult, _ := pizza.AddIngredient()
  expectedText := "Pizza with the following ingredients:"
  if !strings.Contains(pizzaResult, expectedText) {
    t.Errorf("When calling the add ingredient of the pizza decorator it
must return the text %sthe expected text, not '%s'", pizzaResult,
expectedText)
  }
}
```

Now it must compile without problems, so we can check that the test fails:

```
$ go test -v -run=TestPizzaDecorator .
=== RUN   TestPizzaDecorator_AddIngredient
--- FAIL: TestPizzaDecorator_AddIngredient (0.00s)
decorator_test.go:29: Not implemented yet
decorator_test.go:34: When the the AddIngredient method of the pizza
decorator object is called, it must return the text Pizza with the
following ingredients:
    FAIL
    exit status 1
    FAIL
```

Our first test is done, and we can see that the `PizzaDecorator` struct isn't returning anything yet, that's why it fails. We can now move on to the `Onion` type. The test of the `Onion` type is quite similar to that of the `Pizza` decorator, but we must also make sure that we actually add the ingredient to the `IngredientAdd` method and not to a nil pointer:

```
func TestOnion_AddIngredient(t *testing.T) {
  onion := &Onion{}
  onionResult, err := onion.AddIngredient()
  if err == nil {
    t.Errorf("When calling AddIngredient on the onion decorator without" +
"an IngredientAdd on its Ingredient field must return an error, not a
string with '%s'", onionResult)
  }
```

The first half of the preceding test examines the returning error when no
`IngredientAdd` method is passed to the `Onion` struct initializer. As no pizza is available to
add the ingredient, an error must be returned:

```
onion = &Onion{&PizzaDecorator{}}
onionResult, err = onion.AddIngredient()

if err != nil {
  t.Error(err)
}
if !strings.Contains(onionResult, "onion") {
    t.Errorf("When calling the add ingredient of the onion decorator it" +
"must return a text with the word 'onion', not '%s'", onionResult)
  }
}
```

The second part of the `Onion` type test actually passes `PizzaDecorator` structure to the
initializer. Then, we check whether no error is being returned, and also whether the
returning string contains the word `onion` in it. This way, we can ensure that onion has been
added to the pizza.

Finally for the `Onion` type, the console output of this test with our current implementation
will be the following:

```
$ go test -v -run=TestOnion_AddIngredient .
=== RUN   TestOnion_AddIngredient
--- FAIL: TestOnion_AddIngredient (0.00s)
decorator_test.go:48: Not implemented yet
decorator_test.go:52: When calling the add ingredient of the onion
decorator it must return a text with the word 'onion', not ''
    FAIL
    exit status 1
    FAIL
```

The `meat` ingredient is exactly the same, but we change the type to meat instead of onion:

```
func TestMeat_AddIngredient(t *testing.T) {
  meat := &Meat{}
  meatResult, err := meat.AddIngredient()
  if err == nil {
    t.Errorf("When calling AddIngredient on the meat decorator without" +
"an IngredientAdd in its Ingredient field must return an error," + "not a
string with '%s'", meatResult)
  }

  meat = &Meat{&PizzaDecorator{}}
  meatResult, err = meat.AddIngredient()
```

```
  if err != nil {
    t.Error(err)
  }

  if !strings.Contains(meatResult, "meat") {
    t.Errorf("When calling the add ingredient of the meat decorator it" +
"must return a text with the word 'meat', not '%s'", meatResult)
  }
}
```

So, the result of the tests will be similar:

```
go test -v -run=TestMeat_AddIngredient .
=== RUN   TestMeat_AddIngredient
--- FAIL: TestMeat_AddIngredient (0.00s)
decorator_test.go:68: Not implemented yet
decorator_test.go:72: When calling the add ingredient of the meat
decorator it must return a text with the word 'meat', not ''
    FAIL
    exit status 1
    FAIL
```

Finally, we must check the full stack test. Creating a pizza with onion and meat must return the text Pizza with the following ingredients: meat, onion:

```
func TestPizzaDecorator_FullStack(t *testing.T) {
  pizza := &Onion{&Meat{&PizzaDecorator{}}}
  pizzaResult, err := pizza.AddIngredient()
  if err != nil {
    t.Error(err)
  }

  expectedText := "Pizza with the following ingredients: meat, onion"
  if !strings.Contains(pizzaResult, expectedText){
    t.Errorf("When asking for a pizza with onion and meat the returned " +
"string must contain the text '%s' but '%s' didn't have it",
expectedText,pizzaResult)
  }

  t.Log(pizzaResult)
}
```

Our test creates a variable called `pizza` which, like the m*atryoshka dolls*, embeds types of the `IngredientAdd` method in several levels. Calling the `AddIngredient` method executes the method at the "onion" level, which executes the "meat" one, which, finally, executes that of the `PizzaDecorator` struct. After checking that no error had been returned, we check whether the returned text follows the needs of the *acceptance criteria 5*. The tests are run with the following command:

```
go test -v -run=TestPizzaDecorator_FullStack .
=== RUN   TestPizzaDecorator_FullStack
--- FAIL: TestPizzaDecorator_FullStack (0.
decorator_test.go:80: Not implemented yet
decorator_test.go:87: When asking for a pizza with onion and meat the
returned string must contain the text 'Pizza with the following
ingredients: meat, onion' but '' didn't have it
    FAIL
    exit status 1
    FAIL
```

From the preceding output, we can see that the tests now return an empty string for our decorated type. This is, of course, because no implementation has been done yet. This was the last test to check the fully decorated implementation. Let's look closely at the implementation then.

Implementation

We are going to start implementing the `PizzaDecorator` type. Its role is to provide the initial text of the full pizza:

```
type PizzaDecorator struct {
  Ingredient IngredientAdd
}

func (p *PizzaDecorator) AddIngredient() (string, error) {
  return "Pizza with the following ingredients:", nil
}
```

A single line change on the return of the `AddIngredient` method was enough to pass the test:

```
go test -v -run=TestPizzaDecorator_Add .
=== RUN   TestPizzaDecorator_AddIngredient
--- PASS: TestPizzaDecorator_AddIngredient (0.00s)
PASS
ok
```

Moving on to the Onion struct implementation, we must take the beginning of our IngredientAdd returned string, and add the word onion at the end of it in order to get a composed pizza in return:

```
type Onion struct {
    Ingredient IngredientAdd
}

func (o *Onion) AddIngredient() (string, error) {
    if o.Ingredient == nil {
        return "", errors.New("An IngredientAdd is needed in the Ingredient
field of the Onion")
    }
    s, err := o.Ingredient.AddIngredient()
    if err != nil {
        return "", err
    }
    return fmt.Sprintf("%s %s,", s, "onion"), nil
}
```

Checking that we actually have a pointer to IngredientAdd first, we use the contents of the inner IngredientAdd, and check it for errors. If no errors occur, we receive a new string composed of this content, a space, and the word onion (and no errors). Looks good enough to run the tests:

```
go test -v -run=TestOnion_AddIngredient .
=== RUN   TestOnion_AddIngredient
--- PASS: TestOnion_AddIngredient (0.00s)
PASS
ok
```

Implementation of the Meat struct is very similar:

```
type Meat struct {
    Ingredient IngredientAdd
}

func (m *Meat) AddIngredient() (string, error) {
    if m.Ingredient == nil {
        return "", errors.New("An IngredientAdd is needed in the Ingredient
field of the Meat")
    }
    s, err := m.Ingredient.AddIngredient()
    if err != nil {
        return "", err
    }
    return fmt.Sprintf("%s %s,", s, "meat"), nil
```

```
    }
```

And here goes their test execution:

```
go test -v -run=TestMeat_AddIngredient .
=== RUN   TestMeat_AddIngredient
--- PASS: TestMeat_AddIngredient (0.00s)
PASS
ok
```

Okay. So, now all the pieces are to be tested separately. If everything is okay, the test of the *full stacked* solution must be passing smoothly:

```
go test -v -run=TestPizzaDecorator_FullStack .
=== RUN   TestPizzaDecorator_FullStack
--- PASS: TestPizzaDecorator_FullStack (0.00s)
decorator_test.go:92: Pizza with the following ingredients: meat,
onion,
PASS
ok
```

Awesome! With the Decorator pattern, we could keep stacking `IngredientAdds` which call their inner pointer to add functionality to `PizzaDecorator`. We aren't touching the core type either, nor modifying or implementing new things. All the new features are implemented by an external type.

A real-life example – server middleware

By now, you should have understood how the Decorator pattern works. Now we can try a more advanced example using the small HTTP server that we designed in the Adapter pattern section. You learned that an HTTP server can be created by using the `http` package, and implementing the `http.Handler` interface. This interface has only one method called `ServeHTTP(http.ResponseWriter, http.Request)`. Can we use the Decorator pattern to add more functionality to a server? Of course!

We will add a couple of pieces to this server. First, we are going to log every connection made to it to the `io.Writer` interface (for the sake of simplicity, we'll use the `io.Writer` implementation of the `os.Stdout` interface so that it outputs to the console). The second piece will add basic HTTP authentication to every request made to the server. If the authentication passes, a `Hello Decorator!` message will appear. Finally, the user will be able to select the number of decoration items that he/she wants in the server, and the server will be structured and created at runtime.

Starting with the common interface, http.Handler

We already have the common interface that we will decorate using nested types. We first need to create our core type, which is going to be the `Handler` that returns the sentence `Hello Decorator!`:

```
type MyServer struct{}

func (m *MyServer) ServeHTTP(w http.ResponseWriter, r *http.Request) {
    fmt.Fprintln(w, "Hello Decorator!")
}
```

This handler can be attributed to the `http.Handle` method to define our first endpoint. Let's check this now by creating the package's `main` function, and sending a `GET` request to it:

```
func main() {
    http.Handle("/", &MyServer{})

    log.Fatal(http.ListenAndServe(":8080", nil))
}
```

Execute the server using the Terminal to execute the **go run main.go** command. Then, open a new Terminal to make the `GET` request. We'll use the `curl` command to make our requests:

```
$ curl http://localhost:8080
Hello Decorator!
```

We have crossed the first milestone of our decorated server. The next step is to decorate it with logging capabilities. To do so, we must implement the `http.Handler` interface, in a new type, as follows:

```
type LoggerServer struct {
    Handler   http.Handler
    LogWriter io.Writer
}

func (s *LoggerServer) ServeHTTP(w http.ResponseWriter, r *http.Request) {
    fmt.Fprintf(s.LogWriter, "Request URI: %s\n", r.RequestURI)
    fmt.Fprintf(s.LogWriter, "Host: %s\n", r.Host)
    fmt.Fprintf(s.LogWriter, "Content Length: %d\n",
r.ContentLength)
    fmt.Fprintf(s.LogWriter, "Method: %s\n",
r.Method) fmt.Fprintf(s.LogWriter, "--------------------------------\n")

    s.Handler.ServeHTTP(w, r)
```

```
  }
```

We call this type `LoggerServer`. As you can see, it stores not only a `Handler`, but also `io.Writer` to write the output of the log. Our implementation of the `ServeHTTP` method prints the request URI, the host, the content length, and the used method `io.Writer`. Once printing is finished, it calls the `ServeHTTP` function of its inner `Handler` field.

We can decorate `MyServer` with this `LoggerMiddleware`:

```
func main() {
  http.Handle("/", &LoggerServer{
    LogWriter:os.Stdout,
    Handler:&MyServer{},
  })

  log.Fatal(http.ListenAndServe(":8080", nil))
}
```

Now run the **curl** command:

```
$ curl http://localhost:8080
Hello Decorator!
```

Our **curl** command returns the same message, but if you look at the Terminal where you have run the Go application, you can see the logging:

```
$ go run server_decorator.go
Request URI: /
Host: localhost:8080
Content Length: 0
Method: GET
```

We have decorated `MyServer` with logging capabilities without actually modifying it. Can we do the same with authentication? Of course! After logging the request, we will authenticate it by using **HTTP Basic Authentication** as follows:

```
type BasicAuthMiddleware struct {
  Handler  http.Handler
  User     string
  Password string
}
```

The **BasicAuthMiddleware** middleware stores three fields–a handler to decorate like in the previous middlewares, a user, and a password, which will be the only authorization to access the contents on the server. The implementation of the `decorating` method will proceed as follows:

```
func (s *BasicAuthMiddleware) ServeHTTP(w http.ResponseWriter, r
*http.Request) {
  user, pass, ok := r.BasicAuth()

  if ok {
    if user == s.User && pass == s.Password {
      s.Handler.ServeHTTP(w, r)
    }
    else {
      fmt.Fprintf(w, "User or password incorrect\n")
    }
  }
  else {
    fmt.Fprintln(w, "Error trying to retrieve data from Basic auth")
  }
}
```

In the preceding implementation, we use the `BasicAuth` method from `http.Request` to automatically retrieve the user and password from the request, plus an `ok/ko` from the parsing action. Then we check whether the parsing is correct (returning a message to the requester if incorrect, and finishing the request). If no problems have been detected during parsing, we check whether the username and the password match with the ones stored in `BasicAuthMiddleware`. If the credentials are valid, we shall call the decorated type (our server), but if the credentials aren't valid, we receive the `User or password incorrect` message in return, and the request is finished.

Now, we need to provide the user with a way to choose among different types of servers. We will retrieve user input data in the main function. We'll have three options to choose from:

- Simple server
- Server with logging
- Server with logging and authentication

We have to use the `Fscanf` function to retrieve input from the user:

```
func main() {
  fmt.Println("Enter the type number of server you want to launch from the
following:")
  fmt.Println("1.- Plain server")
  fmt.Println("2.- Server with logging")
  fmt.Println("3.- Server with logging and authentication")

  var selection int
  fmt.Fscanf(os.Stdin, "%d", &selection)
```

```
        }
```

The `Fscanf` function needs an `io.Reader` implementor as the first argument (which is going to be the input in the console), and it takes the server selected by the user from it. We'll pass `os.Stdin` as the `io.Reader` interface to retrieve user input. Then, we'll write the type of data it is going to parse. The `%d` specifier refers to an integer number. Finally, we'll write memory direction to store the parsed input, in this case, the memory position of the `selection` variable.

Once the user selects an option, we can take the basic server and decorate it at runtime, switching over to the selected option:

```
switch selection {
case 1:
  mySuperServer = new(MyServer)
case 2:
  mySuperServer = &LoggerMiddleware{
    Handler:   new(MyServer),
    LogWriter: os.Stdout,
  }
case 3:
  var user, password string

  fmt.Println("Enter user and password separated by a space")
  fmt.Fscanf(os.Stdin, "%s %s", &user, &password)

  mySuperServer = &LoggerMiddleware{
  Handler: &SimpleAuthMiddleware{
    Handler:   new(MyServer),
    User:      user,
    Password: password,
  },
    LogWriter: os.Stdout,
  }
default:
  mySuperServer = new(MyServer)
}
```

The first option will be handled by the default `switch` option–a plain `MyServer`. In the case of the second option, we decorate a plain server with logging. The third Option is a bit more developed–we ask the user for a username and a password using `Fscanf` again. Note that you can scan more than one input, as we are doing to retrieve the user and the password. Then, we take the basic server, decorate it with authentication, and finally, with logging.

If you follow the indentation of the nested types of option three, the request passes through the logger, then the authentication middleware, and finally, the `MyServer` argument if everything is okay. The requests will follow the same route.

The end of the main function takes the decorated handler, and launches the server on the 8080 port:

```
http.Handle("/", mySuperServer)
log.Fatal(http.ListenAndServe(":8080", nil))
```

So, let's launch the server with the third option:

```
$go run server_decorator.go
Enter the server type number you want to launch from the following:
1.- Plain server
2.- Server with logging
3.- Server with logging and authentication

Enter user and password separated by a space
mario castro
```

We will first test the plain server by choosing the first option. Run the server with the command **go run server_decorator.go**, and select the first option. Then, in a different Terminal, run the basic request with curl, as follows:

```
$ curl http://localhost:8080
Error trying to retrieve data from Basic auth
```

Uh, oh! It doesn't give us access. We haven't passed any user and password, so it tells us that we cannot continue. Let's try with some random user and password:

```
$ curl -u no:correct http://localhost:8080
User or password incorrect
```

No access! We can also check in the Terminal where we launched the server and where every request is being logged:

```
Request URI: /
Host: localhost:8080
Content Length: 0
Method: GET
```

Finally, enter the correct username and password:

```
$ curl -u packt:publishing http://localhost:8080
Hello Decorator!
```

Here we are! Our request has also been logged, and the server has granted access to us. Now we can improve our server as much as we want by writing more middlewares to decorate the server's functionality.

A few words about Go's structural typing

Go has a feature that most people dislike at the beginning–structural typing. This is when your structure defines your type without explicitly writing it. For example, when you implement an interface, you don't have to write explicitly that you are actually implementing it, contrary to languages such as Java where you have to write the keyword `implements`. If your method follows the signature of the interface, you are actually implementing the interface. This can also lead to accidental implementations of interface, something that could provoke an impossible-to-track mistake, but that is very unlikely.

However, structural typing also allows you to define an interface after defining their implementers. Imagine a `MyPrinter` struct as follows:

```
type MyPrinter struct{}
func(m *MyPrinter)Print(){
  println("Hello")
}
```

Imagine we have been working with the `MyPrinter` type for few months now, but it didn't implement any interface, so it can't be a possible candidate for a Decorator pattern, or maybe it can? What if we wrote an interface that matches its `Print` method after a few months? Consider the following code snippet:

```
type Printer interface {
  Print()
}
```

It actually implements the `Printer` interface, and we can use it to create a Decorator solution.

Structural typing allows a lot of flexibility when writing programs. If you don't know whether a type should be a part of an interface or not, you can leave it and add the interface later, when you are completely sure about it. This way, you can decorate types very easily and with little modification in your source code.

Summarizing the Decorator design pattern – Proxy versus Decorator

You might be wondering, what's the difference between the Decorator pattern and the Proxy pattern? In the Decorator pattern, we decorate a type dynamically. This means that the decoration may or may not be there, or it may be composed of one or many types. If you remember, the Proxy pattern wraps a type in a similar fashion, but it does so at compile time and it's more like a way to access some type.

At the same time, a decorator might implement the entire interface that the type it decorates also implements **or not**. So you can have an interface with 10 methods and a decorator that just implements one of them and it will still be valid. A call on a method not implemented by the decorator will be passed to the decorated type. This is a very powerful feature but also very prone to undesired behaviors at runtime if you forget to implement any interface method.

In this aspect, you may think that the Proxy pattern is less flexible, and it is. But the Decorator pattern is weaker, as you could have errors at runtime, which you can avoid at compile time by using the Proxy pattern. Just keep in mind that the Decorator is commonly used when you want to add functionality to an object at runtime, like in our web server. It's a compromise between what you need and what you want to sacrifice to achieve it.

Facade design pattern

The next pattern we'll see in this chapter is the Facade pattern. When we discussed the Proxy pattern, you got to know that it was a way to wrap an type to hide some of its features of complexity from the user. Imagine that we group many proxies in a single point such as a file or a library. This could be a Facade pattern.

Description

A facade, in architectural terms, is the front wall that hides the rooms and corridors of a building. It protects its inhabitants from cold and rain, and provides them privacy. It orders and divides the dwellings.

The Facade design pattern does the same, but in our code. It shields the code from unwanted access, orders some calls, and hides the complexity scope from the user.

Objectives

You use Facade when you want to hide the complexity of some tasks, especially when most of them share utilities (such as authentication in an API). A library is a form of facade, where someone has to provide some methods for a developer to do certain things in a friendly way. This way, if a developer needs to use your library, he doesn't need to know all the inner tasks to retrieve the result he/she wants.

So, you use the Facade design pattern in the following scenarios:

- When you want to decrease the complexity of some parts of our code. You hide that complexity behind the facade by providing a more easy-to-use method.
- When you want to group actions that are cross-related in a single place.
- When you want to build a library so that others can use your products without worrying about how it all works.

Example

As an example, we are going to take the first steps toward writing our own library that accesses `OpenWeatherMaps` service. In case you are not familiar with `OpenWeatherMap` service, it is an HTTP service that provides you with live information about weather, as well as historical data on it. The **HTTP REST** API is very easy to use, and will be a good example on how to create a Facade pattern for hiding the complexity of the network connections behind the REST service.

Acceptance criteria

The `OpenWeatherMap` API gives lots of information, so we are going to focus on getting live weather data in one city in some geo-located place by using its latitude and longitude values. The following are the requirements and acceptance criteria for this design pattern:

1. Provide a single type to access the data. All information retrieved from `OpenWeatherMap` service will pass through it.
2. Create a way to get the weather data for some city of some country.
3. Create a way to get the weather data for some latitude and longitude position.
4. Only second and thrird point must be visible outside of the package; everything else must be hidden (including all connection-related data).

Unit test

To start with our API Facade, we will need an interface with the methods asked in *acceptance criteria 2* and *acceptance criteria 3*:

```
type CurrentWeatherDataRetriever interface {
  GetByCityAndCountryCode(city, countryCode string) (Weather, error)
  GetByGeoCoordinates(lat, lon float32) (Weather, error)
}
```

We will call *acceptance criteria 2* `GetByCityAndCountryCode`; we will also need a city name and a country code in the string format. A country code is a two-character code, which represents the **International Organization for Standardization (ISO)** name of world countries. It returns a `Weather` value, which we will define later, and an error if something goes wrong.

Acceptance criteria 3 will be called `GetByGeoCoordinates`, and will need latitude and longitude values in the `float32` format. It will also return a `Weather` value and an error. The `Weather` value is going to be defined according to the returned JSON that the `OpenWeatherMap` API works with. You can find the description of this JSON at the webpage `http://openweathermap.org/current#current_JSON`.

If you look at the JSON definition, it has the following type:

```
type Weather struct {
  ID    int     `json:"id"`
  Name string `json:"name"`
  Cod   int     `json:"cod"`
  Coord struct {
    Lon float32 `json:"lon"`
    Lat float32 `json:"lat"`
  } `json:"coord"`
  Weather []struct {
    Id          int     `json:"id"`
    Main        string `json:"main"`
    Description string `json:"description"`
    Icon        string `json:"icon"`
  } `json:"weather"`

  Base string `json:"base"`
  Main struct {
    Temp     float32 `json:"temp"`
    Pressure float32 `json:"pressure"`
    Humidity float32 `json:"humidity"`
    TempMin  float32 `json:"temp_min"`
    TempMax  float32 `json:"temp_max"`
```

```
    } `json:"main"`

Wind struct {
   Speed float32 `json:"speed"`
   Deg   float32 `json:"deg"`
} `json:"wind"`

Clouds struct {
   All int `json:"all"`
} `json:"clouds"`
Rain struct {
   ThreeHours float32 `json:"3h"`
} `json:"rain"`
Dt  uint32 `json:"dt"`
Sys struct {
   Type    int      `json:"type"`
   ID      int      `json:"id"`
   Message float32 `json:"message"`
   Country string  `json:"country"`
   Sunrise int      `json:"sunrise"`
   Sunset  int      `json:"sunset"`
}`json:"sys"`
}
```

It's quite a long struct, but we have everything that a response could include. The struct is called `Weather`, as it is composed of an ID, a name and a Code (`Cod`), and a few anonymous structs, which are: `Coord`, `Weather`, `Base`, `Main`, `Wind`, `Clouds`, `Rain`, `Dt`, and `Sys`. We could write these anonymous structs outside of the `Weather` struct by giving them a name, but it would only be useful if we have to work with them separately.

After every member and struct within our `Weather` struct, you can find a `json:"something"` line. This comes in handy when differentiating between the JSON key name and your member name. If the JSON key is `something`, we aren't forced to call our member `something`. For example, our ID member will be called `id` in the JSON response.

Why don't we give the name of the JSON keys to our types? Well, if your fields in your type are lowercase, the `encoding/json` package won't parse them correctly. Also, that last annotation provides us a certain flexibility, not only in terms of changing the members' names, but also of omitting some key if we don't need it, with the following signature:

```
`json:"something,omitempty"`
```

With `omitempty` at the end, the parse won't fail if this key is not present in the bytes representation of the JSON key.

Okay, our acceptance criteria 1 ask for a single point of access to the API. This is going to be called `CurrentWeatherData`:

```
type CurrentWeatherData struct {
  APIkey string
}
```

The `CurrentWeatherData` type has an API key as public member to work. This is because you have to be a registered user in `OpenWeatherMap` to enjoy their services. Refer to the `OpenWeatherMap` API's webpage for documentation on how to get an API key. We won't need it in our example, because we aren't going to do integration tests.

We need mock data so that we can write a `mock` function to retrieve the data. When sending an HTTP request, the response is contained in a member called body in the form of an `io.Reader`. We have already worked with types that implement the `io.Reader` interface, so this should look familiar to you. Our `mock` function appears like this:

```
func getMockData() io.Reader {
  response := `{
    "coord":{"lon":-3.7,"lat":40.42},"weather :
[{"id":803,"main":"Clouds","description":"broken
clouds","icon":"04n"}],"base":"stations","main":{"temp":303.56,"pressure":1
016.46,"humidity":26.8,"temp_min":300.95,"temp_max":305.93},"wind":{"speed"
:3.17,"deg":151.001},"rain":{"3h":0.0075},"clouds":{"all":68},"dt":14712958
23,"sys":{"type":3,"id":1442829648,"message":0.0278,"country":"ES","sunrise
":1471238808,"sunset":1471288232},"id":3117735,"name":"Madrid","cod":200}`

  r := bytes.NewReader([]byte(response))
  return r
}
```

This preceding mocked data was produced by making a request to `OpenWeatherMap` using an API key. The `response` variable is a string containing a JSON response. Take a close look at the grave accent (`) used to open and close the string. This way, you can use as many quotes as you want without any problem.

Further on, we use a special function in the bytes package called `NewReader`, which accepts an slice of bytes (which we create by converting the type from string), and returns an `io.Reader` implementor with the contents of the slice. This is perfect to mimic the `Body` member of an HTTP response.

We will write a test to try `response parser`. Both methods return the same type, so we can use the same `JSON parser` for both:

```
func TestOpenWeatherMap_responseParser(t *testing.T) {
```

```
    r := getMockData()
    openWeatherMap := CurrentWeatherData{APIkey: ""}

    weather, err := openWeatherMap.responseParser(r)
    if err != nil {
      t.Fatal(err)
    }

    if weather.ID != 3117735 {
      t.Errorf("Madrid id is 3117735, not %d\n", weather.ID)
    }
  }
```

In the preceding test, we first asked for some mock data, which we store in the variable `r`. Later, we created a type of `CurrentWeatherData`, which we called `openWeatherMap`. Finally, we asked for a weather value for the provided `io.Reader` interface that we store in the variable `weather`. After checking for errors, we make sure that the ID is the same as the one stored in the mock data that we got from the `getMockData` method.

We have to declare the `responseParser` method before running tests, or the code won't compile:

```
func (p *CurrentWeatherData) responseParser(body io.Reader) (*Weather,
error) {
  return nil, fmt.Errorf("Not implemented yet")
}
```

With all the aforementioned, we can run this test:

```
go test -v -run=responseParser .
=== RUN   TestOpenWeatherMap_responseParser
--- FAIL: TestOpenWeatherMap_responseParser (0.00s)
        facade_test.go:72: Not implemented yet
FAIL
exit status 1
FAIL
```

Okay. We won't write more tests, because the rest would be merely integration tests, which are outside of the scope of explanation of a structural pattern, and will force us to have an API key as well as an Internet connection. If you want to see what the integration tests look like for this example, refer to the code that comes bundled with the book.

Implementation

First of all, we are going to implement the parser that our methods will use to parse the JSON response from the `OpenWeatherMap` REST API:

```
func (p *CurrentWeatherData) responseParser(body io.Reader) (*Weather,
error) {
  w := new(Weather)
  err := json.NewDecoder(body).Decode(w)
  if err != nil {
    return nil, err
  }

  return w, nil
}
```

And this should be enough to pass the test by now:

```
go test -v -run=responseParser .
=== RUN   TestOpenWeatherMap_responseParser
--- PASS: TestOpenWeatherMap_responseParser (0.00s)
PASS
ok
```

At least we have our parser well tested. Let's structure our code to look like a library. First, we will create the methods to retrieve the weather of a city by its name and its country code, and the method that uses its latitude and longitude:

```
func (c *CurrentWeatherData) GetByGeoCoordinates(lat, lon float32) (weather
*Weather, err error) {
  return c.doRequest(
  fmt.Sprintf("http://api.openweathermap.org/data/2.5/weather
q=%s,%s&APPID=%s", lat, lon, c.APIkey))
}

func (c *CurrentWeatherData) GetByCityAndCountryCode(city, countryCode
string) (weather *Weather, err error) {
  return c.doRequest(
  fmt.Sprintf("http://api.openweathermap.org/data/2.5/weather?lat=%f&lon=%f&A
PPID=%s", city, countryCode, c.APIkey) )
}
```

A piece of cake? Of course! Everything must be as easy as possible, and it is a sign of a good job. The complexity in this facade is to create connections to the `OpenWeatherMap` API, and control the possible errors. This problem is shared between all the Facade methods in our example, so we don't need to write more than one API call right now.

What we do is pass the URL that the REST API needs in order to return the information we desire. This is achieved by the `fmt.Sprintf` function, which formats the strings in each case. For example, to gather the data using a city name and a country code, we use the following string:

```
fmt.Sprintf("http://api.openweathermap.org/data/2.5/weather?lat=%f&lon=%f&A
PPID=%s", city, countryCode, c.APIkey)
```

This takes the pre-formatted string `https://openweathermap.org/api` and formats it by replacing each `%s` specifier with the city, the `countryCode` that we introduced in the arguments, and the API key member of the `CurrentWeatherData` type.

But, we haven't set any API key! Yes, because this is a library, and the users of the library will have to use their own API keys. We are hiding the complexity of creating the URIs, and handling the errors.

Finally, the `doRequest` function is a big fish, so we will see it in detail, step by step:

```
func (o *CurrentWeatherData) doRequest(uri string) (weather *Weather, err
error) {
  client := &http.Client{}
  req, err := http.NewRequest("GET", uri, nil)
  if err != nil {
    return
  }
  req.Header.Set("Content-Type", "application/json")
```

First, the signature tells us that the `doRequest` method accepts a URI string, and returns a pointer to the `Weather` variable and an error. We start by creating an `http.Client` class, which will make the requests. Then, we create a request object, which will use the `GET` method, as described in the `OpenWeatherMap` webpage, and the URI we passed. If we were to use a different method, or more than one, they would have to be brought about by arguments in the signature. Nevertheless, we will use just the `GET` method, so we could hardcode it there.

Then, we check whether the request object has been created successfully, and set a header that says that the content type is a JSON:

```
resp, err := client.Do(req)
if err != nil {
  return
}

if resp.StatusCode != 200 {
  byt, errMsg := ioutil.ReadAll(resp.Body)
```

```
    if errMsg == nil {
        errMsg = fmt.Errorf("%s", string(byt))
    }
    err = fmt.Errorf("Status code was %d, aborting. Error message
was:\n%s\n",resp.StatusCode, errMsg)

    return
}
```

Then we make the request, and check for errors. Because we have given names to our return types, if any error occurs, we just have to return the function, and Go will return the variable `err` and the variable `weather` in the state they were in at that precise moment.

We check the status code of the response, as we only accept 200 as a good response. If 200 isn't returned, we will create an error message with the contents of the body and the status code returned:

```
    weather, err = o.responseParser(resp.Body)
    resp.Body.Close()

    return
}
```

Finally, if everything goes well, we use the `responseParser` function we wrote earlier to parse the contents of Body, which is an `io.Reader` interface. Maybe you are wondering why we aren't controlling `err` from the `response parser` method. It's funny, because we are actually controlling it. `responseParser` and `doRequest` have the same return signature. Both return a `Weather` pointer and an error (if any), so we can return directly whatever the result was.

Library created with the Facade pattern

We have the first milestone for a library for the `OpenWeatherMap` API using the facade pattern. We have hidden the complexity of accessing the `OpenWeatherMap` REST API in the `doRequest` and `responseParser` functions, and the users of our library have an easy-to-use syntax to query the API. For example, to retrieve the weather for Madrid, Spain, a user will only have to introduce arguments and an API key at the beginning:

```
    weatherMap := CurrentWeatherData{*apiKey}

    weather, err := weatherMap.GetByCityAndCountryCode("Madrid", "ES")
    if err != nil {
        t.Fatal(err)
    }
```

```
    fmt.Printf("Temperature in Madrid is %f celsius\n",
  weather.Main.Temp-273.15)
```

The console output for the weather in Madrid at the moment of writing this chapter is the following:

```
$ Temperature in Madrid is 30.600006 celsius
```

A typical summer day!

Flyweight design pattern

Our next pattern is the **Flyweight** design pattern. It's very commonly used in computer graphics and the video game industry, but not so much in enterprise applications.

Description

Flyweight is a pattern which allows sharing the state of a heavy object between many instances of some type. Imagine that you have to create and store too many objects of some heavy type that are fundamentally equal. You'll run out of memory pretty quickly. This problem can be easily solved with the Flyweight pattern, with additional help of the Factory pattern. The factory is usually in charge of encapsulating object creation, as we saw previously.

Objectives

Thanks to the Flyweight pattern, we can share all possible states of objects in a single common object, and thus minimize object creation by using pointers to already created objects.

Example

To give an example, we are going to simulate something that you find on betting webpages. Imagine the final match of the European championship, which is viewed by millions of people across the continent. Now imagine that we own a betting webpage, where we provide historical information about every team in Europe. This is plenty of information, which is usually stored in some distributed database, and each team has, literally, megabytes of information about their players, matches, championships, and so on.

If a million users access information about a team and a new instance of the information is created for each user querying for historical data, we will run out of memory in the blink of an eye. With our Proxy solution, we could make a cache of the *n* most recent searches to speed up queries, but if we return a clone for every team, we will still get short on memory (but faster thanks to our cache). Funny, right?

Instead, we will store each team's information just once, and we will deliver references to them to the users. So, if we face a million users trying to access information about a match, we will actually just have two teams in memory with a million pointers to the same memory direction.

Acceptance criteria

The acceptance criteria for a Flyweight pattern must always reduce the amount of memory that is used, and must be focused primarily on this objective:

1. We will create a `Team` struct with some basic information such as the team's name, players, historical results, and an image depicting their shield.
2. We must ensure correct team creation (note the word *creation* here, candidate for a creational pattern), and not having duplicates.
3. When creating the same team twice, we must have two pointers pointing to the same memory address.

Basic structs and tests

Our `Team` struct will contain other structs inside, so a total of four structs will be created. The `Team` struct has the following signature:

```
type Team struct {
  ID              uint64
  Name            string
```

```
   Shield          []byte
   Players         []Player
   HistoricalData []HistoricalData
}
```

Each team has an ID, a name, some image in an slice of bytes representing the team's shield, a slice of players, and a slice of historical data. This way, we will have two teams' ID:

```
const (
   TEAM_A = iota
   TEAM_B
)
```

We declare two constants by using the `const` and `iota` keywords. The `const` keyword simply declares that the following declarations are constants. `iota` is a untyped integer that automatically increments its value for each new constant between the parentheses.
The `iota` value starts to reset to 0 when we declare `TEAM_A`, so `TEAM_A` is equal to 0. On the `TEAM_B` variable, `iota` is incremented by one so `TEAM_B` is equal to 1.
The `iota` assignment is an elegant way to save typing when declaring constant values that doesn't need specific value (like the *Pi* constant on the `math` package).

Our `Player` and `HistoricalData` are the following:

```
type Player struct {
   Name     string
   Surname  string
   PreviousTeam uint64
   Photo    []byte
}

type HistoricalData struct {
   Year          uint8
   LeagueResults []Match
}
```

As you can see, we also need a `Match` struct, which is stored within `HistoricalData` struct. A `Match` struct, in this context, represents the historical result of a match:

```
type Match struct {
   Date         time.Time
   VisitorID    uint64
   LocalID      uint64
   LocalScore   byte
   VisitorScore byte
   LocalShoots  uint16
```

```
    VisitorShoots uint16
}
```

This is enough to represent a team, and to fulfill *Acceptance Criteria 1*. You have probably guessed that there is a lot of information on each team, as some of the European teams have existed for more than 100 years.

For *Acceptance Criteria 2*, the word *creation* should give us some clue about how to approach this problem. We will build a factory to create and store our teams. Our Factory will consist of a map of years, including pointers to `Teams` as values, and a `GetTeam` function. Using a map will boost the team search if we know their names in advance. We will also dispose of a method to return the number of created objects, which will be called the `GetNumberOfObjects` method:

```
type teamFlyweightFactory struct {
    createdTeams map[string]*Team
}

func (t *teamFlyweightFactory) GetTeam(name string) *Team {
    return nil
}

func (t *teamFlyweightFactory) GetNumberOfObjects() int {
    return 0
}
```

This is enough to write our first unit test:

```
func TestTeamFlyweightFactory_GetTeam(t *testing.T) {
    factory := teamFlyweightFactory{}

teamA1 := factory.GetTeam(TEAM_A)
    if teamA1 == nil {
      t.Error("The pointer to the TEAM_A was nil")
    }

    teamA2 := factory.GetTeam(TEAM_A)
    if teamA2 == nil {
      t.Error("The pointer to the TEAM_A was nil")
    }

    if teamA1 != teamA2 {
      t.Error("TEAM_A pointers weren't the same")
    }

    if factory.GetNumberOfObjects() != 1 {
      t.Errorf("The number of objects created was not 1: %d\n",
```

```
factory.GetNumberOfObjects())
    }
}
```

In our test, we verify all the acceptance criteria. First we create a factory, and then ask for a pointer of TEAM_A. This pointer cannot be nil, or the test will fail.

Then we call for a second pointer to the same team. This pointer can't be nil either, and it should point to the same memory address as the previous one so we know that it has not allocated a new memory.

Finally, we should check whether the number of created teams is only one, because we have asked for the same team twice. We have two pointers but just one instance of the team. Let's run the tests:

```
$ go test -v -run=GetTeam .
=== RUN   TestTeamFlyweightFactory_GetTeam
--- FAIL: TestTeamFlyweightFactory_GetTeam (0.00s)
flyweight_test.go:11: The pointer to the TEAM_A was nil
flyweight_test.go:21: The pointer to the TEAM_A was nil
flyweight_test.go:31: The number of objects created was not 1: 0
FAIL
exit status 1
FAIL
```

Well, it failed. Both pointers were nil and it has not created any object. Interestingly, the function that compares the two pointers doesn't fail; all in all, nil equals nil.

Implementation

Our GetTeam method will need to scan the map field called createdTeams to make sure the queried team is already created, and return it if so. If the team wasn't created, it will have to create it and store it in the map before returning:

```
func (t *teamFlyweightFactory) GetTeam(teamID int) *Team {
  if t.createdTeams[teamID] != nil {
    return t.createdTeams[teamID]
  }

  team := getTeamFactory(teamID)
  t.createdTeams[teamID] = &team

  return t.createdTeams[teamID]
}
```

The preceding code is very simple. If the parameter name exists in the createdTeams map, return the pointer. Otherwise, call a factory for team creation. This is interesting enough to stop for a second and analyze. When you use the Flyweight pattern, it is very common to have a Flyweight factory, which uses other types of creational patterns to retrieve the objects it needs.

So, the getTeamFactory method will give us the team we are looking for, we will store it in the map, and return it. The team factory will be able to create the two teams: TEAM_A and TEAM_B:

```
func getTeamFactory(team int) Team {
  switch team {
    case TEAM_B:
    return Team{
      ID:    2,
      Name: TEAM_B,
    }
    default:
    return Team{
      ID:    1,
      Name: TEAM_A,
    }
  }
}
```

We are simplifying the objects' content so that we can focus on the Flyweight pattern's implementation. Okay, so we just have to define the function to retrieve the number of objects created, which is done as follows:

```
func (t *teamFlyweightFactory) GetNumberOfObjects() int {
  return len(t.createdTeams)
}
```

This was pretty easy. The len function returns the number of elements in an array or slice, the number of characters in a string, and so on. It seems that everything is done, and we can launch our tests again:

```
$ go test -v -run=GetTeam .
=== RUN   TestTeamFlyweightFactory_GetTeam
--- FAIL: TestTeamFlyweightFactory_GetTeam (0.00s)
panic: assignment to entry in nil map [recovered]
        panic: assignment to entry in nil map

goroutine 5 [running]:
panic(0x530900, 0xc0820025c0)
        /home/mcastro/Go/src/runtime/panic.go:481 +0x3f4
```

```
testing.tRunner.func1(0xc082068120)
        /home/mcastro/Go/src/testing/testing.go:467 +0x199
panic(0x530900, 0xc0820025c0)
        /home/mcastro/Go/src/runtime/panic.go:443 +0x4f7
/home/mcastro/go-design-
patterns/structural/flyweight.(*teamFlyweightFactory).GetTeam(0xc08202fec0,
0x0, 0x0)
        /home/mcastro/Desktop/go-design-
patterns/structural/flyweight/flyweight.go:71 +0x159
/home/mcastro/go-design-
patterns/structural/flyweight.TestTeamFlyweightFactory_GetTeam(0xc082068120
)
        /home/mcastro/Desktop/go-design-
patterns/structural/flyweight/flyweight_test.go:9 +0x61
testing.tRunner(0xc082068120, 0x666580)
        /home/mcastro/Go/src/testing/testing.go:473 +0x9f
created by testing.RunTests
        /home/mcastro/Go/src/testing/testing.go:582 +0x899
exit status 2
FAIL
```

Panic! Have we forgotten something? By reading the stack trace on the panic message, we can see some addresses, some files, and it seems that the `GetTeam` method is trying to assign an entry to a nil map on *line 71* of the `flyweight.go` file. Let's look at *line 71* closely (remember, if you are writing code while following this tutorial, that the error will probably be in a different line so look closely at your own stark trace):

```
t.createdTeams[teamName] = &team
```

Okay, this line is on the `GetTeam` method, and, when the method passes through here, it means that it had not found the team on the map-it has created it (the variable team), and is trying to assign it to the map. But the map is nil, because we haven't initialized it when creating the factory. This has a quick solution. In our test, initialize the map where we have created the factory:

```
factory := teamFlyweightFactory{
  createdTeams: make(map[int]*Team,0),
}
```

I'm sure you have seen the problem here already. If we don't have access to the package, we can initialize the variable. Well, we can make the variable public, and that's all. But this would involve every implementer necessarily knowing that they have to initialize the map, and its signature is neither convenient, or elegant. Instead, we are going to create a simple factory builder to do it for us. This is a very common approach in Go:

```
func NewTeamFactory() teamFlyweightFactory {
```

```
    return teamFlyweightFactory{
      createdTeams: make(map[int]*Team),
    }
}
```

So now, in the test, we replace the factory creation with a call to this function:

```
func TestTeamFlyweightFactory_GetTeam(t *testing.T) {
    factory := NewTeamFactory()
    ...
}
```

And we run the test again:

```
$ go test -v -run=GetTeam .
=== RUN   TestTeamFlyweightFactory_GetTeam
--- PASS: TestTeamFlyweightFactory_GetTeam (0.00s)
PASS
ok
```

Perfect! Let's improve the test by adding a second test, just to ensure that everything will be running as expected with more volume. We are going to create a million calls to the team creation, representing a million calls from users. Then, we will simply check that the number of teams created is only two:

```
func Test_HighVolume(t *testing.T) {
    factory := NewTeamFactory()

    teams := make([]*Team, 500000*2)
    for i := 0; i < 500000; i++ {
    teams[i] = factory.GetTeam(TEAM_A)
}

for i := 500000; i < 2*500000; i++ {
    teams[i] = factory.GetTeam(TEAM_B)
}

if factory.GetNumberOfObjects() != 2 {
    t.Errorf("The number of objects created was not 2:
%d\n",factory.GetNumberOfObjects())
    }
}
```

In this test, we retrieve TEAM_A and TEAM_B 500,000 times each to reach a million users. Then, we make sure that just two objects were created:

```
$ go test -v -run=Volume .
=== RUN   Test_HighVolume
```

```
--- PASS: Test_HighVolume (0.04s)
PASS
ok
```

Perfect! We can even check where the pointers are pointing to, and where they are located. We will check with the first three as an example. Add these lines at the end of the last test, and run it again:

```
for i:=0; i<3; i++ {
   fmt.Printf("Pointer %d points to %p and is located in %p\n", i, teams[i],
&teams[i])
}
```

In the preceding test, we use the `Printf` method to print information about pointers. The `%p` flag gives you the memory location of the object that the pointer is pointing to. If you reference the pointer by passing the `&` symbol, it will give you the direction of the pointer itself.

Run the test again with the same command; you will see three new lines in the output with information similar to the following:

```
Pointer 0 points to 0xc082846000 and is located in 0xc082076000
Pointer 1 points to 0xc082846000 and is located in 0xc082076008
Pointer 2 points to 0xc082846000 and is located in 0xc082076010
```

What it tells us is that the first three positions in the map point to the same location, but that we actually have three different pointers, which are, effectively, much lighter than our team object.

What's the difference between Singleton and Flyweight then?

Well, the difference is subtle but it's just there. With the Singleton pattern, we ensure that the same type is created only once. Also, the Singleton pattern is a Creational pattern. With Flyweight, which is a Structural pattern, we aren't worried about how the objects are created, but about how to structure a type to contain heavy information in a light way. The structure we are talking about is the `map[int]*Team` structure in our example. Here, we really didn't care about how we created the object; we have simply written an uncomplicated the `getTeamFactory` method for it. We gave major importance to having a light structure to hold a shareable object (or objects), in this case, the map.

Summary

We have seen several patterns to organize code structures. Structural patterns are concerned about how to create objects, or how they do their business (we'll see this in the behavioral patterns).

Don't feel confused about mixing several patterns. You could end up mixing six or seven quite easily if you strictly follow the objectives of each one. Just keep in mind that over-engineering is as bad as no engineering at all. I remember prototyping a load balancer one evening, and after two hours of crazy over-engineered code, I had such a mess in my head that I preferred to start all over again.

In the next chapter, we'll see behavioral patterns. They are a bit more complex, and they often use Structural and Creational patterns for their objectives, but I'm sure that the reader will find them quite challenging and interesting.

5
Behavioral Patterns - Strategy, Chain of Responsibility, and Command Design Patterns

The last group of common patterns we are going to see are the behavioral patterns. Now, we aren't going to define structures or encapsulate object creation but we are going to deal with behaviors.

What's to deal with in behavior patterns? Well, now we will encapsulate behaviors, for example, algorithms in the Strategy pattern or executions in the command pattern.

Correct Behavior design is the last step after knowing how to deal with object creation and structures. Defining the behavior correctly is the last step of good software design because, all in all, good software design lets us improve algorithms and fix errors easily while the best algorithm implementation will not save us from bad software design.

Strategy design pattern

The Strategy pattern is probably the easiest to understand of the Behavioral patterns. We have used it a few times while developing the previous patterns but without stopping to talk about it. Now we will.

Description

The Strategy pattern uses different algorithms to achieve some specific functionality. These algorithms are hidden behind an interface and, of course, they must be interchangeable. All algorithms achieve the same functionality in a different way. For example, we could have a `Sort` interface and few sorting algorithms. The result is the same, some list is sorted, but we could have used quick sort, merge sort, and so on.

Can you guess when we used a Strategy pattern in the previous chapters? Three, two, one… Well, we heavily used the strategy pattern when we used the `io.Writer` interface. The `io.Writer` interface defines a strategy to write, and the functionality is always the same–to write something. We could write it to the standard out, to some file or to a user-defined type, but we do the same thing at the end–to write. We just change the strategy to write (in this case, we change the place where we write).

Objectives

The objectives of the Strategy pattern are really clear. The pattern should do the following:

- Provide a few algorithms to achieve some specific functionality
- All types achieve the same functionality in a different way but the client of the strategy isn't affected

The problem is that this definition covers a huge spectrum of possibilities. This is because Strategy pattern is actually used for a variety of scenarios and many software engineering solutions come with some kind of strategy within. Therefore it's better to see it in action with a real example.

Rendering images or text

We are going to do something different for this example. Instead of printing text on the console only, we are also going to paint objects on a file.

In this case, we will have two strategies: console and file. But the user of the library won't have to deal with the complexity behind them.

The key feature is that the "caller" doesn't know how the underlying library is working and he just knows the information available on the defined strategy. This is nicely seen on the following diagram:

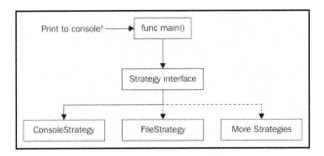

In this diagram, we have chosen to print to console but we won't deal with the **ConsoleStrategy** type directly, we'll always use an interface that represents it. The **ConsoleStrategy** type will hide the implementation details of printing to console to caller in `main` function. **FileStrategy** hides its implementation details as well as any future strategy.

Acceptance criteria

A strategy must have a very clear objective and we will have two ways to achieve it. Our objectives will be as follows:

- Provide a way to show to the user an object (a square) in text or image
- The user must choose between image or text when launching the app
- The app must be able to add more visualization strategies (audio, for example)
- If the user selects text, the word *Square* must be printed in the console
- If the user selects image, an image of a white square on a black background will be printed on a file

Implementation

We aren't going to write tests for this example as it will be quite complicated to check that an image has appeared on the screen (although not impossible by using **OpenCV**, an impressive library for computer vision). We will start directly by defining our strategy interface that each printing strategy must implement (in our case, the file and console types):

```
type PrintStrategy interface {
  Print() error
}
```

That's all. Our strategy defines a simple `Print()` method that returns an `error` (the error-returning type is mandatory when dealing with files, for example). The types that needs to implement `PrintStrategy` will be called `ConsoleSquare` and a `ImageSquare` type:

```
type ConsoleSquare struct {}

type ImageSquare struct {
  DestinationFilePath string
}
```

The `ConsoleSquare` struct doesn't need any inner field because it will always print the word `Square` to the console. The `ImageSquare` struct will store a field for the destination of the image file where we will print the square. We will start with the implementation of the `ConsoleSquare` type as it is the simplest:

```
func(c *ConsoleSquare) Print() error {
  println("Square")
  return nil
}
```

Very easy, but the image is more complex. We won't spend too much time in explaining in detail how the `image` package works because the code is easily understandable:

```
func (t *ImageSquare) Print() error {
  width := 800
  height := 600

  origin := image.Point{0, 0}

  bgImage := image.NewRGBA(image.Rectangle{
    Min: origin,
    Max: image.Point{X: width, Y: height},
  })
```

```
bgColor := image.Uniform{color.RGBA{R: 70, G: 70, B: 70, A:0}}
quality := &jpeg.Options{Quality: 75}

draw.Print(bgImage, bgImage.Bounds(), &bgColor, origin, draw.Src)
```

However, here is a short explanation:

- We define a size for the image (`width` and `height` variables) of 800 pixels of width and 600 pixels of height. Those are going to be the size limits of our image and anything that we write outside of that size won't be visible.

- The `origin` variable stores an `image.Point`, a type to represent a position in any two-dimensional space. We set the position of this point at *(0, 0)*, the upper-left corner of the image.

- We need a bitmap that will represent our background, here we called it `bgImage`. We have a very handy function in the image package to create the `image.RGBA` types called `image.NewRGBA`. We need to pass a rectangle to this function so that it knows the bounds of the image. A rectangle is represented by two `image.Point` types–its upper left corner point (the `Min` field) and its lower right corner point (the `Max` field). We use `origin` as the upper-left and a new point with the values of `width` and `height` as the lower-right point.

- The image will have a gray background color (`bgColor`). This is done by instancing a type of `image.Uniform`, which represents a uniform color (hence the name). The `image.Uniform` type needs an instance of a `color.Color` interface. A `color.Color` type is any type that implements the `RGBA()` (`r, g, b, a uint32`) method to return a `uint32` value for red, green, blue, and alpha colors (RGBA). Alpha is a value for the transparency of a pixel. The `color` package conveniently provides a type called `color.RGBA` for this purpose (in case we don't need to implement our own, which is our case).

- When storing an image in certain formats, we have to specify the quality of the image. It will affect not only the quality but the size of the file, of course. Here, it is defined as 75; 100 is the maximum quality possible that we can set. As you can see, we are using the `jpeg` package here to set the value of a type called `Options` that simply stores the value of the quality, it doesn't have more values to apply.

- Finally, the `draw.Print` function writes the pixels on the supplied image (bgImage) with the characteristics that we have defined on the bounds defined by the same image. The first argument of the `draw.Print` method takes the destination image, where we used `bgImage`. The second argument is the bounds of the object to draw in the destination image, we used the same bounds of the image but we could use any other if we wanted a smaller rectangle. The third argument is the color to use to colorize the bounds. The `Origin` variable is used to tell where the upper-left corner of the bound must be placed. In this case, the bounds are the same size as the image so we need to set it to the origin. The last argument specified is the operation type; just leave it in the `draw.Src` argument.

Now we have to draw the square. The operation is essentially the same as to draw the background but, in this case, we are drawing a square over the previously drawn `bgImage`:

```
squareWidth := 200
squareHeight := 200
squareColor := image.Uniform{color.RGBA{R: 255, G: 0, B: 0, A: 1}}
square := image.Rect(0, 0, squareWidth, squareHeight)
square = square.Add(image.Point{
  X: (width / 2) - (squareWidth / 2),
  Y: (height / 2) - (squareHeight / 2),
})
squareImg := image.NewRGBA(square)

draw.Print(bgImage, squareImg.Bounds(), &squareColor, origin, draw.Src)
```

The square will be of 200*200 pixels of red color. When using the method `Add`, the `Rect` type origin is translated to the supplied point; this is to center the square on the image. We create an image with the square `Rect` and call the `Print` function on the `bgImage` image again to draw the red square over it:

```
w, err := os.Create(t.DestinationFilePath)
if err != nil {
  return fmt.Errorf("Error opening image")
}
defer w.Close()

if err = jpeg.Encode(w, bgImage, quality); err != nil {
  return fmt.Errorf("Error writing image to disk")
}

return nil
}
```

Finally, we will create a file to store the contents of the image. The file will be stored in the path supplied in the `DestinationFilePath` field of the `ImageSquare` struct. To create a file, we use `os.Create` that returns the `*os.File`. As with every file, it must be closed after using it so don't forget to use the `defer` keyword to ensure that you close it when the method finishes.

To defer, or not to defer?
Some people ask why the use of `defer` at all? Wouldn't it be the same to simply write it without `defer` at the end of the function? Well, actually not. If any error occurs during the method execution and you return this error, the `Close` method won't be executed if it's at the end of the function. You can close the file before returning but you'll have to do it in every error check. With `defer`, you don't have to worry about this because the deferred function is executed always (with or without error). This way, we ensure that the file is closed.

To parse the arguments, we'll use the `flag` package. We have used it before but let's recall its usage. A flag is a command that the user can pass when executing our app. We can define a flag by using the `flag.[type]` methods defined in the `flag` package. We want to read the output that the user wants to use from the console. This flag will be called `output`. A flag can have a default value; in this case, it will have the value `console` that will be used when printing to console. So, if the user executes the program without arguments, it prints to console:

```
var output = flag.String("output", "console", "The output to use between
'console' and 'image' file")
```

Our final step is to write the main function:

```
func main(){
    flag.Parse()
```

Remember that the first thing to do in the main when using flags is to parse them using the `flag.Parse()` method! It's very common to forget this step:

```
var activeStrategy PrintStrategy

switch *output {
case "console":
  activeStrategy = &TextSquare{}
case "image":
  activeStrategy = &ImageSquare{"/tmp/image.jpg"}
default:
  activeStrategy = &TextSquare{}
}
```

We define a variable for the strategy that the user has chosen, called `activeStrategy`. But check that the `activeStrategy` variable has the `PrintStrategy` type so it can be populated with any implementation of the `PrintStrategy` variable. We will set `activeStrategy` to a new instance of `TextSquare` when the user writes the **--output=console** command and an `ImageSquare` when we write the **--output=image** command.

Finally, here is the design pattern execution:

```
    err := activeStrategy.Print()
    if err != nil {
      log.Fatal(err)
    }
}
```

Our `activeStrategy` variable is a type implementing `PrintStrategy` and either the `TextSquare` or `ImageSquare` classes. The user will choose at runtime which strategy he wants to use for each particular case. Also, we could have written a factory method pattern to create strategies, so that the strategy creation will also be uncoupled from the main function and abstracted in a different independent package. Think about it: if we have the strategy creation in a different package, it will also allow us to use this project as a library and not only as a standalone app.

Now we will execute both strategies; the `TextSquare` instance will give us a square by printing the word `Square` on the console:

```
$ go run main.go --output=console
Square
```

It has worked as expected. Recalling how flags work, we have to use the `--` (double dash) and the defined flag, `output` in our case. Then you have two options–using = (equals) and immediately writing the value for the flag or writing <space> and the value for the flag. In this case, we have defined the default value of output to the console so the following three executions are equivalent:

```
$ go run main.go --output=console
Square
$ go run main.go --output console
Square
$ go run main.go
Square
```

Now we have to try the file strategy. As defined before, the file strategy will print a red square to a file as an image with dark gray background:

```
$ go run main.go --output image
```

Nothing happened? But everything worked correctly. This is actually bad practice. Users must always have some sort of feedback when using your app or your library. Also, if they are using your code as a library, maybe they have a specific format for output so it won't be nice to directly print to the console. We will solve this issue later. Right now, open the folder `/tmp` with your favourite file explorer and you will see a file called `image.jpg` with our red square in a dark grey background.

Solving small issues in our library

We have a few issues in our code:

- It cannot be used as a library. We have critical code written in the `main` package (strategy creation).
  Solution: Abstract to two different packages the strategy creation from the command-line application.
- None of the strategies are doing any logging to file or console. We must provide a way to read some logs that an external user can integrate in their logging strategies or formats.
  Solution: Inject an `io.Writer` interface as dependency to act as a logging sink.

- Our `TextSquare` class is always writing to the console (an implementer of the `io.Writer` interface) and the `ImageSquare` is always writing to file (another implementer of the `io.Writer` interface). This is too coupled.
  Solution: Inject an `io.Writer` interface so that the `TextSquare` and `ImageSquare` can write to any of the `io.Writer` implementations that are available (file and console, but also bytes buffer, binary encoders, `JSON` handlers... dozens of packages).

So, to use it as a library and solve the first issue, we will follow a common approach in Go file structures for apps and libraries. First, we will place our main package and function outside of the root package; in this case, in a folder called `cli`. It is also common to call this folder `cmd` or even `app`. Then, we will place our `PrintStrategy` interface in the root package, which now will be called the `strategy` package. Finally, we will create a `shapes` package in a folder with the same name where we will put both text and image strategies. So, our file structure will be like this:

- **Root package**: strategy

    File: `print_strategy.go`

- **SubPackage**: shapes

    Files: `image.go`, `text.go`, `factory.go`

- **SubPackage**: cli

    File: `main.go`

We are going to modify our interface a bit to fit the needs we have written previously:

```
type PrintStrategy interface {
  Print() error
  SetLog(io.Writer)
  SetWriter(io.Writer)
}
```

We have added the `SetLog(io.Writer)` method to add a logger strategy to our types; this is to provide feedback to users. Also, it has a `SetWriter` method to set the `io.Writer` strategy. This interface is going to be located on the root package in the `print_strategy.go` file. So the final schema looks like this:

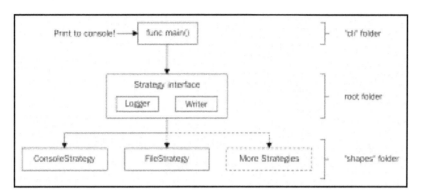

Both the `TextSquare` and `ImageSquare` strategies have to satisfy the `SetLog` and `SetWriter` methods which simply store some object on their fields so, instead of implementing the same twice, we can create a struct that implements them and embed this struct in the strategies. By the way, this would be the composite pattern we have seen previously:

```
type PrintOutput struct {
    Writer    io.Writer
    LogWriter io.Writer
}

func(d *PrintOutput) SetLog(w io.Writer) {
    d.LogWriter = w
}

func(d *PrintOutput) SetWriter(w io.Writer) {
    d.Writer = w
}
```

So now each strategy must have the `PrintOutput` struct embedded if we want to modify their `Writer` and `logger` fields.

We also need to modify our strategy implementation. The TextSquare struct now needs a field to store the output io.Writer (the place where it is going to write instead of writing always to the console) and the log writer. These two fields can be provided by embedding the PrintOutput struct. The TextSquare struct is also stored in the file text.go within the shapes package. So, the struct is now like this:

```
package shapes

type TextSquare struct {
    strategy.PrintOutput
}
```

So now the Print() method is slightly different because, instead of writing directly to the console by using the println function, we have to write whichever io.Writer is stored in the Writer field:

```
func (t *TextSquare) Print() error {
    r := bytes.NewReader([]byte("Circle"))
    io.Copy(t.Writer, r)
    return nil
}
```

The bytes.NewReader is a very useful function that takes an array of bytes and converts them to an io.Reader interface. We need an io.Reader interface to use the io.Copy function. The io.Copy function is also incredibly useful as it takes an io.Reader (as the second parameter) and pipes it to an io.Writer (its first parameter). So, we won't return an error in any case. However, it's easier to do so using directly the Write method of t.Writer:

```
func (t *TextSquare) Print() error {
    t.Writer.Write([]byte("Circle"))
    return nil
}
```

You can use whichever method you like more. Usually, you will use the Write method but it's nice to know the bytes.NewReader function too.

Did you realize that when we use t.Writer, we are actually accessing PrintOutput.Writer? The TextSquare type has a Writer field because the PrintOutput struct has it and it's embedded on the TextSquare struct.

Embedding is not inheritance. We have embedded the
PrintOutput struct on the TextSquare struct. Now we can access
PrintOutput fields as if they were in TextSquare fields. This feels a bit
like inheritance but there is a very important difference here: TextSquare
is not a PrintOutput value but it has a PrintOutput in its composition.
What does it mean? That if you have a function that expects a
PrintOutput, you cannot a pass TextSquare just because it has a
PrintOutput embedded.
But, if you have a function that accepts an interface that PrintOutput
implements, you can pass TextSquare if it has a PrintOutput
embedded. This is what we are doing in our example.

The ImageSquare struct is now like the TextSquare, with a PrintOutput embedded:

```
type ImageSquare struct {
  strategy.PrintOutput
}
```

The Print method also needs to be modified. Now, we aren't creating a file from the Print
method, as it was breaking the single responsibility principle. A file implements an
io.Writer so we will open the file outside of the ImageSquare struct and inject it on the
Writer field. So, we just need to modify the end of the Print() method where we wrote to
the file:

```
draw.Print(bgImage, squareImg.Bounds(), &squareColor, origin, draw.Src)

if i.Writer == nil {
  return fmt.Errorf("No writer stored on ImageSquare")
}
if err := jpeg.Encode(i.Writer, bgImage, quality); err != nil {
  return fmt.Errorf("Error writing image to disk")
}

if i.LogWriter != nil {
  io.Copy(i.LogWriter, "Image written in provided writer\n")
}

return nil
```

If you check our previous implementation, after using `draw`, you can see that we used the `Print` method, we created a file with `os.Create` and passed it to the `jpeg.Encode` function. We have deleted this part about creating the file and we have replaced it with a check looking for a `Writer` in the fields (`if i.Writer != nil`). Then, on `jpeg.Encode` we can replace the file value we were using previously with the content of the `i.Writer` field. Finally, we are using `io.Copy` again to log some message to the `LogWriter` if a logging strategy is provided.

We also have to abstract the knowledge needed from the user to create instances of implementors of the `PrintStrategy` for which we are going to use a Factory method:

```
const (
  TEXT_STRATEGY  = "text"
  IMAGE_STRATEGY = "image"
)

func NewPrinter(s string) (strategy.Output, error) {
  switch s {
  case TEXT_STRATEGY:
    return &TextSquare{
      PrintOutput: strategy.PrintOutput{
        LogWriter: os.Stdout,
      },
    }, nil
  case IMAGE_STRATEGY:
    return &ImageSquare{
      PrintOutput: strategy.PrintOutput{
        LogWriter: os.Stdout,
      },
    }, nil
  default:
    return nil, fmt.Errorf("Strategy '%s' not found\n", s)
  }
}
```

We have two constants, one of each of our strategies: `TEXT_STRATEGY` and `IMAGE_STRATEGY`. Those are the constants that must be provided to the factory to retrieve each square drawer strategy. Our factory method receives an argument `s`, which is a string with one of the previous constants.

Each strategy has a `PrintOutput` type embedded with a default logger to `stdout` but you can override it later by using the `SetLog(io.Writer)` methods. This approach could be considered a Factory of prototypes. If it is not a recognized strategy, a proper message error will be returned.

What we have now is a library. We have all the functionality we need between the strategy and shapes packages. Now we will write the main package and function in a new folder called cli:

```
var output = flag.String("output", "text", "The output to use between "+
  "'console' and 'image' file")

func main() {
  flag.Parse()
```

Again, like before, the main function starts by parsing the input arguments on the console to gather the chosen strategy. We can use the variable output now to create a strategy without Factory:

```
activeStrategy, err := shapes.NewPrinter(*output)
if err != nil {
  log.Fatal(err)
}
```

With this snippet, we have our strategy or we stop program execution in the log.Fatal method if any error is found (such as an unrecognized strategy).

Now we will implement the business needs by using our library. For the purpose of the TextStrategy, we want to write, for example, to stdout. For the purpose of the image, we will write to /tmp/image.jpg. Just like before. So, following the previous statements, we can write:

```
switch *output {
case shapes.TEXT_STRATEGY:
  activeStrategy.SetWriter(os.Stdout)
case shapes.IMAGE_STRATEGY:
  w, err := os.Create("/tmp/image.jpg")
  if err != nil {
    log.Fatal("Error opening image")
  }
  defer w.Close()

  activeStrategy.SetWriter(w)
}
```

In the case of TEXT_STRATEGY, we use SetWriter to set the io.Writer to os.Stdout. In the case of IMAGE_STRATEGY, we create an image in any of our folders and pass the file variable to the SetWriter method. Remember that os.File implements the io.Reader and io.Writer interfaces, so it's perfectly legal to pass it as an io.Writer to the SetWriter method:

```
err = activeStrategy.Print()
if err != nil {
  log.Fatal(err)
}
```

Finally, we call the `Print` method of whichever strategy was chosen by the user and check for possible errors. Let's try the program now:

```
$ go run main.go --output text
Circle
```

It has worked as expected. What about the image strategy?

```
$ go run main.go --output image
Image written in provided writer
```

If we check in `/tmp/image.jpg`, we can find our red square on the dark background.

Final words on the Strategy pattern

We have learned a powerful way to encapsulate algorithms in different structs. We have also used embedding instead of inheritance to provide cross-functionality between types, which will come in handy very often in our apps. You'll find yourself combining strategies here and there as we have seen in the second example, where we have strategies for logging and writing by using the `io.Writer` interface, a strategy for byte-streaming operations.

Chain of responsibility design pattern

Our next pattern is called **chain of responsibility**. As its name implies, it consists of a chain and, in our case, each link of the chain follows the single responsibility principle.

Description

The single responsibility principle implies that a type, function, method, or any similar abstraction must have one single responsibility only and it must do it quite well. This way, we can apply many functions that achieve one specific thing each to some struct, slice, map, and so on.

When we apply many of these abstractions in a logical way very often, we can chain them to execute in order such as, for example, a logging chain.

A logging chain is a set of types that logs the output of some program to more than one `io.Writer` interface. We could have a type that logs to the console, a type that logs to a file, and a type that logs to a remote server. You can make three calls every time you want to do some logging, but it's more elegant to make only one and provoke a chain reaction.

But also, we could have a chain of checks and, in case one of them fails, break the chain and return something. This is the authentication and authorization middleware works.

Objectives

The objective of the chain of responsibility is to provide to the developer a way to chain actions at runtime. The actions are chained to each other and each link will execute some action and pass the request to the next link (or not). The following are the objectives followed by this pattern:

- Dynamically chain the actions at runtime based on some input
- Pass a request through a chain of processors until one of them can process it, in which case the chain could be stopped

A multi-logger chain

We are going to develop a multi-logger solution that we can chain in the way we want. We will use two different console loggers and one general-purpose logger:

1. We need a simple logger that logs the text of a request with a prefix *First logger* and passes it to the next link in the chain.
2. A second logger will write on the console if the incoming text has the word `hello` and pass the request to a third logger. But, if not, the chain will be broken and it will return immediately.
3. A third logger type is a general purpose logger called `WriterLogger` that uses an `io.Writer` interface to log.
4. A concrete implementation of the `WriterLogger` writes to a file and represents the third link in the chain.

The implementation of these steps is described in the following figure:

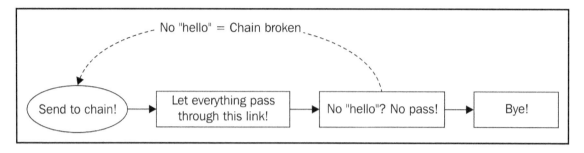

Unit test

The very first thing to do for the chain is, as usual, to define the interface. A chain of responsibility interface will usually have, at least, a `Next()` method. The `Next()` method is the one that executes the next link in the chain, of course:

```
type ChainLogger interface {
   Next(string)
}
```

The `Next` method on our example's interface takes the message we want to log and passes it to the following link in the chain. As written in the acceptance criteria, we need three loggers:

```
type FirstLogger struct {
   NextChain ChainLogger
}

func (f *FirstLogger) Next(s string) {}

type SecondLogger struct {
   NextChain ChainLogger
}

func (f *SecondLogger) Next(s string) {}

type WriterLogger struct {
   NextChain ChainLogger
   Writer    io.Writer
}
func (w *WriterLogger) Next(s string) {}
```

The FirstLogger and SecondLogger types have exactly the same structure–both implement ChainLogger and have a NextChain field that points to the next ChainLogger.
The WriterLogger type is equal to the FirstLogger and SecondLogger types but also has a field to write its data to, so you can pass any io.Writer interface to it.
As we have done before, we'll implement an io.Writer struct to use in our testing. In our test file, we define the following struct:

```
type myTestWriter struct {
  receivedMessage string
}

func (m *myTestWriter) Write(p []byte) (int, error) {
  m.receivedMessage += string(p)
  return len(p), nil
}

func(m *myTestWriter) Next(s string){
  m.Write([]byte(s))
}
```

We will pass an instance of the myTestWriter struct to WriterLogger so we can track what's being logged on testing. The myTestWriter class implements the common Write([]byte) (int, error) method from the io.Writer interface. Remember, if it has the Write method, it can be used as io.Writer. The Write method simply stored the string argument to the receivedMessage field so we can check later its value on tests.

This is the beginning of the first test function:

```
func TestCreateDefaultChain(t *testing.T) {
  //Our test ChainLogger
  myWriter := myTestWriter{}

  writerLogger := WriterLogger{Writer: &myWriter}
  second := SecondLogger{NextChain: &writerLogger}
  chain := FirstLogger{NextChain: &second}
```

Let's describe these few lines a bit as they are quite important. We create a variable with a default myTestWriter type that we'll use as an io.Writer interface in the last link of our chain. Then we create the last piece of the link chain, the writerLogger interface. When implementing the chain, you usually start with the last piece on the link and, in our case, it is a WriterLogger. The WriterLogger writes to an io.Writer so we pass myWriter as io.Writer interface.

Then we have created a `SecondLogger`, the middle link in our chain, with a pointer to the `writerLogger`. As we mentioned before, `SecondLogger` just logs and passes the message in case it contains the word `hello`. In a production app, it could be an error-only logger.

Finally, the first link in the chain has the variable name chain. It points to the second logger. So, to resume, our chain looks like this: `FirstLogger | SecondLogger | WriterLogger`.

This is going to be our default setup for our tests:

```
  t.Run("3 loggers, 2 of them writes to console, second only if it founds " +
    "the word 'hello', third writes to some variable if second found
  'hello'",
    func(t *testing.T){
      chain.Next("message that breaks the chain\n")

      if myWriter.receivedMessage != "" {
        t.Fatal("Last link should not receive any message")
      }

      chain.Next("Hello\n")

      if !strings.Contains(myWriter.receivedMessage, "Hello") {
        t.Fatal("Last link didn't received expected message")
      }
  })
```

Continuing with Go 1.7 or later testing signatures, we define an inner test with the following description: *three loggers, two of them write to console, the second only if it finds the word 'hello', the third writes to some variable if the second found 'hello'*. It's quite descriptive and very easy to understand if someone else has to maintain this code.

First, we use a message on the `Next` method that will not reach the third link in the chain as it doesn't contain the word `hello`. We check the contents of the `receivedMessage` variable, that by default is empty, to see if it has changed because it shouldn't.

Next, we use the chain variable again, our first link in the chain, and pass the message `"Hello\n"`. According to the description of the test, it should log using `FirstLogger`, then in `SecondLogger` and finally in `WriterLogger` because it contains the word `hello` and the `SecondLogger` will let it pass.

The test checks that `myWriter`, the last link in the chain that stored the past message in a variable called `receivedMessage`, has the word that we passed first in the chain: hello. Let's run it so it fails:

```
go test -v .
=== RUN   TestCreateDefaultChain
=== RUN
TestCreateDefaultChain/3_loggers,_2_of_them_writes_to_console,_second_only_
if_it_founds_the_word_'hello',_third_writes_to_some_variable_if_second_foun
d_'hello'
    --- FAIL: TestCreateDefaultChain (0.00s)
    --- FAIL:
TestCreateDefaultChain/3_loggers,_2_of_them_writes_to_console,_second_only_
if_it_founds_the_word_'hello',_third_writes_to_some_variable_if_second_foun
d_'hello' (0.00s)
        chain_test.go:33: Last message didn't received expected message
FAIL
exit status 1
FAIL
```

The test passed for the first check of the test and didn't for the second check. Well... ideally no check should pass before any implementation is done. Remember that in test-driven development, tests must fail on the first launch because the code they are testing isn't implemented yet. Go zero-initialization misleads us with this passed check on the test. We can solve this in two ways:

- Making the signature of the `ChainLogger` to return an error: `Next(string)` `error`. This way, we would break the chain returning an error. This is a much more convenient way in general, but it will introduce quite a lot of boilerplate right now.
- Changing the `receivedMessage` field to a pointer. A default value of a pointer is nil, instead of an empty string.

We will use the second option now, as it's much simpler and quite effective too. So let's change the signature of the `myTestWriter` struct to the following:

```go
type myTestWriter struct {
  receivedMessage *string
}

func (m *myTestWriter) Write(p []byte) (int, error) {
  if m.receivedMessage == nil {
        m.receivedMessage = new(string)
  }
  tempMessage := fmt.Sprintf("%s%s", m.receivedMessage, p)
```

```
    m.receivedMessage = &tempMessage
    return len(p), nil
}

func (m *myTestWriter) Next(s string) {
  m.Write([]byte(s))
}
```

Check that the type of `receivedMessage` has the asterisk (*) now to indicate that it's a pointer to a string. The `Write` function needed to change too. Now we have to check the contents of the `receivedMessage` field because, as every pointer, it's initialized to nil. Then we have to store the message in a variable first, so we can take the address in the next line on the assignment (`m.receivedMessage = &tempMessage`).

So now our test code should change a bit too:

```
t.Run("3 loggers, 2 of them writes to console, second only if it founds "+
  "the word 'hello', third writes to some variable if second found 'hello'",
func(t *testing.T) {
  chain.Next("message that breaks the chain\n")

  if myWriter.receivedMessage != nil {
    t.Error("Last link should not receive any message")
  }

  chain.Next("Hello\n")

  if myWriter.receivedMessage == "" ||
!strings.Contains(*myWriter.receivedMessage, "Hello") {
    t.Fatal("Last link didn't received expected message")
  }
})
```

Now we are checking that `myWriter.receivedMessage` is actually `nil`, so no content has been written for sure on the variable. Also, we have to change the second if to check first that the member isn't nil before checking its contents or it can throw a panic on test. Let's test it again:

```
go test -v .
=== RUN    TestCreateDefaultChain
=== RUN
TestCreateDefaultChain/3_loggers,_2_of_them_writes_to_console,_second_only_
if_it_founds_the_word_'hello',_third_writes_to_some_variable_if_second_foun
d_'hello'
--- FAIL: TestCreateDefaultChain (0.00s)
--- FAIL:
TestCreateDefaultChain/3_loggers,_2_of_them_writes_to_console,_second_only_
```

```
if_it_founds_the_word_'hello',_third_writes_to_some_variable_if_second_foun
d_'hello' (0.00s)
        chain_test.go:40: Last link didn't received expected message
FAIL
exit status 1
FAIL
```

It fails again and, again, the first half of the test passes correctly without implemented code. So what should we do now? We have change the signature of the `myWriter` type to make the test fail in both checks and, again, just fail in the second. Well, in this case we can pass this small issue. When writing tests, we must be very careful to not get too crazy about them; unit tests are tools to help us write and maintain code, but our target is to write functionality, not tests. This is important to keep in mind as you can get really crazy engineering unit tests.

Implementation

Now we have to implement the first, second, and third loggers called `FirstLogger`, `SecondLogger`, and `WriterLogger` respectively. The `FirstLogger` logger is the easiest one as described in the first acceptance criterion: *We need a simple logger that logs the text of a request with a prefix First logger: and passes it to the next link in the chain*. So let's do it:

```go
type FirstLogger struct {
  NextChain ChainLogger
}

func (f *FirstLogger) Next(s string) {
  fmt.Printf("First logger: %s\n", s)

  if f.NextChain != nil {
    f.NextChain.Next(s)
  }
}
```

The implementation is quite easy. Using the `fmt.Printf` method to format and print the incoming string, we appended the text `First Logger:` text. Then, we check that the `NextChain` type has actually some content and pass the control to it by calling its `Next(string)` method. The test shouldn't pass yet so we'll continue with the `SecondLogger` logger:

```go
type SecondLogger struct {
  NextChain ChainLogger
}
```

```
func (se *SecondLogger) Next(s string) {
  if strings.Contains(strings.ToLower(s), "hello") {
    fmt.Printf("Second logger: %s\n", s)

    if se.NextChain != nil {
      se.NextChain.Next(s)
    }

    return
  }

  fmt.Printf("Finishing in second logging\n\n")
}
```

As mentioned in the second acceptance criterion, the `SecondLogger` description is: *A second logger will write on the console if the incoming text has the word "hello" and pass the request to a third logger.* First of all, it checks whether the incoming text contains the text `hello`. If it's true, it prints the message to the console, appending the text `Second logger:` and passes the message to the next link in the chain (check previous instance that a third link exists).

But if it doesn't contain the text `hello`, the chain is broken and it prints the message `Finishing in second logging`.

We'll finalize with the `WriterLogger` type:

```
type WriterLogger struct {
  NextChain ChainLogger
  Writer    io.Writer
}

func (w *WriterLogger) Next(s string) {
  if w.Writer != nil {
    w.Writer.Write([]byte("WriterLogger: " + s))
  }

  if w.NextChain != nil {
    w.NextChain.Next(s)
  }
}
```

The `WriterLogger` struct's `Next` method checks that there is an existing `io.Writer` interface stored in the `Writer` member and writes there the incoming message appending the text `WriterLogger:` to it. Then, like the previous links, check that there are more links to pass the message.

Now the tests will pass successfully:

```
go test -v .
=== RUN   TestCreateDefaultChain
=== RUN
TestCreateDefaultChain/3_loggers,_2_of_them_writes_to_console,_second_only_
if_it_founds_the_word_'hello',_third_writes_to_some_variable_if_second_foun
d_'hello'
    First logger: message that breaks the chain
    Finishing in second logging
    First logger: Hello
    Second logger: Hello
    --- PASS: TestCreateDefaultChain (0.00s)
        --- PASS:
TestCreateDefaultChain/3_loggers,_2_of_them_writes_to_console,_second_only_
if_it_founds_the_word_'hello',_third_writes_to_some_variable_if_second_foun
d_'hello' (0.00s)
    PASS
    ok
```

The first half of the test prints two messages–the `First logger:` message that breaks the chain, which is the expected message for the `FirstLogger`. But it halts in the `SecondLogger` because no `hello` word has been found on the incoming message; that's why it prints the `Finishing in second logging` string.

The second half of the test receives the message `Hello`. So the `FirstLogger` prints and the `SecondLogger` prints too. The third logger doesn't print to console at all but to our `myWriter.receivedMessage` line defined in the test.

What about a closure?

Sometimes it can be useful to define an even more flexible link in the chain for quick debugging. We can use closures for this so that the link functionality is defined by the caller. What does a closure link look like? Similar to the `WriterLogger` logger:

```go
type ClosureChain struct {
  NextChain ChainLogger
  Closure   func(string)
}

func (c *ClosureChain) Next(s string) {
  if c.Closure != nil {
    c.Closure(s)
  }
```

```
        if c.NextChain != nil {
          c.Next(s)
        }
      }
```

The `ClosureChain` type has a `NextChain`, as usual, and a `Closure` member. Look at the signature of the `Closure`: `func(string)`. This means it is a function that takes a `string` and returns nothing.

The `Next(string)` method for `ClosureChain` checks that the `Closure` member is stored and executes it with the incoming string. As usual, the link checks for more links to pass the message as every link in the chain.

So, how do we use it now? We'll define a new test to show its functionality:

```
    t.Run("2 loggers, second uses the closure implementation", func(t
    *testing.T) {
      myWriter = myTestWriter{}
      closureLogger := ClosureChain{
        Closure: func(s string) {
          fmt.Printf("My closure logger! Message: %s\n", s)
          myWriter.receivedMessage = &s
        },
      }

      writerLogger.NextChain = &closureLogger

      chain.Next("Hello closure logger")

      if *myWriter.receivedMessage != "Hello closure logger" {
        t.Fatal("Expected message wasn't received in myWriter")
      }
    })
```

The description of this test makes it clear: `"2 loggers, second uses the closure implementation"`. We simply use two `ChainLogger` implementations and we use the `closureLogger` in the second link. We have created a new `myTestWriter` to store the contents of the message. When defining the `ClosureChain`, we defined an anonymous function directly on the `Closure` member when creating `closureLogger`. It prints `"My closure logger! Message: %s\n"` with the incoming message replacing `"%s"`. Then, we store the incoming message on `myWriter`, to check later.

After defining this new link, we use the third link from the previous test, add the closure as the fourth link, and passed the message `Hello closure logger`. We use the word `Hello` at the beginning so that we ensure that the message will pass the `SecondLogger`.

Finally, the contents of `myWriter.receivedMessage` must contain the pased text: `Hello closure logger`. This is quite a flexible approach with one drawback: when defining a closure like this, we cannot test its contents in a very elegant way. Let's run the tests again:

```
go test -v .
=== RUN   TestCreateDefaultChain
=== RUN
TestCreateDefaultChain/3_loggers,_2_of_them_writes_to_console,_second_only_
if_it_founds_the_word_'hello',_third_writes_to_some_variable_if_second_foun
d_'hello'
First logger: message that breaks the chain
Finishing in second logging

First logger: Hello
Second logger: Hello
=== RUN
TestCreateDefaultChain/2_loggers,_second_uses_the_closure_implementation
First logger: Hello closure logger
Second logger: Hello closure logger
My closure logger! Message: Hello closure logger
--- PASS: TestCreateDefaultChain (0.00s)
    --- PASS:
TestCreateDefaultChain/3_loggers,_2_of_them_writes_to_console,_second_only_
if_it_founds_the_word_'hello',_third_writes_to_some_variable_if_second_foun
d_'hello' (0.00s)
    --- PASS:
TestCreateDefaultChain/2_loggers,_second_uses_the_closure_implementation
(0.00s)
PASS
ok
```

Look at the third `RUN`: the message passes correctly through the first, second, and third links to arrive at the closure that prints the expected `My closure logger! Message: Hello closure logger` message.

It's very useful to add a closure method implementation to some interfaces as it provides quite a lot of flexibility when using the library. You can find this approach very often in Go code, being the most known the one of package `net/http`. The `HandleFunc` function which we used previously in the structural patterns to define a handler for an HTTP request.

Putting it together

We learned a powerful tool to achieve dynamic processing of actions and state handling. The Chain of responsibility pattern is widely used, also to create **Finite State Machines (FSM)**. It is also used interchangeably with the Decorator pattern with the difference that when you decorate, you change the structure of an object while with the chain you define a behavior for each link in the chain that can break it too.

Command design pattern

To finish with this chapter, we will see also the **Command** pattern–a tiny design pattern but still frequently used. You need a way to connect types that are really unrelated? So design a Command for them.

Description

The Command design pattern is quite similar to the Strategy design pattern but with key differences. While in the strategy pattern we focus on changing algorithms, in the Command pattern, we focus on the invocation of something or on the abstraction of some type.

A Command pattern is commonly seen as a container. You put something like the info for user interaction on a UI that could be `click on login` and pass it as a command. You don't need to have the complexity related to the `click on login` action in the command but simply the action itself.

An example for the organic world would be a box for a delivery company. We can put anything on it but, as a delivery company, we are interested in managing the box instead of its contents directly.

The command pattern will be used heavily when dealing with channels. With channels you can send any message through it but, if we need a response from the receiving side of the channel, a common approach is to create a command that has a second, response channel attached where we are listening.

Similarly, a good example would be a multi-player video game, where every stroke of each user can be sent as commands to the rest of the users through the network.

Objectives

When using the Command design pattern, we are trying to encapsulate some sort of action or information in a light package that must be processed somewhere else. It's similar to the Strategy pattern but, in fact, a Command could trigger a preconfigured Strategy somewhere else, so they are not the same. The following are the objectives for this design pattern:

- Put some information into a box. Just the receiver will open the box and know its contents.
- Delegate some action somewhere else.

The behavior is also explained in the following diagram:

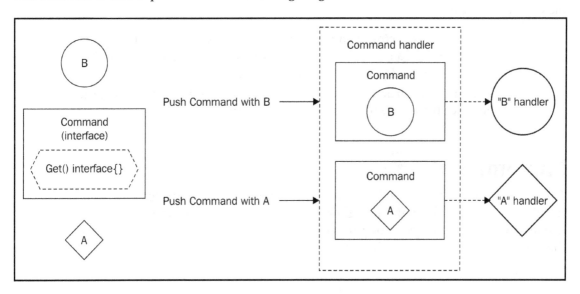

There we have a **Command** interface with a **Get() interface{}** method. We have a type **A** and a type **B**. The idea is that **A** and **B** implement the **Command** interface to return themselves as an `interface{}`. As now they implement **Command**, they can be used in a **Command handler** which doesn't care very much about the underlying type. Now **A** and **B** can travel through functions that handles commands or store Commands freely. But **B** handler can take an object from any **Command** handler to "unwrap" it and take its **B** content as well as **A** command handler with its `A` content.

We put the information in a box (the **Command**) and delegate what to do with it to the handlers of Commands.

A simple queue

Our first example is going to be pretty small. We will put some information into a Command implementer and we will have a queue. We will create many instances of a type implementing a Command pattern and we will pass them to a queue that will store the commands until three of them are in the queue, at which time it will process them.

Acceptance criteria

So the ideal acceptance criteria to understand well the implications of the Command should reflect somehow the creation of a box that can accept unrelated types and the execution of the Command itself:

- We need a constructor of console printing commands. When using this constructor with a `string`, it will return a command that will print it. In this case, the handler is inside the command that acts as a box and as a handler.
- We need a data structure that stores incoming commands in a queue and prints them once the queue reaches the length of three.

Implementation

This pattern is quite simple and we will write a few different examples so we'll implement the library directly to keep things light and short. The classical Command design pattern usually has a common type structure with an `Execute` method. We are also going to use this structure as it's quite flexible and simple:

```
type Command interface {
   Execute()
}
```

This is generic enough to fill a lot of unrelated types! Think about it–we are going to create a type that prints to console when using the `Execute()` method but it could print a number or launch a rocket as well! The key here is to focus on invocations because the handlers are also in Command. So we need some type implementing this interface and printing to the console some sort of message:

```
type ConsoleOutput struct {
   message string
}

func (c *ConsoleOutput) Execute() {
```

```
        fmt.Println(c.message)
    }
```

The `ConsoleOutput` type implements the `Command` interface and prints to the console the member called `message`.

As defined in the first acceptance criterion, we need a `Command` constructor that accepts a message string and returns the `Command` interface. It will have the signature `func CreateCommand(s string) Command`:

```
    func CreateCommand(s string) Command {
        fmt.Println("Creating command")

        return &ConsoleOutput{
            message: s,
        }
    }
```

For the command `queue`, we'll define a very simple type called `CommandQueue` to store in a queue any type implementing the `Command` interface:

```
    type CommandQueue struct {
        queue []Command
    }

    func (p *CommandQueue) AddCommand(c Command) {
        p.queue = append(p.queue, c)

        if len(p.queue) == 3 {
            for _, command := range p.queue {
                command.Execute()
            }

            p.queue = make([]Command, 3)
        }
    }
```

The `CommandQueue` type stores an array of the `Commands` interface. When the queue array reaches three items, it executes all the commands stored in the queue field. If it hasn't reached the required length yet, it just stores the command.

We will create five commands, enough to trigger the command queue mechanism, and add them to the queue. Each time a command is created, the message `Creating command` will be printed to the console. When we create the third command, the automatic command executor will be launched, printing the first three messages. We create and add two commands more, but because we haven't reached the third command again, they won't be printed and just the `Creating command` messages will be printed:

```
func main() {
  queue := CommandQueue{}

  queue.AddCommand(CreateCommand("First message"))
  queue.AddCommand(CreateCommand("Second message"))
  queue.AddCommand(CreateCommand("Third message"))

  queue.AddCommand(CreateCommand("Fourth message"))
  queue.AddCommand(CreateCommand("Fifth message"))
}
```

Let's run the `main` program. Our definition said that the commands are processed once every three messages and we will create a total of five messages. The first three messages must be printed but not the fourth and fifth because we didn't reach a sixth message to trigger the command processing:

```
$go run command.go
Creating command
Creating command
Creating command
First message
Second message
Third message
Creating command
Creating command
```

As you can see, the fourth and fifth messages aren't printed, as expected, but we know that the commands were created and stored on the array. They just weren't processed because the queue was waiting for one command more to trigger the processor.

More examples

The previous example shows how to use a Command handler that executes the content of the command. But a common way to use a Command pattern is to delegate the information, instead of the execution, to a different object.

For example, instead of printing to the console, we will create a command that extracts information:

```
type Command interface {
    Info() string
}
```

In this case, our `Command` interface will have a method named `Info` that will retrieve some information from its implementor. We will create two implementations; one will return the time passed since the creation of the command to its execution:

```
type TimePassed struct {
    start time.Time
}

func (t *TimePassed) Info() string {
    return time.Since(t.start).String()
}
```

The `time.Since` function returns the time elapsed since the time stored in the provided parameter. We returned the string representation of the passed time by calling the `String()` method on the `time.Time` type. The second implementation of our new `Command` will return the message `Hello World!`:

```
type HelloMessage struct{}

func (h HelloMessage) Info() string {
    return "Hello world!"
}
```

And our `main` function will simply create an instance of each type, then waits for a second and print the info returned from each `Command`:

```
func main() {
    var timeCommand Command
    timeCommand = &TimePassed{time.Now()}

    var helloCommand Command
    helloCommand = &HelloMessage{}

    time.Sleep(time.Second)
    fmt.Println(timeCommand.Info())
    fmt.Println(helloCommand.Info())
}
```

The `time.Sleep` function stops the execution of the current goroutine for the specified period (a second). So, to recall–the `timeCommand` variable stores the time when the program was started and its `Info()` method returns a string representation of the time that passed since we give a value to the type to the moment were we called the `Info()` method on it. The `helloCommand` variable returns the message `Hello World!` when we call its `Info()` method. Here we haven't implemented a `Command` handler again to keep things simple but we can consider the console as the handler because we can only print ASCII characters on it like the ones retrieved by the `Info()` method.

Let's run the `main` function:

```
go run command.go
1.000216755s
Hello world!
```

Here we are. In this case, we retrieve some information by using the Command pattern. One type stores `time` information while the other stores nothing and it simply returns the same simple string. Each time we run the `main` function will return a different elapsed time, so don't worry if the time doesn't match with the one in the example.

Chain of responsibility of commands

Do you remember the chain of responsibility design pattern? We were passing a `string` message between links to print its contents. But we could be using the previous Command to retrieve information for logging to the console. We'll mainly reuse the code that we have written already.

The `Command` interface will be from the type interface that returns a `string` from the previous example:

```
type Command interface {
  Info() string
}
```

We will use the `Command` implementation of the `TimePassed` type too:

```
type TimePassed struct {
  start time.Time
}

func (t *TimePassed) Info() string {
  return time.Since(t.start).String()
}
```

Remember that this type returns the elapsed time from the object creation on its `Info()` string method. We also need the `ChainLogger` interface from the *Chain of responsibility design pattern* section of this chapter but, this time, it will pass Commands on its `Next` method instead of `string`:

```
type ChainLogger interface {
   Next(Command)
}
```

We'll use just the same type for two links in the chain for simplicity. This link is very similar to the `FirstLogger` type from the chain of responsibility example, but this time it will append the message `Elapsed time from creation:` and it will wait 1 second before printing. We'll call it `Logger` instead of `FirstLogger`:

```
type Logger struct {
   NextChain ChainLogger
}

func (f *Logger) Next(c Command) {
   time.Sleep(time.Second)

   fmt.Printf("Elapsed time from creation: %s\n", c.Info())

   if f.NextChain != nil {
      f.NextChain.Next(c)
   }
}
```

Finally, we need a `main` function to execute the chain that takes `Command` pointers:

```
func main() {
   second := new(Logger)
   first := Logger{NextChain: second}

   command := &TimePassed{start: time.Now()}

   first.Next(command)
}
```

Line by line, we create a variable called `second` with a pointer to a `Logger`; this is going to be the second link in our chain. Then we create a variable called `first`, that will be the first link in the chain. The first link points to the `second` variable, the second link in the chain.

Then, we create an instance of `TimePassed` to use it as the `Command` type. The start time of this command is the execution time (the `time.Now()` method returns the time in the moment of the execution).

Finally, we pass the `Command` interface to the chain on the `first.Next(command)` statement. The output of this program is the following:

```
go run chain_command.go
Elapsed time from creation: 1.0003419s
Elapsed time from creation: 2.000682s
```

The resulting output is reflected in the following diagram: The command with the time field is pushed to the first link that knows how to execute Commands of any type. Then it passes the Command to the second link that also knows how to execute Commands:

This approach hides the complexity behind each `Command` execution from the Command handlers on each link. The functionality hidden behind a Command can be simple or incredibly complex but the idea here is to reuse the handler to manage many types of unrelated implementations.

Rounding-up the Command pattern up

Command is a very tiny design pattern; its functionality is quite easy to understand but it's widely used for its simplicity. It looks very similar to the Strategy pattern but remember that Strategy is about having many algorithms to achieve some specific task, but all of them achieve the same task. In the Command pattern, you have many tasks to execute, and not all of them need to be equal.

So, in short, the Command pattern is about execution encapsulation and delegation so that just the receiver or receivers trigger that execution.

Summary

We have taken our first steps in the Behavioral patterns. The objective of this chapter was to introduce the reader to the concept of algorithm and execution encapsulation using proper interfaces and structures. With the strategy, we have encapsulated algorithms, with the chain of responsibility handlers and with the Command design pattern executions.

Now, with the knowledge we have acquired about the strategy pattern, we can uncouple heavily our applications from their algorithms, just for testing, this is a very useful feature to inject mocks in different types that would be almost impossible to test. But also for anything that could need different approaches based on some context (such as shorting a list; some algorithms perform better depending on the distribution of the list).

The Chain of Responsibility pattern opens the door of middleware of any type and plugin-like libraries to improve the functionality of some part. Many open source projects uses a Chain of Responsibility to handler HTTP requests and responses to extract information to the end user (such as cookies info) or check authentication details (I'll let you pass to the next link only if I have you on my database).

Finally, the Command pattern is the most common pattern for UI handling but also very useful in many other scenarios where we need some type of handling between many unrelated types that are travelling through the code (such as a message passed through a channel).

6
Behavioral Patterns - Template, Memento, and Interpreter Design Patterns

In this chapter, we will see the next three Behavioral design patterns. The difficulty is being raised as now we will use combinations of Structural and Creational patterns to better solve the objective of some of the Behavioral patterns.

We will start with Template design pattern, a pattern that looks very similar to the Strategy pattern but that provides greater flexibility. Memento design pattern is used in 99% of applications we use every day to achieve undo functions and transactional operations. Finally, we will write a reverse polish notation interpreter to perform simple mathematical operations.

Let's start with the Template design pattern.

Template design pattern

The **Template** pattern is one of those widely used patterns that are incredibly useful, especially when writing libraries and frameworks. The idea is to provide a user some way to execute code within an algorithm.

In this section, we will see how to write idiomatic Go Template patterns and see some Go source code where it's wisely used. We will write an algorithm of three steps where the second step is delegated to the user while the first and third aren't. The first and third steps on the algorithm represent the template.

Description

While with the Strategy pattern we were encapsulating algorithm implementation in different strategies, with the Template pattern we will try to achieve something similar but with just part of the algorithm.

The Template design pattern lets the user write a part of an algorithm while the rest is executed by the abstraction. This is common when creating libraries to ease in some complex task or when reusability of some algorithm is compromised by only a part of it.

Imagine, for example, that we have a long transaction of HTTP requests. We have to perform the following steps:

1. Authenticate user.
2. Authorize him.
3. Retrieve some details from a database.
4. Make some modification.
5. Send the details back in a new request.

It wouldn't make sense to repeat steps 1 to 5 in the user's code every time he needs to modify something on the database. Instead, steps 1, 2, 3, and 5 will be abstracted in the same algorithm that receives an interface with whatever the fifth step needs to finish the transaction. It doesn't need to be a interface either, it could be a callback.

Objectives

The Template design pattern is all about reusability and giving responsibilities to the user. So the objectives for this pattern are following:

- Defer a part of an algorithm of the library to a the user
- Improve reusability by abstracting the parts of the code that are not common between executions

Example – a simple algorithm with a deferred step

In our first example, we are going to write an algorithm that is composed of three steps and each of them returns a message. The first and third steps are controlled by the Template and just the second step is deferred to the user.

Requirements and acceptance criteria

A brief description of what the Template pattern has to do is to define a template for an algorithm of three steps that defers the implementation of the second step to the user:

1. Each step in the algorithm must return a string.
2. The first step is a method called `first()` and returns the string `hello`.
3. The third step is a method called `third()` and returns the string `template`.
4. The second step is whatever string the user wants to return but it's defined by the `MessageRetriever` interface that has a `Message()` `string` method.
5. The algorithm is executed sequentially by a method called `ExecuteAlgorithm` and returns the strings returned by each step joined in a single string by a space.

Unit tests for the simple algorithm

We will focus on testing the public methods only. This is a very common approach. All in all, if your private methods aren't called from some level of the public ones, they aren't called at all. We need two interfaces here, one for the Template implementors and one for the abstract step of the algorithm:

```
type MessageRetriever interface {
  Message()string
}

type Template interface {
    first() string
    third() string
    ExecuteAlgorithm(MessageRetriever) string
}
```

A Template implementor will accept a `MessageRetriever` interface to execute as part of its execution algorithm. We need a type that implements this interface called `Template`, we will call it `TemplateImpl`:

```
type TemplateImpl struct{}

func (t *TemplateImpl) first() string {
  return ""
}

func (t *TemplateImpl) third() string {
  return ""
}
```

```
func (t *TemplateImpl) ExecuteAlgorithm(m MessageRetriever) string {
    return ""
}
```

So our first test checks the fourth and fifth acceptance criteria. We will create the TestStruct type that implements the MessageRetriever interface returning the string world and has embedded the Template so that it can call the ExecuteAlgorithm method. It will act as the Template and the abstraction:

```
type TestStruct struct {
    Template
}

func (m *TestStruct) Message() string {
    return "world"
}
```

First, we will define the TestStruct type. In this case, the part of the algorithm deferred to us is going to return the world text. This is the string we will look for later in the test doing a check of type "is the word world present on this string?".

Take a close look, the TestStruct embeds a type called Template which represents the Template pattern of our algorithm.

When we implement the Message() method, we are implicitly implementing the MessageRetriever interface. So now we can use TestStruct type as a pointer to a MessageRetriever interface:

```
func TestTemplate_ExecuteAlgorithm(t *testing.T) {
    t.Run("Using interfaces", func(t *testing.T){
        s := &TestStruct{}
        res := s.ExecuteAlgorithm(s)
      expected := "world"

        if !strings.Contains(res, expected) {
            t.Errorf("Expected string '%s' wasn't found on returned string\n",
expected)
        }
    })
}
```

In the test, we will use the type we have just created. When we call the ExecuteAlgorithm method, we need to pass the MessageRetriever interface. As the TestStruct type also implements the MessageRetriever interface, we can pass it as an argument, but this is not mandatory, of course.

The result of the `ExecuteAlgorithm` method, as defined in the fifth acceptance criterion, must return a string that contains the returned value of the `first()` method, the returned value of `TestStruct` (the `world` string) and the returned value of the `third()` method separated by a space. Our implementation is on the second place; that's why we checked that a space is prefixed and suffixed on the string `world`.

So, if the returned string, when calling the `ExecuteAlgorithm` method, doesn't contain the string `world`, the test fails.

This is enough to make the project compile and run the tests that should fail:

```
go test -v .
=== RUN    TestTemplate_ExecuteAlgorithm
=== RUN    TestTemplate_ExecuteAlgorithm/Using_interfaces
--- FAIL: TestTemplate_ExecuteAlgorithm (0.00s)
      --- FAIL: TestTemplate_ExecuteAlgorithm/Using_interfaces (0.00s)
          template_test.go:47: Expected string ' world ' was not found on
returned string
    FAIL
    exit status 1
    FAIL
```

Time to pass to the implementation of this pattern.

Implementing the Template pattern

As defined in the acceptance criteria, we have to return the string `hello` in the `first()` method and the string `template` in the `third()` method. That's pretty easy to implement:

```
type Template struct{}

func (t *Template) first() string {
  return "hello"
}

func (t *Template) third() string {
  return "template"
}
```

With this implementation, we should be covering the *second* and *third* acceptance criteria and partially covering the *first* criterion (each step in the algorithm must return a string).

To cover the *fifth* acceptance criterion, we define an `ExecuteAlgorithm` method that accepts the `MessageRetriever` interface as argument and returns the full algorithm: a single string done by joining the strings returned by the `first()`, `Message()` string and `third()` methods:

```
func (t *Template) ExecuteAlgorithm(m MessageRetriever) string {
    return strings.Join([]string{t.first(), m.Message(), t.third()},  " ")
}
```

The `strings.Join` function has the following signature:

```
func Join([]string,string) string
```

It takes an array of strings and joins them, placing the second argument between each item in the array. In our case, we create a string array on the fly to pass it as the first argument. Then we pass a whitespace as the second argument.

With this implementation, the tests must be passing already:

```
go test -v .
=== RUN   TestTemplate_ExecuteAlgorithm
=== RUN   TestTemplate_ExecuteAlgorithm/Using_interfaces
--- PASS: TestTemplate_ExecuteAlgorithm (0.00s)
    --- PASS: TestTemplate_ExecuteAlgorithm/Using_interfaces (0.00s)
PASS
ok
```

The tests passed. The test has checked that the string `world` is present in the returned result, which is the `hello world template` message. The `hello` text was the string returned by the `first()` method, the `world` string was returned by our `MessageRetriever` implementation, and `template` was the string returned by the `third()` method. The whitespaces are inserted by Go's `strings.Join` function. But any use of the `TemplateImpl.ExecuteAlgorithm` type will always return "hello [something] template" in its result.

Anonymous functions

This is not the only way to achieve the Template design pattern. We can also use an anonymous function to give our implementation to the `ExecuteAlgorithm` method.

Let's write a test in the same method that was used previously just after the test (marked in bold):

```go
func TestTemplate_ExecuteAlgorithm(t *testing.T) {
  t.Run("Using interfaces", func(t *testing.T){
    s := &TestStruct{}
    res := s.ExecuteAlgorithm(s)

    expectedOrError(res, " world ", t)
  })

  t.Run("Using anonymous functions", func(t *testing.T)
  {
    m := new(AnonymousTemplate)
    res := m.ExecuteAlgorithm(func() string {
      return "world"
    })
    expectedOrError(res, " world ", t)
  })
}

func expectedOrError(res string, expected string, t *testing.T){
  if !strings.Contains(res, expected) {
    t.Errorf("Expected string '%s' was not found on returned string\n",
expected)
  }
}
```

Our new test is called *Using anonymous functions*. We have also extracted the checking on the test to an external function to reuse it in this test. We have called this function `expectedOrError` because it will fail with an error if the expected value isn't received.

In our test, we will create a type called `AnonymousTemplate` that replaces the previous `Template` type. The `ExecuteAlgorithm` method of this new type accepts the `func()` method `string` type that we can implement directly in the test to return the string `world`.

The `AnonymousTemplate` type will have the following structure:

```go
type AnonymousTemplate struct{}

func (a *AnonymousTemplate) first() string {
  return ""
}

func (a *AnonymousTemplate) third() string {
  return ""
}
```

```
func (a *AnonymousTemplate) ExecuteAlgorithm(f func() string) string {
  return ""
}
```

The only difference with the `Template` type is that the `ExecuteAlgorithm` method accepts a function that returns a string instead of a `MessageRetriever` interface. Let's run the new test:

```
go test -v .
=== RUN    TestTemplate_ExecuteAlgorithm
=== RUN    TestTemplate_ExecuteAlgorithm/Using_interfaces
=== RUN    TestTemplate_ExecuteAlgorithm/Using_anonymous_functions
--- FAIL: TestTemplate_ExecuteAlgorithm (0.00s)
    --- PASS: TestTemplate_ExecuteAlgorithm/Using_interfaces (0.00s)
    --- FAIL: TestTemplate_ExecuteAlgorithm/Using_anonymous_functions
(0.00s)
        template_test.go:47: Expected string ' world ' was not found on
returned string
    FAIL
    exit status 1
    FAIL
```

As you can read in the output of the test execution, the error is thrown on the *Using anonymous functions* test, which is what we were expecting. Now we will write the implementation as follows:

```
type AnonymousTemplate struct{}

func (a *AnonymousTemplate) first() string {
  return "hello"
}

func (a *AnonymousTemplate) third() string {
  return "template"
}

func (a *AnonymousTemplate) ExecuteAlgorithm(f func() string) string {
  return strings.Join([]string{a.first(), f(), a.third()}, " ")
}
```

The implementation is quite similar to the one in the `Template` type. However, now we have passed a function called `f` that we will use as the second item in the string array we used on `Join` function. As `f` is simply a function that returns a string, the only thing we need to do with it is to execute it in the proper place (the second position in the array).

Run the tests again:

```
go test -v .
=== RUN    TestTemplate_ExecuteAlgorithm
=== RUN    TestTemplate_ExecuteAlgorithm/Using_interfaces
=== RUN    TestTemplate_ExecuteAlgorithm/Using_anonymous_functions
--- PASS: TestTemplate_ExecuteAlgorithm (0.00s)
    --- PASS: TestTemplate_ExecuteAlgorithm/Using_interfaces (0.00s)
    --- PASS: TestTemplate_ExecuteAlgorithm/Using_anonymous_functions
(0.00s)
PASS
ok
```

Awesome! Now we know two ways to implement the Template design pattern.

How to avoid modifications on the interface

The problem of the previous approach is that now we have two templates to maintain and we could end duplicating code. What can we do in the situation that we cannot change the interface are we using? Our interface was `MessageRetriever` but we want to use an anonymous function now.

Well, do you remember the Adapter design pattern? We just have to create an `Adapter` type that, accepting a `func() string` type, returns an implementation of the `MessageRetriever` interface. We will call this type `TemplateAdapter`:

```
type TemplateAdapter struct {
  myFunc func() string
}

func (a *TemplateAdapter) Message() string {
  return ""
}

func MessageRetrieverAdapter(f func() string) MessageRetriever {
  return nil
}
```

As you can see, the `TemplateAdapter` type has a field called `myFunc` which is of type `func() string`. We have also defined adapter as private because it shouldn't be used without a function defined in the `myFunc` field. We have created a public function called the `MessageRetrieverAdapter` to achieve this. Our test should look more or less like this:

```
t.Run("Using anonymous functions adapted to an interface", func(t
*testing.T){
```

```
messageRetriever := MessageRetrieverAdapter(func() string {
  return "world"
})

if messageRetriever == nil {
  t.Fatal("Can not continue with a nil MessageRetriever")
}

template := Template{}
res := template.ExecuteAlgorithm(messageRetriever)

expectedOrError(res, " world ", t)
})
```

Look at the statement where we called the `MessageRetrieverAdapter` method. We passed an anonymous function as an argument defined as `func() string`. Then, we reuse the previously defined `Template` type from our first test to pass the `messageRetriever` variable. Finally, we checked again with the `expectedOrError` method. Take a look at the `MessageRetrieverAdapter` method, it will return a function that has nil value. If strictly following the test-driven development rules, we must do tests first and they must not pass before implementation is done. That's why we returned nil on the `MessageRetrieverAdapter` function.

So, let's run the tests:

```
go test -v .
=== RUN    TestTemplate_ExecuteAlgorithm
=== RUN    TestTemplate_ExecuteAlgorithm/Using_interfaces
=== RUN    TestTemplate_ExecuteAlgorithm/Using_anonymous_functions
=== RUN
TestTemplate_ExecuteAlgorithm/Using_anonymous_functions_adapted_to_an_inter
face
   --- FAIL: TestTemplate_ExecuteAlgorithm (0.00s)
      --- PASS: TestTemplate_ExecuteAlgorithm/Using_interfaces (0.00s)
      --- PASS: TestTemplate_ExecuteAlgorithm/Using_anonymous_functions
(0.00s)
      --- FAIL:
TestTemplate_ExecuteAlgorithm/Using_anonymous_functions_adapted_to_an_inter
face (0.00s)
         template_test.go:39: Can not continue with a nil MessageRetriever
   FAIL
   exit status 1
   FAIL
```

The test fails on *line 39* of the code and it doesn't continue (again, depending on how you wrote your code, the line representing your error could be somewhere else). We stop test execution because we will need a valid MessageRetriever interface when we call the ExecuteAlgorithm method.

For the implementation of the adapter for our Template pattern, we will start with MessageRetrieverAdapter method:

```
func MessageRetrieverAdapter(f func() string) MessageRetriever {
    return &adapter{myFunc: f}
}
```

It's very easy, right? You could be wondering what happens if we pass nil value for the f argument. Well, we will cover this issue by calling the myFunc function.

The adapter type is finished with this implementation:

```
type adapter struct {
    myFunc func() string
}

func (a *adapter) Message() string {
    if a.myFunc != nil {
        return a.myFunc()
    }

    return ""
}
```

When calling the Message() function, we check that we actually have something stored in the myFunc function before calling. If nothing was stored, we return an empty string.

Now, our third implementation of the Template type, using the Adapter pattern, is done:

```
go test -v .
=== RUN   TestTemplate_ExecuteAlgorithm
=== RUN   TestTemplate_ExecuteAlgorithm/Using_interfaces
=== RUN   TestTemplate_ExecuteAlgorithm/Using_anonymous_functions
=== RUN
TestTemplate_ExecuteAlgorithm/Using_anonymous_functions_adapted_to_an_inter
face
    --- PASS: TestTemplate_ExecuteAlgorithm (0.00s)
        --- PASS: TestTemplate_ExecuteAlgorithm/Using_interfaces (0.00s)
        --- PASS: TestTemplate_ExecuteAlgorithm/Using_anonymous_functions
(0.00s)
            --- PASS:
TestTemplate_ExecuteAlgorithm/Using_anonymous_functions_adapted_to_an_inter
```

```
face (0.00s)
    PASS
    ok
```

Looking for the Template pattern in Go's source code

The `Sort` package in Go's source code can be considered a Template implementation of a sort algorithm. As defined in the package itself, the `Sort` package provides primitives for sorting slices and user-defined collections.

Here, we can also find a good example of why Go authors aren't worried about implementing generics. Sorting the lists is maybe the best example of generic usage in other languages. The way that Go deals with this is very elegant too-it deals with this issue with an interface:

```
type Interface interface {
    Len() int
    Less(i, j int) bool
    Swap(i, j int)
}
```

This is the interface for lists that need to be sorted by using the `sort` package. In the words of Go's authors:

> *"A type, typically, is a collection that satisfies sort. Interface can be sorted by the routines in this package. The methods require that the elements of the collection be enumerated by an integer index."*

In other words, write a type that implements this `Interface` so that the `Sort` package can be used to sort any slice. The sorting algorithm is the template and we must define how to retrieve values in our slice.

If we peek in the `sort` package, we can also find an example of how to use the sorting template but we will create our own example:

```
package main

import (
    "sort"
    "fmt"
)
```

```
type MyList []int

func (m MyList) Len() int {
    return len(m)
}

func (m MyList) Swap(i, j int) {
    m[i], m[j] = m[j], m[i]
}

func (m MyList) Less(i, j int) bool {
    return m[i] < m[j]
}
```

First, we have done a very simple type that stores an int list. This could be any kind of list, usually a list of some kind of struct. Then we have implemented the sort.Interface interface by defining the Len, Swap, and Less methods.

Finally, the main function creates an unordered list of numbers of the MyList type:

```
func main() {
    var myList MyList = []int{6,4,2,8,1}

    fmt.Println(myList)
    sort.Sort(myList)
    fmt.Println(myList)
}
```

We print the list that we created (unordered) and then we sort it (the sort.Sort method actually modifies our variable instead of returning a new list so beware!). Finally, we print again the resulting list. The console output of this main method is the following:

```
go run sort_example.go
[6 4 2 8 1]
[1 2 4 6 8]
```

The sort.Sort function has sorted our list in a transparent way. It has a lot of code written and delegates Len, Swap and Less methods to an interface, like we did in our template delegating to the MessageRetriever interface.

Summarizing the Template design pattern

We wanted to put a lot of focus on this pattern because it is very important when developing libraries and frameworks and allows a lot of flexibility and control to users of our library.

We have also seen again that it's very common to mix patterns to provide flexibility to the users, not only in a behavioral way but also structural. This will come very handy when working with concurrent apps where we need to restrict access to parts of our code to avoid races.

Memento design pattern

Let's now look at a pattern with a fancy name. If we check a dictionary to see the meaning of *memento*, we will find the following description:

> *"An object kept as a reminder of a person or event."*

Here, the key word is **reminder** as we will remember actions with this design pattern.

Description

The meaning of memento is very similar to the functionality it provides in design patterns. Basically, we'll have a type with some state and we want to be able to save milestones of its state. Having a finite amount of states saved, we can recover them if necessary for a variety of tasks-undo operations, historic, and so on.

The Memento design pattern usually has three players (usually called **actors**):

- **Memento**: A type that stores the type we want to save. Usually, we won't store the business type directly and we provide an extra layer of abstraction through this type.
- **Originator**: A type that is in charge of creating mementos and storing the current active state. We said that the Memento type wraps states of the business type and we use originator as the creator of mementos.
- **Care Taker**: A type that stores the list of mementos that can have the logic to store them in a database or to not store more than a specified number of them.

Objectives

Memento is all about a sequence of actions over time, say to undo one or two operations or to provide some kind of transactionality to some application.

Memento provides the foundations for many tasks, but its main objectives could be defined as follows:

- Capture an object state without modifying the object itself
- Save a limited amount of states so we can retrieve them later

A simple example with strings

We will develop a simple example using a string as the state we want to save. This way, we will focus on the common Memento pattern implementations before making it a bit more complex with a new example.

The string, stored in a field of a `State` instance, will be modified and we will be able to undo the operations done in this state.

Requirements and acceptance criteria

We are constantly talking about state; all in all, the Memento pattern is about storing and retrieving states. Our acceptance criteria must be all about states:

1. We need to store a finite amount of states of type string.
2. We need a way to restore the current stored state to one of the state list.

With these two simple requirements, we can already start writing some tests for this example.

Unit test

As mentioned previously, the Memento design pattern is usually composed of three actors: state, memento, and originator. So we will need three types to represent these actors:

```
type State struct {
  Description string
}
```

The `State` type is the core business object we will be using during this example. It's any kind of object that we want to track:

```
type memento struct {
   state State
}
```

The `memento` type has a field called `state` representing a single value of a `State` type. Our `states` will be containerized within this type before storing them into the `care taker` type. You could be wondering why we don't store directly `State` instances. Basically, because it will couple the `originator` and the `careTaker` to the business object and we want to have as little coupling as possible. It will also be less flexible, as we will see in the second example:

```
type originator struct {
   state State
}

func (o *originator) NewMemento() memento {
   return memento{}
}

func (o *originator) ExtractAndStoreState(m memento) {
   //Does nothing
}
```

The `originator` type also stores a state. The `originator` struct's objects will take states from mementos and create new mementos with their stored state.

> What's the difference between the originator object and the Memento pattern? Why don't we use Originator pattern's object directly? Well, if the Memento contains a specific state, the `originator` type contains the state that is currently loaded. Also, to save the state of something could be as simple as to take some value or as complex as to maintain the state of some distributed application.

The Originator will have two public methods–the `NewMemento()` method and the `ExtractAndStoreState(m memento)` method. The `NewMemento` method will return a new Memento built with `originator` current `State` value. The `ExtractAndStoreState` method will take the state of a Memento and store it in the `Originator`'s state field:

```
type careTaker struct {
   mementoList []memento
}
```

```
func (c *careTaker) Add(m memento) {
  //Does nothing
}

func (c *careTaker) Memento(i int) (memento, error) {
  return memento{}, fmt.Errorf("Not implemented yet")
}
```

The `careTaker` type stores the Memento list with all the states we need to save. It also stores an `Add` method to insert a new Memento on the list and a Memento retriever that takes an index on the Memento list.

So let's start with the `Add` method of the `careTaker` type. The `Add` method must take a `memento` object and add it to the `careTaker` object's list of Mementos:

```
func TestCareTaker_Add(t *testing.T) {
  originator := originator{}
  originator.state = State{Description:"Idle"}

  careTaker := careTaker{}
  mem := originator.NewMemento()
  if mem.state.Description != "Idle" {
    t.Error("Expected state was not found")
  }
```

At the beginning of our test, we created two basic actors for memento–the `originator` and the `careTaker`. We set a first state on the originator with the description `Idle`.

Then, we create the first Memento calling the `NewMemento` method. This should wrap the current originator's state in a `memento` type. Our first check is very simple–the state description of the returned Memento must be like the state description we pass to the originator, that is, the `Idle` description.

The last step to check whether our Memento's `Add` method works correctly is to see whether the Memento list has grown after adding one item:

```
currentLen := len(careTaker.mementoList)
careTaker.Add(mem)

if len(careTaker.mementoList) != currentLen+1 {
  t.Error("No new elements were added on the list")
}
```

We also have to test the `Memento(int) memento` method. This should take a `memento` value from the `careTaker` list. It takes the index you want to retrieve from the list so, as usual with lists, we must check that it behaves correctly against negative numbers and out of index values:

```
func TestCareTaker_Memento(t *testing.T) {
    originator := originator{}
    careTaker := careTaker{}

    originator.state = State{"Idle"}
    careTaker.Add(originator.NewMemento())
```

We have to start like we did in our previous test–creating an `originator` and `careTaker` objects and adding the first Memento to the `caretaker`:

```
mem, err := careTaker.Memento(0)
if err != nil {
  t.Fatal(err)
}

if mem.state.Description != "Idle" {
  t.Error("Unexpected state")
}
```

Once we have the first object on the `careTaker` object, we can ask for it using `careTaker.Memento(0)`. Index 0 on the `Memento(int)` method retrieves the first item on the slice (remember that slices start with 0). No error should be returned because we have already added a value to the `caretaker` object.

Then, after retrieving the first memento, we checked that the description matches the one that we passed at the beginning of the test:

```
mem, err = careTaker.Memento(-1)
if err == nil {
  t.Fatal("An error is expected when asking for a negative number but no
error was found")
  }
}
```

The last step on this test involves using a negative number to retrieve some value. In this case, an error must be returned that shows that no negative numbers can be used. It is also possible to return the first index when you pass negative numbers but here we will return an error.

The last function to check is the `ExtractAndStoreState` method. This function must take a Memento and extract all its state information to set it in the `Originator` object:

```
func TestOriginator_ExtractAndStoreState(t *testing.T) {
  originator := originator{state:State{"Idle"}}
  idleMemento := originator.NewMemento()

  originator.ExtractAndStoreState(idleMemento)
  if originator.state.Description != "Idle" {
    t.Error("Unexpected state found")
  }
}
```

This test is simple. We create a default `originator` variable with an `Idle` state. Then, we retrieve a new Memento object to use it later. We change the state of the `originator` variable to the `Working` state to ensure that the new state will be written.

Finally, we have to call the `ExtractAndStoreState` method with the `idleMemento` variable. This should restore the state of the originator to the `idleMemento` state's value, something that we checked in the last `if` statement.

Now it's time to run the tests:

```
go test -v .
=== RUN   TestCareTaker_Add
--- FAIL: TestCareTaker_Add (0.00s)
  memento_test.go:13: Expected state was not found
  memento_test.go:20: No new elements were added on the list
=== RUN   TestCareTaker_Memento
--- FAIL: TestCareTaker_Memento (0.00s)
  memento_test.go:33: Not implemented yet
=== RUN   TestOriginator_ExtractAndStoreState
--- FAIL: TestOriginator_ExtractAndStoreState (0.00s)
  memento_test.go:54: Unexpected state found
FAIL
exit status 1
FAIL
```

Because the three tests fail, we can continue with the implementation.

Implementing the Memento pattern

The Memento pattern's implementation is usually very simple if you don't get too crazy. The three actors (`memento`, `originator`, and `care taker`) have a very defined role in the pattern and their implementation is very straightforward:

```
type originator struct {
  state State
```

```
}

func (o *originator) NewMemento() memento {
  return memento{state: o.state}
}

func (o *originator) ExtractAndStoreState(m memento) {
  o.state = m.state
}
```

The `Originator` object needs to return a new values of Memento types when calling the `NewMemento` method. It also needs to store the value of a `memento` object in the state field of the struct as needed for the `ExtractAndStoreState` method:

```
type careTaker struct {
  mementoList []memento
}

func (c *careTaker) Push(m memento) {
  c.mementoList = append(c.mementoList, m)
}

func (c *careTaker) Memento(i int) (memento, error) {
  if len(c.mementoList) < i || i < 0 {
    return memento{}, fmt.Errorf("Index not found\n")
  }
  return c.mementoList[i], nil
}
```

The `careTaker` type is also straightforward. When we call the `Add` method, we overwrite the `mementoList` field by calling the `append` method with the value passed in the argument. This creates a new list with the new value included.

When calling the `Memento` method, we have to do a couple of checks beforehand. In this case, we check that the index is not outside of the range of the slice and that the index is not a negative number in the `if` statement, in which case we return an error. If everything goes fine, it just returns the specified `memento` object and no errors.

A note about method and function naming conventions.
You could find some people that like to give slightly more descriptive names to methods such as `Memento`. An example would be to use a name such as `MementoOrError` method, clearly showing that you return two objects when calling this function or even `GetMementoOrError` method. This could be a very explicit approach for naming and it's not necessarily bad, but you won't find it very common in Go's source code.

Time to check the test results:

```
go test -v .
=== RUN    TestCareTaker_Add
--- PASS: TestCareTaker_Add (0.00s)
=== RUN    TestCareTaker_Memento
--- PASS: TestCareTaker_Memento (0.00s)
=== RUN    TestOriginator_ExtractAndStoreState
--- PASS: TestOriginator_ExtractAndStoreState (0.00s)
PASS
ok
```

That was enough to reach 100% of coverage. While this is far from being a perfect metric, at least we know that we are reaching every corner of our source code and that we haven't cheated in our tests to achieve it.

Another example using the Command and Facade patterns

The previous example is good and simple enough to understand the functionality of the Memento pattern. However, it is more commonly used in conjunction with the Command pattern and a simple Facade pattern.

The idea is to use a Command pattern to encapsulate a set of different types of states (those that implement a `Command` interface) and provide a small facade to automate the insertion in the `caretaker` object.

We are going to develop a small example of a hypothetical audio mixer. We are going to use the same Memento pattern to save two types of states: `Volume` and `Mute`. The `Volume` state is going to be a byte type and the `Mute` state a Boolean type. We will use two completely different types to show the flexibility of this approach (and its drawbacks).

As a side note, we can also ship each `Command` interface with their own serialization methods on the interface. This way, we can give the ability to the caretaker to store states in some kind of storage without really knowing what's storing.

Our `Command` interface is going to have one method to return the value of its implementer. It's very simple, every command in our audio mixer that we want to undo will have to implement this interface:

```
type Command interface {
    GetValue() interface{}
}
```

There is something interesting in this interface. The `GetValue` method returns an interface to a value. This also means that the return type of this method is... well... untyped? Not really, but it returns an interface that can be a representation of any type and we will need to typecast it later if we want to use its specific type. Now we have to define the `Volume` and `Mute` types and implement the `Command` interface:

```
type Volume byte

func (v Volume) GetValue() interface{} {
  return v
}

type Mute bool

func (m Mute) GetValue() interface{} {
  return m
}
```

They are both quite easy implementations. However, the `Mute` type will return a `bool` type on the `GetValue()` method and `Volume` will return a `byte` type.

As in the previous example, we'll need a `Memento` type that will hold a `Command`. In other words, it will store a pointer to a `Mute` or a `Volume` type:

```
type Memento struct {
  memento Command
}
```

The `originator` type works as in the previous example but uses the `Command` keyword instead of the `state` keyword:

```
type originator struct {
  Command Command
}

func (o *originator) NewMemento() Memento {
  return Memento{memento: o.Command}
}

func (o *originator) ExtractAndStoreCommand(m Memento) {
  o.Command = m.memento
}
```

And the `caretaker` object is almost the same, but this time we'll use a stack instead of a simple list and we will store a command instead of a state:

```
type careTaker struct {
```

```
    mementoList []Memento
}

func (c *careTaker) Add(m Memento) {
    c.mementoList = append(c.mementoList, m)
}

func (c *careTaker) Pop() Memento {
    if len(c.mementoStack) > 0 {
        tempMemento := c.mementoStack[len(c.mementoStack)-1]
        c.mementoStack = c.mementoStack[0:len(c.mementoStack)-1]
        return tempMemento
    }

    return Memento{}
}
```

However, our `Memento` list is replaced with a `Pop` method. It also returns a `memento` object but it will return them acting as a stack (last to enter, first to go out). So, we take the last element on the stack and store it in the `tempMemento` variable. Then we replace the stack with a new version that doesn't contain the last element on the next line. Finally, we return the `tempMemento` variable.

Until now, everything looks almost like in the previous example. We also talked about automating some tasks by using the Facade pattern, so let's do it. This is going to be called the `MementoFacade` type and will have the `SaveSettings` and `RestoreSettings` methods. The `SaveSettings` method takes a `Command`, stores it in an inner originator, and saves it in an inner `careTaker` field. The `RestoreSettings` method makes the opposite flow-restores an index of the `careTaker` and returns the `Command` inside the `Memento` object:

```
type MementoFacade struct {
    originator originator
    careTaker  careTaker
}

func (m *MementoFacade) SaveSettings(s Command) {
    m.originator.Command = s
    m.careTaker.Add(m.originator.NewMemento())
}

func (m *MementoFacade) RestoreSettings(i int) Command {
    m.originator.ExtractAndStoreCommand(m.careTaker.Memento(i))
    return m.originator.Command
}
```

Our Facade pattern will hold the contents of the originator and the care taker and will provide those two easy-to-use methods to save and restore settings.

So, how do we use this?

```
func main(){
    m := MementoFacade{}

    m.SaveSettings(Volume(4))
    m.SaveSettings(Mute(false))
```

First, we get a variable with a Facade pattern. Zero-value initialization will give us zero-valued `originator` and `caretaker` objects. They don't have any unexpected field so everything will initialize correctly (if any of them had a pointer, for example, it would be initialized to `nil` as mentioned in the *Zero initialization* section of `Chapter 1`, *Ready... Steady... Go!*).

We create a `Volume` value with `Volume(4)` and, yes, we have used parentheses. The `Volume` type does not have any inner field like structs so we cannot use curly braces to set its value. The way to set it is to use parentheses (or create a pointer to the type `Volume` and then set the value of the pointed space). We also save a value of the type `Mute` using the Facade pattern.

We don't know what `Command` type is returned here, so we need to make a type assertion. We will make a small function to help us with this that checks the type and prints an appropriate value:

```
func assertAndPrint(c Command){
    switch cast := c.(type) {
    case Volume:
        fmt.Printf("Volume:\t%d\n", cast)
    case Mute:
        fmt.Printf("Mute:\t%t\n", cast)
    }
}
```

The `assertAndPrint` method takes a `Command` type and casts it to the two possible types-`Volume` or `Mute`. In each case, it prints a message to the console with a personalized message. Now we can continue and finish the `main` function, which will look like this:

```
func main() {
    m := MementoFacade{}

    m.SaveSettings(Volume(4))
    m.SaveSettings(Mute(false))
```

```
    assertAndPrint(m.RestoreSettings(0))
    assertAndPrint(m.RestoreSettings(1))
}
```

The part highlighted in bold shows the new changes within the `main` function. We took the index 0 from the `careTaker` object and passed it to the new function and the same with the index 1. Running this small program, we should get the `Volume` and `Mute` values on the console:

```
$ go run memento_command.go
Mute:    false
Volume: 4
```

Great! In this small example, we have combined three different design patterns to keep getting comfortable using various patterns. Keep in mind that we could have abstracted the creation of `Volume` and `Mute` states to a Factory pattern too so this is not where would stop.

Last words on the Memento pattern

With the Memento pattern, we have learned a powerful way to create undoable operations that are very useful when writing UI applications but also when you have to develop transactional operations. In any case, the situation is the same: you need a `Memento`, an `Originator`, and a `caretaker` actor.

 A **transaction operation** is a set of atomic operations that must all be done or fail. In other words, if you have a transaction composed of five operations and just one of them fails, the transaction cannot be completed and every modification done by the other four must be undone.

Interpreter design pattern

Now we are going to dig into a quite complex pattern. The **Interpreter** pattern is, in fact, widely used to solve business cases where it's useful to have a language to perform common operations. Let's see what we mean by language.

Description

The most famous interpreter we can talk about is probably SQL. It's defined as a special-purpose programming language for managing data held in relational databases. SQL is quite complex and big but, all in all, is a set of words and operators that allow us to perform operations such as insert, select, or delete.

Another typical example is musical notation. It's a language itself and the interpreter is the musician who knows the connection between a note and its representation on the instrument they are playing.

In computer science, it can be useful to design a small language for a variety of reasons: repetitive tasks, higher-level languages for non-developers, or **Interface Definition Languages (IDL)** such as **Protocol buffers** or **Apache Thrift**.

Objectives

Designing a new language, big or small, can be a time consuming task so it's very important to have the objectives clear before investing time and resources on writing an interpreter of it:

- Provide syntax for very common operations in some scope (such as playing notes).
- Have a intermediate language to translate actions between two systems. For example, the apps that generate the **Gcode** needed to print with 3D printers.
- Ease the use of some operations in an easier-to-use syntax.

SQL allows the use of relational databases in a very easy-to-use syntax (that can become incredibly complex too) but the idea is to not need to write your own functions to make insertions and searches.

Example – a polish notation calculator

A very typical example of an interpreter is to create a reverse polish notation calculator. For those who don't know what polish notation is, it's a mathematical notation to make operations where you write your operation first (sum) and then the values (3 4), so + 3 4 is equivalent to the more common 3 + 4 and its result would be 7. So, for a reverse polish notation, you put first the values and then the operation, so 3 4 + would also be 7.

Acceptance criteria for the calculator

For our calculator, the acceptance criteria we should pass to consider it done are as follows:

1. Create a language that allows making common arithmetic operations (sums, subtractions, multiplications, and divisions). The syntax is `sum` for sums, `mul` for multiplications, `sub` for subtractions, and `div` for divisions.
2. It must be done using reverse polish notation.
3. The user must be able to write as many operations in a row as they want.
4. The operations must be performed from left to right.

So the `3 4 sum 2 sub` notation is the same than *(3 + 4) – 2* and result would be *5*.

Unit test of some operations

In this case, we will only have a public method called `Calculate` that takes an operation with its values defined as a string and will return a value or an error:

```
func Calculate(o string) (int, error) {
    return 0, fmt.Errorf("Not implemented yet")
}
```

So, we will send a string like "3 4 +" to the `Calculate` method and it should return *7, nil*. Two tests more will check the correct implementation:

```
func TestCalculate(t *testing.T) {
    tempOperation = "3 4 sum 2 sub"
    res, err = Calculate(tempOperation)
    if err != nil {
        t.Error(err)
    }

    if res != 5 {
        t.Errorf("Expected result not found: %d != %d\n", 5, res)
    }
}
```

First, we are going to make the operation we have used as an example. The `3 4 sum 2 sub` notation is part of our language and we use it in the `Calculate` function. If an error is returned, the test fails. Finally, the result must be equal to 5 and we check it on the last lines. The next test checks the rest of the operators on slightly more complex operations:

```
tempOperation := "5 3 sub 8 mul 4 sum 5 div"
res, err := Calculate(tempOperation)
```

```
  if err != nil {
    t.Error(err)
  }

  if res != 4 {
    t.Errorf("Expected result not found: %d != %d\n", 4, res)
  }
}
```

Here, we repeated the preceding process with a longer operation, the *(((5 – 3) * 8) + 4) / 5* notation which is equal to *4*. From left to right, it would be as follows:

```
(((5 - 3) * 8) + 4) / 5
  ((2 * 8) + 4) / 5
    (16 + 4) / 5
      20 / 5
        4
```

The test must fail, of course!

```
$ go test -v .
  interpreter_test.go:9: Not implemented yet
  interpreter_test.go:13: Expected result not found: 4 != 0
  interpreter_test.go:19: Not implemented yet
  interpreter_test.go:23: Expected result not found: 5 != 0
exit status 1
FAIL
```

Implementation

Implementation is going to be longer than testing this time. To start, we will define our possible operators in constants:

```
const (
  SUM = "sum"
  SUB = "sub"
  MUL = "mul"
  DIV = "div"
)
```

Interpreter patterns are usually implemented using an abstract syntax tree, something that is commonly achieved using a stack. We have created stacks before during the book so this should be already familiar to readers:

```
type polishNotationStack []int
```

```
func (p *polishNotationStack) Push(s int) {
  *p = append(*p, s)
}

func (p *polishNotationStack) Pop() int {
  length := len(*p)

  if length > 0 {
    temp := (*p)[length-1]
    *p = (*p)[:length-1]
    return temp
  }

  return 0
}
```

We have two methods–the `Push` method to add elements to the top of the stack and the `Pop` method to remove elements and return them. In case you are thinking that the line `*p = (*p)[:length-1]` is a bit cryptic, we'll explain it.

The value stored in the direction of `p` will be overridden with the actual value in the direction of `p` (`*p`) but taking only the elements from the beginning to the penultimate element of the array (`:length-1`).

So, now we will go step by step with the `Calculate` function, creating more functions as far as we need them:

```
func Calculate(o string) (int, error) {
  stack := polishNotationStack{}
  operators := strings.Split(o, " ")
```

The first two things we need to do are to create the stack and to get all different symbols from the incoming operation (in this case, we aren't checking that it isn't empty). We split the incoming string operations by the space to get a nice slice of symbols (values and operators).

Next, we will iterate over every symbol by using range but we need a function to know whether the incoming symbol is a value or an operator:

```
func isOperator(o string) bool {
  if o == SUM || o == SUB || o == MUL || o == DIV {
    return true
  }

  return false
}
```

If the incoming symbol is any of the ones defined in our constants, the incoming symbol is an operator:

```
func Calculate(o string) (int, error) {
    stack := polishNotationStack{}
    operators := strings.Split(o, " ")

    for _, operatorString := range operators {
        if isOperator(operatorString) {
            right := stack.Pop()
            left := stack.Pop()
        }
        else
        {
            //Is a value
        }
    }
}
```

If it is an operator, we consider that we have already passed two values so what we have to do is to take those two values from the stack. The first value taken would be the rightmost and the second the leftmost (remember that in subtractions and divisions, the order of the operands is important). Then, we need some function to get the operation we want to perform:

```
func getOperationFunc(o string) func(a, b int) int {
    switch o {
    case SUM:
        return func(a, b int) int {
            return a + b
        }
    case SUB:
        return func(a, b int) int {
            return a - b
        }
    case MUL:
        return func(a, b int) int {
            return a * b
        }
    case DIV:
        return func(a, b int) int {
            return a / b
        }
    }
    return nil
}
```

The `getOperationFunc` functions returns a two-argument function that returns an integer. We check the incoming operator and we return an anonymous function that performs the specified operation. So, now our `for range` continues like this:

```
func Calculate(o string) (int, error) {
    stack := polishNotationStack{}
    operators := strings.Split(o, " ")

    for _, operatorString := range operators {
        if isOperator(operatorString) {
            right := stack.Pop()
            left := stack.Pop()
            mathFunc := getOperationFunc(operatorString)          res :=
mathFunc(left, right)          stack.Push(res)
        } else {
            //Is a value
        }
    }
}
```

The `mathFunc` variable is returned by the function. We use it immediately to perform the operation on the left and right values taken from the stack and we store its result in a new variable called `res`. Finally, we need to push this new value to the stack to keep operating with it later.

Now, here is the implementation when the incoming symbol is a value:

```
func Calculate(o string) (int, error) {
    stack := polishNotationStack{}
    operators := strings.Split(o, " ")

    for _, operatorString := range operators {
        if isOperator(operatorString) {
            right := stack.Pop()
            left := stack.Pop()
            mathFunc := getOperationFunc(operatorString)
            res := mathFunc(left, right)
            stack.Push(res)
        } else {
            val, err := strconv.Atoi(operatorString)
            if err != nil {
                return 0, err
            }
            stack.Push(val)
        }
    }
}
```

What we need to do every time we get a symbol is to push it to the stack. We have to parse the string symbol to a usable `int` type. This is commonly done with the `strconv` package by using its `Atoi` function. The `Atoi` function takes a string and returns an integer from it or an error. If everything goes well, the value is pushed into the stack.

At the end of the `range` statement, just one value must be stored on it, so we just need to return it and the function is done:

```
func Calculate(o string) (int, error) {
  stack := polishNotationStack{}
  operators := strings.Split(o, " ")

for _, operatorString := range operators {
    if isOperator(operatorString) {
      right := stack.Pop()
      left := stack.Pop()
      mathFunc := getOperationFunc(operatorString)
      res := mathFunc(left, right)
      stack.Push(res)
    } else {
      val, err := strconv.Atoi(operatorString)
      if err != nil {
        return 0, err
      }

      stack.Push(val)
    }
  }
  return int(stack.Pop()), nil}
```

Time to run the tests again:

```
$ go test -v .
ok
```

Great! We have just created a reverse polish notation interpreter in a very simple and easy way (we still lack the parser, but that's another story).

Complexity with the Interpreter design pattern

In this example, we haven't used any interfaces. This is not exactly how the Interpreter design pattern is defined in more object-oriented languages. However, this example is the simplest example possible to understand the objectives of the language and the next level is inevitably much more complex and not intended for beginner users.

With a more complex example, we will have to define a type containing more types of itself, a value, or nothing. With a parser, you create this abstract syntax tree to interpret it later.

The same example, done by using interfaces, would be as in the following description section.

Interpreter pattern again – now using interfaces

The main interface we are going to use is called the `Interpreter` interface. This interface has a `Read()` method that every symbol (value or operator) must implement:

```
type Interpreter interface {
    Read() int
}
```

We will implement only the sum and the subtraction from the operators and a type called `Value` for the numbers:

```
type value int

func (v *value) Read() int {
    return int(*v)
}
```

The `Value` is a type `int` that, when implementing the `Read` method, just returns its value:

```
type operationSum struct {
    Left   Interpreter
    Right  Interpreter
}

func (a *operationSum) Read() int {
    return a.Left.Read() + a.Right.Read()
}
```

The `operationSum` struct has the `Left` and `Right` fields and its `Read` method returns the sum of each of their `Read` methods. The `operationSubtract` struct is the same but subtracting:

```
type operationSubtract struct {
    Left   Interpreter
    Right  Interpreter
}

func (s *operationSubtract) Read() int {
```

```
    return s.Left.Read() - s.Right.Read()
}
```

We also need a Factory pattern to create operators; we will call it the `operatorFactory` method. The difference now is that it not only accepts the symbol but also the `Left` and `Right` values taken from the stack:

```
func operatorFactory(o string, left, right Interpreter) Interpreter {
    switch o {
    case SUM:
        return &operationSum{
            Left: left,
            Right: right,
        }
    case SUB:
        return &operationSubtract{
            Left: left,
            Right: right,
        }
    }

    return nil
}
```

As we have just mentioned, we also need a stack. We can reuse the one from the previous example by changing its type:

```
type polishNotationStack []Interpreter

func (p *polishNotationStack) Push(s Interpreter) {
    *p = append(*p, s)
}

func (p *polishNotationStack) Pop() Interpreter {
    length := len(*p)

    if length > 0 {
        temp := (*p)[length-1]
        *p = (*p)[:length-1]
        return temp
    }

    return nil
}
```

Now the stack works with Interpreter pointers instead of `int` but its functionality is the same. Finally, our `main` method also looks similar to our previous example:

```go
func main() {
  stack := polishNotationStack{}
  operators := strings.Split("3 4 sum 2 sub", " ")

  for _, operatorString := range operators {
    if operatorString == SUM || operatorString == SUB {
      right := stack.Pop()
      left := stack.Pop()
      mathFunc := operatorFactory(operatorString, left, right)
      res := value(mathFunc.Read())
      stack.Push(&res)
    } else {
      val, err := strconv.Atoi(operatorString)
      if err != nil {
        panic(err)
      }

      temp := value(val)
      stack.Push(&temp)
    }
  }

  println(int(stack.Pop().Read()))
}
```

Like before, we check whether the symbol is operator or value first. When it's a value, it pushes it into the stack.

When the symbol is an operator, we also take the right and left values from the stack, we call the Factory pattern using the current operator and the left and right values that we just took from the stack. Once we have the operator type, we just need to call its `Read` method to push the returned value to the stack too.

Finally, just one example must be left on the stack, so we print it:

```
$ go run interpreter.go
5
```

The power of the Interpreter pattern

This pattern is extremely powerful but it must also be used carefully. To create a language, it generates a strong coupling between its users and the functionality it provides. One can fall into the error of trying to create a too flexible language that is incredibly complex to use and maintain. Also, one can create a fairly small and useful language that doesn't interpret correctly sometimes and it could be a pain for its users.

In our example, we have omitted quite a lot of error-checking to focus on the implementation of the Interpreter. However, you'll need quite a lot of error checking and verbose output on errors to help the user correct its syntax errors. So, have fun writing your language but be nice to your users.

Summary

This chapter has dealt with three extremely powerful patterns that require a lot of practice before using them in production code. It's a very good idea to make some exercises with them by simulating typical production problems:

- Create a simple REST server that reuses most of the error-checking and connection functionality to provide an easy-to-use interface to practice the Template pattern
- Make a small library that can write to different databases but only in the case that all writes were OK, or delete the newly created writes to practice Memento for example
- Write your own language, to make simple things such as answering simple questions like bots usually do so you can practice a bit of the Interpreter pattern

The idea is to practice coding and reread any section until you get comfortable with each pattern.

7

Behavioral Patterns - Visitor, State, Mediator, and Observer Design Patterns

This is the last chapter about Behavioral patterns and it also closes this book's section about common, well known design patterns in Go language.

In this chapter, we are going to look at three more design patterns. Visitor pattern is very useful when you want to abstract away some functionality from a set of objects.

State is used commonly to build **Finite State Machines** (**FSM**) and, in this section, we will develop a small *guess the number* game.

Finally, the Observer pattern is commonly used in event-driven architectures and is gaining a lot of traction again, especially in the microservices world.

After this chapter, we'll need to feel very comfortable with common design patterns before digging in concurrency and the advantages (and complexity), it brings to design patterns.

Visitor design pattern

In the next design pattern, we are going to delegate some logic of an object's type to an external type called the visitor that will visit our object to perform operations on it.

Description

In the Visitor design pattern, we are trying to separate the logic needed to work with a specific object outside of the object itself. So we could have many different visitors that do some things to specific types.

For example, imagine that we have a log writer that writes to console. We could make the logger "visitable" so that you can prepend any text to each log. We could write a Visitor pattern that prepends the date, the time, and the hostname to a field stored in the object.

Objectives

With Behavioral design patterns we are mainly dealing with algorithms. Visitor patterns are not an exception. The objectives that we are trying to achieve are as follows:

- To separate the algorithm of some type from its implementation within some other type
- To improve the flexibility of some types by using them with little or no logic at all so all new functionality can be added without altering the object structure
- To fix a structure or behavior that would break the open/closed principle in a type

You might be thinking what the open/closed principle is. In computer science, the open/closed principle states that: *entities should be open for extension but closed for modification*. This simple state has lots of implications that allows building more maintainable software and less prone to errors. And the Visitor pattern helps us to delegate some commonly changing algorithm from a type that we need it to be "stable" to an external type that can change often without affecting our original one.

A log appender

We are going to develop a simple log appender as an example of the Visitor pattern. Following the approach we have had in previous chapters, we will start with an extremely simple example to clearly understand how the Visitor design pattern works before jumping to a more complex one. We have already developed similar examples modifying texts too, but in slightly different ways.

For this particular example, we will create a Visitor that appends different information to the types it "visits".

Acceptance criteria

To effectively use the Visitor design pattern, we must have two roles–a visitor and a visitable. The Visitor is the type that will act within a Visitable type. So a Visitable interface implementation has an algorithm detached to the Visitor type:

1. We need two message loggers: MessageA and MessageB that will print a message with an A: or a B: respectively before the message.
2. We need a Visitor able to modify the message to be printed. It will append the text "Visited A" or "Visited B" to them, respectively.

Unit tests

As we mentioned before, we will need a role for the Visitor and the Visitable interfaces. They will be interfaces. We also need the MessageA and MessageB structs:

```go
package visitor

import (
  "io"
  "os"
  "fmt"
)

type MessageA struct {
  Msg string
  Output io.Writer
}

type MessageB struct {
  Msg string
  Output io.Writer
}

type Visitor interface {
  VisitA(*MessageA)
  VisitB(*MessageB)
}

type Visitable interface {
  Accept(Visitor)
}

type MessageVisitor struct {}
```

The types `MessageA` and `MessageB` structs both have an `Msg` field to store the text that they will print. The output `io.Writer` will implement the `os.Stdout` interface by default or a new `io.Writer` interface, like the one we will use to check that the contents are correct.

The `Visitor` interface has a `Visit` method, one for each of `Visitable` interface's `MessageA` and `MessageB` type. The `Visitable` interface has a method called `Accept(Visitor)` that will execute the decoupled algorithm.

Like in previous examples, we will create a type that implements the `io.Writer` package so that we can use it in tests:

```
package visitor

import "testing"

type TestHelper struct {
  Received string
}

func (t *TestHelper) Write(p []byte) (int, error) {
  t.Received = string(p)
  return len(p), nil
}
```

The `TestHelper` struct implements the `io.Writer` interface. Its functionality is quite simple; it stores the written bytes on the `Received` field. Later we can check the contents of `Received` to test against our expected value.

We will write just one test that will check the overall correctness of the code. Within this test, we will write two sub tests: one for `MessageA` and one for `MessageB` types:

```
func Test_Overall(t *testing.T) {
  testHelper := &TestHelper{}
  visitor := &MessageVisitor{}
  ...
}
```

We will use a `TestHelper` struct and a `MessageVisitor` struct on each test for each message type. First, we will test the `MessageA` type:

```
func Test_Overall(t *testing.T) {
  testHelper := &TestHelper{}
  visitor := &MessageVisitor{}

  t.Run("MessageA test", func(t *testing.T){
    msg := MessageA{
```

```
        Msg: "Hello World",
        Output: testHelper,
      }

    msg.Accept(visitor)
    msg.Print()

    expected := "A: Hello World (Visited A)"
    if testHelper.Received !=  expected {
      t.Errorf("Expected result was incorrect. %s != %s",
      testHelper.Received, expected)
    }
  })
  ...
}
```

This is the full first test. We created `MessageA` struct, giving it a value `Hello World` for the `Msg` field and the pointer to `TestHelper`, which we created at the beginning of the test. Then, we execute its `Accept` method. Inside the `Accept(Visitor)` method on the `MessageA` struct, the `VisitA(*MessageA)` method is executed to alter the contents of the `Msg` field (that's why we passed the pointer to `VisitA` method, without a pointer the contents won't be persisted).

To test if the `Visitor` type has done its job within the `Accept` method, we must call the `Print()` method on the `MessageA` type later. This way, the `MessageA` struct must write the contents of `Msg` to the provided `io.Writer` interface (our `TestHelper`).

The last part of the test is the check. According to the description of *acceptance criteria 2*, the output text of `MessageA` type must be prefixed with the text `A:`, the stored message and the text `" (Visited)"` just at the end. So, for the `MessageA` type, the expected text must be `"A: Hello World (Visited)"`, this is the check that we did in the `if` section.

The `MessageB` type has a very similar implementation:

```
    t.Run("MessageB test", func(t *testing.T){
      msg := MessageB {
        Msg: "Hello World",
        Output: testHelper,
      }

    msg.Accept(visitor)
    msg.Print()

    expected := "B: Hello World (Visited B)"
    if testHelper.Received !=  expected {
        t.Errorf("Expected result was incorrect. %s != %s",
```

```
          testHelper.Received, expected)
      }
   })
  }
```

In fact, we have just changed the type from MessageA to MessageB and the expected text now is "B: Hello World (Visited B)". The Msg field is also "Hello World" and we also used the TestHelper type.

We still lack the correct implementations of the interfaces to compile the code and run the tests. The MessageA and MessageB structs have to implement the Accept(Visitor) method:

```
func (m *MessageA) Accept(v Visitor) {
  //Do nothing
}

func (m *MessageB) Accept(v Visitor) {
  //Do nothing
}
```

We need the implementations of the VisitA(*MessageA) and VisitB(*MessageB) methods that are declared on the Visitor interface. The MessageVisitor interface is the type that must implement them:

```
func (mf *MessageVisitor) VisitA(m *MessageA){
  //Do nothing
}
func (mf *MessageVisitor) VisitB(m *MessageB){
  //Do nothing
}
```

Finally, we will create a Print() method for each message type. This is the method that we will use to test the contents of the Msg field on each type:

```
func (m *MessageA) Print(){
  //Do nothing
}

func (m *MessageB) Print(){
  //Do nothing
}
```

Now we can run the tests to really check if they are failing yet:

```
go test -v .
=== RUN   Test_Overall
```

```
=== RUN    Test_Overall/MessageA_test
=== RUN    Test_Overall/MessageB_test
--- FAIL: Test_Overall (0.00s)
    --- FAIL: Test_Overall/MessageA_test (0.00s)
        visitor_test.go:30: Expected result was incorrect.   != A: Hello
World (Visited A)
    --- FAIL: Test_Overall/MessageB_test (0.00s)
        visitor_test.go:46: Expected result was incorrect.   != B: Hello
World (Visited B)
FAIL
exit status 1
FAIL
```

The outputs of the tests are clear. The expected messages were incorrect because the contents were empty. It's time to create the implementations.

Implementation of Visitor pattern

We will start completing the implementation of the `VisitA(*MessageA)` and `VisitB(*MessageB)` methods:

```
func (mf *MessageVisitor) VisitA(m *MessageA){
  m.Msg = fmt.Sprintf("%s %s", m.Msg, "(Visited A)")
}
func (mf *MessageVisitor) VisitB(m *MessageB){
  m.Msg = fmt.Sprintf("%s %s", m.Msg, "(Visited B)")
}
```

Its functionality is quite straightforward–the `fmt.Sprintf` method returns a formatted string with the actual contents of `m.Msg`, a white space, and the message, `Visited`. This string will be stored on the `Msg` field, overriding the previous contents.

Now we will develop the `Accept` method for each message type that must execute the corresponding Visitor:

```
func (m *MessageA) Accept(v Visitor) {
  v.VisitA(m)
}

func (m *MessageB) Accept(v Visitor) {
  v.VisitB(m)
}
```

This small code has some implications on it. In both cases, we are using a `Visitor`, which in our example is exactly the same as the `MessageVisitor` interface, but they could be completely different. The key is to understand that the Visitor pattern executes an algorithm in its `Visit` method that deals with the `Visitable` object. What could the `Visitor` be doing? In this example, it alters the `Visitable` object, but it could be simply fetching information from it. For example, we could have a `Person` type with lots of fields: name, surname, age, address, city, postal code, and so on. We could write a Visitor to fetch just the name and surname from a person as a unique string, a visitor to fetch the address info for a different section of an app, and so on.

Finally, there is the `Print()` method, which will help us to test the types. We mentioned before that it must print to the `Stdout` call by default:

```
func (m *MessageA) Print() {
  if m.Output == nil {
    m.Output = os.Stdout
  }

  fmt.Fprintf(m.Output, "A: %s", m.Msg)
}

func (m *MessageB) Print() {
  if m.Output == nil {
    m.Output = os.Stdout
  }
  fmt.Fprintf(m.Output, "B: %s", m.Msg)
}
```

It first checks the content of the `Output` field to assign the output of the `os.Stdout` call in case it is null. In our tests, we are storing a pointer there to our `TestHelper` type so this line is never executed in our test. Finally, each message type prints to the `Output` field, the full message stored in the `Msg` field. This is done by using the `Fprintf` method, which takes an `io.Writer` package as the first argument and the text to format as the next arguments.

Our implementation is now complete and we can run the tests again to see if they all pass now:

```
go test -v .
=== RUN   Test_Overall
=== RUN   Test_Overall/MessageA_test
=== RUN   Test_Overall/MessageB_test
--- PASS: Test_Overall (0.00s)
  --- PASS: Test_Overall/MessageA_test (0.00s)
  --- PASS: Test_Overall/MessageB_test (0.00s)
PASS
```

```
ok
```

Everything is OK! The Visitor pattern has done its job flawlessly and the message contents were altered after calling their `Visit` methods. The very important thing here is that we can add more functionality to both the structs, `MessageA` and `MessageB`, without altering their types. We can just create a new Visitor type that does everything on the `Visitable`, for example, we can create a `Visitor` to add a method that prints the contents of the `Msg` field:

```go
type MsgFieldVisitorPrinter struct {}

func (mf *MsgFieldVisitorPrinter) VisitA(m *MessageA){
  fmt.Printf(m.Msg)
}
func (mf *MsgFieldVisitorPrinter) VisitB(m *MessageB){
  fmt.Printf(m.Msg)
}
```

We have just added some functionality to both types without altering their contents! That's the power of the Visitor design pattern.

Another example

We will develop a second example, this one a bit more complex. In this case, we will emulate an online shop with a few products. The products will have plain types, with just fields and we will make a couple of visitors to deal with them in the group.

First of all, we will develop the interfaces. The `ProductInfoRetriever` type has a method to get the price and the name of the product. The `Visitor` interface, like before, has a `Visit` method that accepts the `ProductInfoRetriever` type. Finally, `Visitable` interface is exactly the same; it has an `Accept` method that takes a `Visitor` type as an argument:

```go
type ProductInfoRetriever interface {
  GetPrice() float32
  GetName() string
}

type Visitor interface {
  Visit(ProductInfoRetriever)
}

type Visitable interface {
  Accept(Visitor)
}
```

All the products of the online shop must implement the `ProductInfoRetriever` type. Also, most products will have some commons fields, such as name or price (the ones defined in the `ProductInfoRetriever` interface). We created the `Product` type, implemented the `ProductInfoRetriever` and the `Visitable` interfaces, and embedded it on each product:

```go
type Product struct {
  Price float32
  Name  string
}

func (p *Product) GetPrice() float32 {
  return p.Price
}

func (p *Product) Accept(v Visitor) {
  v.Visit(p)
}

func (p *Product) GetName() string {
  return p.Name
}
```

Now we have a very generic `Product` type that can store the information about almost any product of the shop. For example, we could have a `Rice` and a `Pasta` product:

```go
type Rice struct {
  Product
}

type Pasta struct {
  Product
}
```

Each has the `Product` type embedded. Now we need to create a couple of `Visitors` interfaces, one that sums the price of all products and one that prints the name of each product:

```go
type PriceVisitor struct {
  Sum float32
}

func (pv *PriceVisitor) Visit(p ProductInfoRetriever) {
  pv.Sum += p.GetPrice()
}

type NamePrinter struct {
```

```
    ProductList string
  }

  func (n *NamePrinter) Visit(p ProductInfoRetriever) {
    n.Names = fmt.Sprintf("%s\n%s", p.GetName(), n.ProductList)
  }
```

The `PriceVisitor` struct takes the value of the `Price` variable of the `ProductInfoRetriever` type, passed as an argument, and adds it to the `Sum` field. The `NamePrinter` struct stores the name of the `ProductInfoRetriever` type, passed as an argument, and appends it to a new line on the `ProductList` field.

Time for the `main` function:

```
func main() {
  products := make([]Visitable, 2)
  products[0] = &Rice{
    Product: Product{
      Price: 32.0,
      Name:  "Some rice",
    },
  }
  products[1] = &Pasta{
    Product: Product{
      Price: 40.0,
      Name:  "Some pasta",
    },
  }

  //Print the sum of prices
  priceVisitor := &PriceVisitor{}

  for _, p := range products {
    p.Accept(priceVisitor)
  }

  fmt.Printf("Total: %f\n", priceVisitor.Sum)

  //Print the products list
  nameVisitor := &NamePrinter{}

  for _, p := range products {
    p.Accept(nameVisitor)
  }

  fmt.Printf("\nProduct list:\n-------------\n%s",
nameVisitor.ProductList)
```

```
}
```

We create a slice of two `Visitable` objects: a `Rice` and a `Pasta` type with some arbitrary names. Then we iterate for each of them using a `PriceVisitor` instance as an argument. We print the total price after the range for. Finally, we repeat this operation with the `NamePrinter` and print the resulting `ProductList`. The output of this `main` function is as follows:

```
go run visitor.go
Total: 72.000000
Product list:
-------------
Some pasta
Some rice
```

Ok, this is a nice example of the Visitor pattern but... what if there are special considerations about a product? For example, what if we need to sum 20 to the total price of a fridge type? OK, let's write the `Fridge` structure:

```
type Fridge struct {
  Product
}
```

The idea here is to just override the `GetPrice()` method to return the product's price plus 20:

```
type Fridge struct {
  Product
}

func (f *Fridge) GetPrice() float32 {
  return f.Product.Price + 20
}
```

Unfortunately, this isn't enough for our example. The `Fridge` structure is not of a `Visitable` type. The `Product` struct is of a `Visitable` type and the `Fridge` struct has a `Product` struct embedded but, as we mentioned in earlier chapters, a type that embeds a second type cannot be considered of that latter type, even when it has all its fields and methods. The solution is to also implement the `Accept(Visitor)` method so that it can be considered as a `Visitable`:

```
type Fridge struct {
  Product
}

func (f *Fridge) GetPrice() float32 {
```

```
    return f.Product.Price + 20
}

func (f *Fridge) Accept(v Visitor) {
    v.Visit(f)
}
```

Let's rewrite the `main` function to add this new `Fridge` product to the slice:

```
func main() {
    products := make([]Visitable, 3)
    products[0] = &Rice{
        Product: Product{
            Price: 32.0,
            Name:  "Some rice",
        },
    }
    products[1] = &Pasta{
        Product: Product{
            Price: 40.0,
            Name:  "Some pasta",
        },
    }
    products[2] = &Fridge{
        Product: Product{
            Price: 50,
            Name:  "A fridge",
        },
    }
    ...
}
```

Everything else continues the same. Running this new `main` function produces the following output:

```
$ go run visitor.go
Total: 142.000000
Product list:
-------------
A fridge
Some pasta
Some rice
```

As expected, the total price is higher now, outputting the sum of the rice (32), the pasta (40), and the fridge (50 of the product plus 20 of the transport, so 70). We could be adding visitors forever to this products, but the idea is clear–we decoupled some algorithms outside of the types to the visitors.

Visitors to the rescue!

We have seen a powerful abstraction to add new algorithms to some types. However, because of the lack of overloading in Go, this pattern could be limiting in some aspects (we have seen it in the first example, where we had to create the `VisitA` and `VisitB` implementations). In the second example, we haven't dealt with this limitation because we have used an interface to the `Visit` method of the `Visitor` struct, but we just used one type of visitor (`ProductInfoRetriever`) and we would have the same problem if we implemented a `Visit` method for a second type, which is one of the objectives of the original *Gang of Four* design patterns.

State design pattern

State patterns are directly related to FSMs. An FSM, in very simple terms, is something that has one or more states and travels between them to execute some behaviors. Let's see how the State pattern helps us to define FSM.

Description

A light switch is a common example of an FSM. It has two states–on and off. One state can transit to the other and vice versa. The way that the State pattern works is similar. We have a `State` interface and an implementation of each state we want to achieve. There is also usually a context that holds cross-information between the states.

With FSM, we can achieve very complex behaviors by splitting their scope between states. This way we can model pipelines of execution based on any kind of inputs or create event-driven software that responds to particular events in specified ways.

Objectives

The main objectives of the State pattern is to develop FSM are as follows:

- To have a type that alters its own behavior when some internal things have changed
- Model complex graphs and pipelines can be upgraded easily by adding more states and rerouting their output states

A small guess the number game

We are going to develop a very simple game that uses FSM. This game is a number guessing game. The idea is simple–we will have to guess some number between 0 and 10 and we have just a few attempts or we'll lose.

We will leave the player to choose the level of difficulty by asking how many tries the user has before losing. Then, we will ask the player for the correct number and keep asking if they don't guess it or if the number of tries reaches zero.

Acceptance criteria

For this simple game, we have five acceptance criteria that basically describe the mechanics of the game:

1. The game will ask the player how many tries they will have before losing the game.
2. The number to guess must be between 0 and 10.
3. Every time a player enters a number to guess, the number of retries drops by one.
4. If the number of retries reaches zero and the number is still incorrect, the game finishes and the player has lost.
5. If the player guesses the number, the player wins.

Implementation of State pattern

The idea of unit tests is quite straightforward in a State pattern so we will spend more time explaining in detail the mechanism to use it, which is a bit more complex than usual.

First of all, we need the interface to represent the different states and a game context to store the information between states. For this game, the context needs to store the number of retries, if the user has won or not, the secret number to guess, and the current state. The state will have an `executeState` method that accepts one of these contexts and returns `true` if the game has finished, or `false` if not:

```
type GameState interface {
    executeState(*GameContext) bool
}

type GameContext struct {
    SecretNumber int
```

```
    Retries int
    Won bool
    Next GameState
}
```

As described in *acceptance criteria 1,* the player must be able to introduce the number of retries they want. This will be achieved by a state called `StartState`. Also, the `StartState` struct must prepare the game, setting the context to its initial value before the player:

```
type StartState struct{}
func(s *StartState) executeState(c *GameContext) bool {
  c.Next = &AskState{}

  rand.Seed(time.Now().UnixNano())
  c.SecretNumber = rand.Intn(10)

  fmt.Println("Introduce a number a number of retries to set the
difficulty:")
  fmt.Fscanf(os.Stdin, "%d\n", &c.Retries)

  return true
}
```

First of all, the `StartState` struct implements the `GameState` structure because it has the `executeState(*Context)` method of Boolean type on its structure. At the beginning of this state, it sets the only state possible after executing this one–the `AskState` state. The `AskState` struct is not declared yet, but it will be the state where we ask the player for a number to guess.

In the next two lines, we use the `Rand` package of Go to generate a random number. In the first line, we feed the random generator with the `int64` type number returned by the current moment, so we ensure a random feed in each execution (if you put a constant number here, the randomizer will also generate the same number too). The `rand.Intn(int)` method returns an integer number between zero and the specified number, so here we cover *acceptance criteria 2.*

Next, a message asking for a number of retries to set precedes the `fmt.Fscanf` method, a powerful function where you can pass it an `io.Reader` (the standard input of the console), a format (number), and an interface to store the contents of the reader, in this case, the `Retries` field of the context.

Finally, we return `true` to tell the engine that the game must continue. Let's see the `AskState` struct, which we have used at the beginning of the function:

```
type AskState struct {}
func (a *AskState) executeState(c *GameContext) bool{
   fmt.Printf("Introduce a number between 0 and 10, you have %d tries
left\n", c.Retries)

   var n int
   fmt.Fscanf(os.Stdin, "%d", &n)
   c.Retries = c.Retries - 1

   if n == c.SecretNumber {
     c.Won = true
     c.Next = &FinishState{}
   }

   if c.Retries == 0 {
     c.Next = &FinishState{}
   }

   return true
}
```

The `AskState` structure also implements the `GameState` state, as you have probably guessed already. This states starts with a message for the player, asking them to insert a new number. In the next three lines, we create a local variable to store the contents of the number that the player will introduce. We used the `fmt.Fscanf` method again, as we did in `StartState` struct to capture the player's input and store it in the variable `n`. Then, we have one retry less in our counter, so we have to subtract one to the number of retries represented in the `Retries` field.

Then, there are two checks: one that checks if the user has entered the correct number, in which case the context field `Won` is set to `true` and the next state is set to the `FinishState` struct (not declared yet).

The second check is controlling that the number of retries has not reached zero, in which case it won't let the player ask again for a number and it will send the player to the `FinishState` struct directly. After all, we have to tell the game engine again that the game must continue by returning `true` in the `executeState` method.

Finally, we define the `FinishState` struct. It controls the exit status of the game, checking the contents of the `Won` field in the context object:

```
type FinishState struct{}
```

```
func(f *FinishState) executeState(c *GameContext) bool {
  if c.Won {
    println("Congrats, you won")
  }
  else {
    println("You lose")
  }
  return false
}
```

The `TheFinishState` struct also implements the `GameState` state by having `executeState` method in its structure. The idea here is very simple–if the player has won (this field is set previously in the `AskState` struct), the `FinishState` structure will print the message `Congrats, you won`. If the player has not won (remember that the zero value of the Boolean variable is `false`), the `FinishState` prints the message `You lose`.

In this case, the game can be considered finished, so we return `false` to say that the game must not continue.

We just need the `main` method to play our game:

```
func main() {
  start := StartState{}
  game := GameContext{
    Next:&start,
  }
  for game.Next.executeState(&game) {}
}
```

Well, yes, it can't be simpler. The game must begin with the `start` method, although it could be abstracted more outside in case that the game needs more initialization in the future, but in our case it is fine. Then, we create a context where we set the `Next` state as a pointer to the `start` variable. So the first state that will be executed in the game will be the `StartState` state.

The last line of the `main` function has a lot of things just there. We create a loop, without any statement inside it. As with any loop, it keeps looping after the condition is not satisfied. The condition we are using is the returned value of the `GameStates` structure, `true` as soon as the game is not finished.

So, the idea is simple: we execute the state in the context, passing a pointer to the context to it. Each state returns `true` until the game has finished and the `FinishState` struct will return `false`. So our for loop will keep looping, waiting for a `false` condition sent by the `FinishState` structure to end the application.

Let's play once:

```
go run state.go
Introduce a number a number of retries to set the difficulty:
5
Introduce a number between 0 and 10, you have 5 tries left
8
Introduce a number between 0 and 10, you have 4 tries left
2
Introduce a number between 0 and 10, you have 3 tries left
1
Introduce a number between 0 and 10, you have 2 tries left
3
Introduce a number between 0 and 10, you have 1 tries left
4
You lose
```

We lost! We set the number of retries to 5. Then we kept inserting numbers, trying to guess the secret number. We entered 8, 2, 1, 3, and 4, but it wasn't any of them. I don't even know what the correct number was; let's fix this!

Go to the definition of the `FinishState` struct and change the line where it says `You lose`, and replace it with the following:

```
fmt.Printf("You lose. The correct number was: %d\n", c.SecretNumber)
```

Now it will show the correct number. Let's play again:

```
go run state.go
Introduce a number a number of retries to set the difficulty:
3
Introduce a number between 0 and 10, you have 3 tries left
6
Introduce a number between 0 and 10, you have 2 tries left
2
Introduce a number between 0 and 10, you have 1 tries left
1
You lose. The correct number was: 9
```

This time we make it a little harder by setting only three tries... and we lost again. I entered 6, 2, and 1, but the correct number was 9. Last try:

```
go run state.go
Introduce a number a number of retries to set the difficulty:
5
Introduce a number between 0 and 10, you have 5 tries left
3
Introduce a number between 0 and 10, you have 4 tries left
```

```
4
Introduce a number between 0 and 10, you have 3 tries left
5
Introduce a number between 0 and 10, you have 2 tries left
6
Congrats, you won
```

Great! This time we lowered the difficulty, allowing up to five tries and we won! we even had one more try left, but we guessed the number in the fourth try after entering 3, 4, 5. The correct number was 6, which was my fourth try.

A state to win and a state to lose

Have you realized that we could have a winning and a lose state instead of printing the messages directly in the `FinishState` struct? This way we could, for example, check some hypothetical scoreboard in the win section to see if we have set a record. Let's refactor our game. First we need a `WinState` and a `LoseState` struct:

```
type WinState struct{}

func (w *WinState) executeState(c *GameContext) bool {
  println("Congrats, you won")

  return false
}

type LoseState struct{}

func (l *LoseState) executeState(c *GameContext) bool {
  fmt.Printf("You lose. The correct number was: %d\n", c.SecretNumber)
  return false
}
```

These two new states have nothing new. They contain the same messages that were previously in the `FinishState` state that, by the way, must be modified to use these new states:

```
func (f *FinishState) executeState(c *GameContext) bool {
  if c.Won {
    c.Next = &WinState{}
  } else {
    c.Next = &LoseState{}
  }
  return true
}
```

Now, the finish state doesn't print anything and, instead, delegates this to the next state in the chain–the `WinState` structure, if the user has won and the `LoseState` struct, if not. Remember that the game doesn't finish on the `FinishState` struct now, and we must return `true` instead of `false` to notify to the engine that it must keep executing states in the chain.

The game built using the State pattern

You must be thinking now that you can extend this game forever with new states, and it's true. The power of the State pattern is not only the capacity to create a complex FSM, but also the flexibility to improve it as much as you want by adding new states and modifying some old states to point to the new ones without affecting the rest of the FSM.

Mediator design pattern

Let's continue with the Mediator pattern. As its name implies, it's a pattern that will be in between two types to exchange information. But, why will we want this behavior at all? Let's look at this in detail.

Description

One of the key objectives of any design pattern is to avoid tight coupling between objects. This can be done in many ways, as we have seen already.

But one particularly effective method when the application grows a lot is the Mediator pattern. The Mediator pattern is the perfect example of a pattern that is commonly used by every programmer without thinking very much about it.

Mediator pattern will act as the type in charge of exchanging communication between two objects. This way, the communicating objects don't need to know each other and can change more freely. The pattern that maintains which objects give what information is the Mediator.

Objectives

As previously described, the main objectives of the Mediator pattern are about loose coupling and encapsulation. The objectives are:

- To provide loose coupling between two objects that must communicate between them
- To reduce the amount of dependencies of a particular type to the minimum by passing these needs to the Mediator pattern

A calculator

For the Mediator pattern, we are going to develop an extremely simple arithmetic calculator. You're probably thinking that a calculator is so simple that it does not need any pattern. But we will see that this is not exactly true.

Our calculator will only do two very simple operations: sum and subtract.

Acceptance criteria

It sounds quite funny to talk about acceptance criteria to define a calculator, but let's do it anyway:

1. Define an operation called Sum that takes a number and adds it to another number.
2. Define an operation called Subtract that takes a number and substracts it to another number.

Well, I don't know about you, but I really need a rest after this *complex* criteria. So why are we defining this so much? Patience, you will have the answer soon.

Implementation

We have to jump directly to the implementation because we cannot test that the sum will be correct (well, we can, but we will be testing if Go is correctly written!). We could test that we pass the acceptance criteria, but it's a bit of an overkill for our example.

So let's start by implementing the necessary types:

```
package main

type One struct{}
type Two struct{}
type Three struct{}
type Four struct{}
```

```
type Five struct{}
type Six struct{}
type Seven struct{}
type Eight struct{}
type Nine struct{}
type Zero struct{}
```

Well… this look quite awkward. We already have numeric types in Go to perform these operations, we don't need a type for each number!

But let's continue for a second with this insane approach. Let's implement the One struct:

```
type One struct{}

func (o *One) OnePlus(n interface{}) interface{} {
  switch n.(type) {
  case One:
    return &Two{}
  case Two:
    return &Three{}
  case Three:
    return &Four{}
  case Four:
    return &Five{}
  case Five:
    return &Six{}
  case Six:
    return &Seven{}
  case Seven:
    return &Eight{}
  case Eight:
    return &Nine{}
  case Nine:
    return [2]interface{}{&One{}, &Zero{}}
  default:
    return fmt.Errorf("Number not found")
  }
}
```

OK , I'll stop here. What is wrong with this implementation? This is completely crazy! It's overkill to make every operation possible between numbers to make sums! Especially when we have more than one digit.

Well, believe it or not, this is how a lot of software is commonly designed today. A small app where an object uses two or three objects grows, and it ends up using dozens of them. It becomes an absolute hell to simply add or remove a type from the application because it is hidden in some of this craziness.

So what can we do in this calculator? Use a Mediator type that frees all the cases:

```go
func Sum(a, b interface{}) interface{}{
  switch a := a.(type) {
    case One:
    switch b.(type) {
      case One:
        return &Two{}
      case Two:
        return &Three{}
      default:
        return fmt.Errorf("Number not found")
    }
    case Two:
    switch b.(type) {
      case One:
        return &Three{}
      case Two:
        return &Four{}
      default:
      return fmt.Errorf("Number not found")

    }
    case int:
    switch b := b.(type) {
      case One:
        return &Three{}
      case Two:
        return &Four{}
      case int:
        return a + b
      default:
      return fmt.Errorf("Number not found")

    }
    default:
    return fmt.Errorf("Number not found")
  }
}
```

We have just developed a couple of numbers to keep things short. The `Sum` function acts as a mediator between two numbers. First it checks the type of the first number named `a`. Then, for each type of the first number, it checks the type of the second number named `b` and returns the resulting type.

While the solution still looks very crazy now, the only one that knows about all possible numbers in the calculator is the `Sum` function. But take a closer look and you'll see that we have added a type case for the `int` type. We have cases `One`, `Two`, and `int`. Inside the `int` case, we also have another `int` case for the `b` number. What do we do here? If both types are of the `int` case, we can return the sum of them.

Do you think that this will work? Let's write a simple `main` function:

```
func main(){
    fmt.Printf("%#v\n", Sum(One{}, Two{}))
    fmt.Printf("%d\n", Sum(1,2))
}
```

We print the sum of type `One` and type `Two`. By using the `"%#v"` format, we ask to print information about the type. The second line in the function uses `int` types, and we also print the result. This in the console produces the following output:

```
$go run mediator.go
&main.Three{}
7
```

Not very impressive, right? But let's think for a second. By using the Mediator pattern, we have been able to refactor the initial calculator, where we have to define every operation on every type to a Mediator pattern, the `Sum` function.

The nice thing is that, thanks to the Mediator pattern, we have been able to start using integers as values for our calculator. We have just defined the simplest example by adding two integers, but we could have done the same with an integer and the `type`:

```
case One:
    switch b := b.(type) {
    case One:
        return &Two{}
    case Two:
        return &Three{}
    case int:
        return b+1
    default:
        return fmt.Errorf("Number not found")
    }
```

With this small modification, we can now use type `One` with an `int` as number `b`. If we keep working on this Mediator pattern, we could achieve a lot of flexibility between types, without having to implement every possible operation between them, generating a tight coupling.

We'll add a new `Sum` method in the main function to see this in action:

```
func main(){
  fmt.Printf("%#v\n", Sum(One{}, Two{}))
  fmt.Printf("%d\n", Sum(1,2))
  fmt.Printf("%d\n", Sum(One{},2))
}
$go run mediator.go&main.Three{}33
```

Nice. The Mediator pattern is in charge of knowing about the possible types and returns the most convenient type for our case, which is an integer. Now we could keep growing this `Sum` function until we completely get rid of using the numeric types we have defined.

Uncoupling two types with the Mediator

We have carried out a disruptive example to try to think outside the box and reason deeply about the Mediator pattern. Tight coupling between entities in an app can become really complex to deal with in the future and allow more difficult refactoring if needed.

Just remember that the Mediator pattern is there to act as a managing type between two types that don't know about each other so that you can take one of the types without affecting the other and replace a type in a more easy and convenient way.

Observer design pattern

We will finish the common *Gang of Four* design patterns with my favorite: the Observer pattern, also known as publish/subscriber or publish/listener. With the State pattern, we defined our first event-driven architecture, but with the Observer pattern we will really reach a new level of abstraction.

Description

The idea behind the Observer pattern is simple–to subscribe to some event that will trigger some behavior on many subscribed types. Why is this so interesting? Because we uncouple an event from its possible handlers.

For example, imagine a login button. We could code that when the user clicks the button, the button color changes, an action is executed, and a form check is performed in the background. But with the Observer pattern, the type that changes the color will subscribe to the event of the clicking of the button. The type that checks the form and the type that performs an action will subscribe to this event too.

Objectives

The Observer pattern is especially useful to achieve many actions that are triggered on one event. It is also especially useful when you don't know how many actions are performed after an event in advance or there is a possibility that the number of actions is going to grow in the near future. To resume, do the following:

- Provide an event-driven architecture where one event can trigger one or more actions
- Uncouple the actions that are performed from the event that triggers them
- Provide more than one event that triggers the same action

The notifier

We will develop the simplest possible application to fully understand the roots of the Observer pattern. We are going to make a `Publisher` struct, which is the one that triggers an event so it must accept new observers and remove them if necessary. When the `Publisher` struct is triggered, it must notify all its observers of the new event with the data associated.

Acceptance criteria

The requirements must tell us to have some type that triggers some method in one or more actions:

1. We must have a publisher with a `NotifyObservers` method that accepts a message as an argument and triggers a `Notify` method on every observer subscribed.
2. We must have a method to add new subscribers to the publisher.
3. We must have a method to remove new subscribers from the publisher.

Unit tests

Maybe you have realized that our requirements defined almost exclusively the `Publisher` type. This is because the action performed by the observer is irrelevant for the Observer pattern. It should simply execute an action, in this case the `Notify` method, that one or many types will implement. So let's define this only interface for this pattern:

```
type Observer interface {
  Notify(string)
}
```

The `Observer` interface has a `Notify` method that accepts a `string` type that will contain the message to spread. It does not need to return anything, but we could return an error if we want to check if all observers have been reached when calling the `publish` method of the `Publisher` structure.

To test all the acceptance criteria, we just need a structure called `Publisher` with three methods:

```
type Publisher struct {
  ObserversList []Observer
}

func (s *Publisher) AddObserver(o Observer) {}

func (s *Publisher) RemoveObserver(o Observer) {}

func (s *Publisher) NotifyObservers(m string) {}
```

The `Publisher` structure stores the list of subscribed observers in a slice field called `ObserversList`. Then it has the three methods mentioned on the acceptance criteria-the `AddObserver` method to subscribe a new observer to the publisher, the `RemoveObserver` method to unsubscribe an observer, and the `NotifyObservers` method with a string that acts as the message we want to spread between all observers.

With these three methods, we have to set up a root test to configure the `Publisher` and three subtests to test each method. We also need to define a test type structure that implements the `Observer` interface. This structure is going to be called `TestObserver`:

```
type TestObserver struct {
  ID      int
  Message string
}
func (p *TestObserver) Notify(m string) {
  fmt.Printf("Observer %d: message '%s' received \n", p.ID, m)
```

```
    p.Message = m
}
```

The `TestObserver` structure implements the Observer pattern by defining a `Notify(string)` method in its structure. In this case, it prints the received message together with its own observer ID. Then, it stores the message in its `Message` field. This allows us to check later if the content of the `Message` field is as expected. Remember that it could also be done by passing the `testing.T` pointer and the expected message and checking within the `TestObserver` structure.

Now we can set up the `Publisher` structure to execute the three tests. We will create three instances of the `TestObserver` structure:

```
func TestSubject(t *testing.T) {
    testObserver1 := &TestObserver{1, ""}
    testObserver2 := &TestObserver{2, ""}
    testObserver3 := &TestObserver{3, ""}
    publisher := Publisher{}
```

We have given a different ID to each observer so that we can see later that each of them has printed the expected message. Then, we have added the observers by calling the `AddObserver` method on the `Publisher` structure.

Let's write an `AddObserver` test, it must add a new observer to the `ObserversList` field of the `Publisher` structure:

```
    t.Run("AddObserver", func(t *testing.T) {
        publisher.AddObserver(testObserver1)
        publisher.AddObserver(testObserver2)
        publisher.AddObserver(testObserver3)

        if len(publisher.ObserversList) != 3 {
            t.Fail()
        }
    })
```

We have added three observers to the `Publisher` structure, so the length of the slice must be 3. If it's not 3, the test will fail.

The `RemoveObserver` test will take the observer with ID 2 and remove it from the list:

```
    t.Run("RemoveObserver", func(t *testing.T) {
        publisher.RemoveObserver(testObserver2)

        if len(publisher.ObserversList) != 2 {
            t.Errorf("The size of the observer list is not the " +
```

```
            "expected. 3 != %d\n", len(publisher.ObserversList))
    }
    for _, observer := range publisher.ObserversList {
        testObserver, ok := observer.(TestObserver)
        if !ok {
            t.Fail()
        }
        if testObserver.ID == 2 {
            t.Fail()
        }
    }
})
```

After removing the second observer, the length of the `Publisher` structure must be 2 now. We also check that none of the observers left have the `ID` 2 because it must be removed.

The last method to test is the `Notify` method. When using the `Notify` method, all instances of `TestObserver` structure must change their `Message` field from empty to the passed message (`Hello World!` in this case). First we will check that all the `Message` fields are, in fact, empty before calling the `NotifyObservers` test:

```
t.Run("Notify", func(t *testing.T) {
    for _, observer := range publisher.ObserversList {
        printObserver, ok := observer.(*TestObserver)
        if !ok {
            t.Fail()
            break
        }

        if printObserver.Message != "" {
            t.Errorf("The observer's Message field weren't " + "  empty: %s\n",
printObserver.Message)
        }
    }
```

Using a `for` statement, we are iterating over the `ObserversList` field to slice in the `publisher` instance. We need to make a type casting from a pointer to an observer, to a pointer to the `TestObserver` structure, and check that the casting has been done correctly. Then, we check that the `Message` field is actually empty.

The next step is to create a message to send–in this case, it will be `"Hello World!"` and then pass this message to the `NotifyObservers` method to notify every observer on the list (currently observers 1 and 3 only):

```
...
message := "Hello World!"
```

```
publisher.NotifyObservers(message)

for _, observer := range publisher.ObserversList {
  printObserver, ok := observer.(*TestObserver)
  if !ok {
    t.Fail()
    break
  }

  if printObserver.Message != message {
    t.Errorf("Expected message on observer %d was " +
      "not expected: '%s' != '%s'\n", printObserver.ID,
      printObserver.Message, message)
  }
  }
 }
})
}
```

After calling the `NotifyObservers` method, each `TestObserver` tests in the `ObserversList` field must have the message `"Hello World!"` stored in their `Message` field. Again, we use a `for` loop to iterate over every observer of the `ObserversList` field and we typecast each to a `TestObserver` test (remember that `TestObserver` structure doesn't have any field as it's an interface). We could avoid type casting by adding a new `Message()` method to `Observer` instance and implementing it in the `TestObserver` structure to return the contents of the `Message` field. Both methods are equally valid. Once we have type casted to a `TestObserver` method called `printObserver` variable as a local variable, we check that each instance in the `ObserversList` structure has the string `"Hello World!"` stored in their `Message` field.

Time to run the tests that must fail all to check their effectiveness in the later implementation:

```
go test -v
=== RUN    TestSubject
=== RUN    TestSubject/AddObserver
=== RUN    TestSubject/RemoveObserver
=== RUN    TestSubject/Notify
--- FAIL: TestSubject (0.00s)
    --- FAIL: TestSubject/AddObserver (0.00s)
    --- FAIL: TestSubject/RemoveObserver (0.00s)
        observer_test.go:40: The size of the observer list is not the
expected. 3 != 0
    --- PASS: TestSubject/Notify (0.00s)
FAIL
exit status 1
FAIL
```

Something isn't working as expected. How is the `Notify` method passing the tests if we haven't implemented the function yet? Take a look at the test of the `Notify` method again. The test iterates over the `ObserversList` structure and each `Fail` call is inside this for loop. If the list is empty, it won't iterate, so it won't execute any `Fail call`.

Let's fix this issue by adding a small non-empty list check at the beginning of the `Notify` test:

```
if len(publisher.ObserversList) == 0 {
    t.Errorf("The list is empty. Nothing to test\n")
}
```

And we will rerun the tests to see if the `TestSubject/Notify` method is already failing:

```
go test -v
=== RUN    TestSubject
=== RUN    TestSubject/AddObserver
=== RUN    TestSubject/RemoveObserver
=== RUN    TestSubject/Notify
--- FAIL: TestSubject (0.00s)
    --- FAIL: TestSubject/AddObserver (0.00s)
    --- FAIL: TestSubject/RemoveObserver (0.00s)
        observer_test.go:40: The size of the observer list is not the
expected. 3 != 0
    --- FAIL: TestSubject/Notify (0.00s)
        observer_test.go:58: The list is empty. Nothing to test
FAIL
exit status 1
FAIL
```

Nice, all of them are failing and now we have some guarantee on our tests. We can proceed to the implementation.

Implementation

Our implementation is just to define the `AddObserver`, the `RemoveObserver`, and the `NotifyObservers` methods:

```
func (s *Publisher) AddObserver(o Observer) {
    s.ObserversList = append(s.ObserversList, o)
}
```

The `AddObserver` method adds the `Observer` instance to the `ObserversList` structure by appending the pointer to the current list of pointers. This one was very easy. The `AddObserver` test must be passing now (but not the rest or we could have done something wrong):

```
go test -v
=== RUN    TestSubject
=== RUN    TestSubject/AddObserver
=== RUN    TestSubject/RemoveObserver
=== RUN    TestSubject/Notify
--- FAIL: TestSubject (0.00s)
    --- PASS: TestSubject/AddObserver (0.00s)
    --- FAIL: TestSubject/RemoveObserver (0.00s)
        observer_test.go:40: The size of the observer list is not the
expected. 3 != 3
    --- FAIL: TestSubject/Notify (0.00s)
        observer_test.go:87: Expected message on observer 1 was not
expected: 'default' != 'Hello World!'
        observer_test.go:87: Expected message on observer 2 was not
expected: 'default' != 'Hello World!'
        observer_test.go:87: Expected message on observer 3 was not
expected: 'default' != 'Hello World!'
    FAIL
    exit status 1
    FAIL
```

Excellent. Just the `AddObserver` method has passed the test, so we can now continue to the `RemoveObserver` method:

```
func (s *Publisher) RemoveObserver(o Observer) {
  var indexToRemove int

  for i, observer := range s.ObserversList {
    if observer == o {
      indexToRemove = i
      break
    }
  }

  s.ObserversList = append(s.ObserversList[:indexToRemove],
s.ObserversList[indexToRemove+1:]...)
}
```

The `RemoveObserver` method will iterate for each element in the `ObserversList` structure, comparing the `Observer` object's `o` variable with the ones stored in the list. If it finds a match, it saves the index in the local variable, `indexToRemove`, and stops the iteration. The way to remove indexes on a slice in Go is a bit tricky:

1. First, we need to use slice indexing to return a new slice containing every object from the beginning of the slice to the index we want to remove (not included).
2. Then, we get another slice from the index we want to remove (not included) to the last object in the slice
3. Finally, we join the previous two new slices into a new one (the `append` function)

For example, in a list from 1 to 10 in which we want to remove the number 5, we have to create a new slice, joining a slice from 1 to 4 and a slice from 6 to 10.

This index removal is done with the `append` function again because we are actually appending two lists together. Just take a closer look at the three dots at the end of the second argument of the `append` function. The `append` function adds an element (the second argument) to a slice (the first), but we want to append an entire list. This can be achieved using the three dots, which translate to something like *keep adding elements until you finish the second array*.

Ok, let's run this test now:

```
go test -v
=== RUN    TestSubject
=== RUN    TestSubject/AddObserver
=== RUN    TestSubject/RemoveObserver
=== RUN    TestSubject/Notify
--- FAIL: TestSubject (0.00s)
    --- PASS: TestSubject/AddObserver (0.00s)
    --- PASS: TestSubject/RemoveObserver (0.00s)
    --- FAIL: TestSubject/Notify (0.00s)
        observer_test.go:87: Expected message on observer 1 was not
expected: 'default' != 'Hello World!'
        observer_test.go:87: Expected message on observer 3 was not
expected: 'default' != 'Hello World!'
FAIL
exit status 1
FAIL
```

We continue in the good path. The `RemoveObserver` test has been fixed without fixing anything else. Now we have to finish our implementation by defining the `NotifyObservers` method:

```
func (s *Publisher) NotifyObservers(m string) {
```

```
      fmt.Printf("Publisher received message '%s' to notify observers\n", m)
      for _, observer := range s.ObserversList {
        observer.Notify(m)
      }
  }
```

The `NotifyObservers` method is quite simple because it prints a message to the console to announce that a particular message is going to be passed to the `Observers`. After this, we use a for loop to iterate over `ObserversList` structure and execute each `Notify(string)` method by passing the argument `m`. After executing this, all observers must have the message `Hello World!` stored in their `Message` field. Let's see if this is true by running the tests:

```
go test -v
=== RUN    TestSubject
=== RUN    TestSubject/AddObserver
=== RUN    TestSubject/RemoveObserver
=== RUN    TestSubject/Notify
Publisher received message 'Hello World!' to notify observers
Observer 1: message 'Hello World!' received
Observer 3: message 'Hello World!' received
--- PASS: TestSubject (0.00s)
    --- PASS: TestSubject/AddObserver (0.00s)
    --- PASS: TestSubject/RemoveObserver (0.00s)
    --- PASS: TestSubject/Notify (0.00s)
PASS
ok
```

Excellent! We can also see the outputs of the `Publisher` and `Observer` types on the console. The `Publisher` structure prints the following message:

```
hey! I have received the message  'Hello World!' and I'm going to pass the
same message to the observers
```

After this, all observers print their respective messages as follows:

```
hey, I'm observer 1 and I have received the message 'Hello World!'
```

And the same for the third observer.

Summary

We have unlocked the power of event-driven architectures with the State pattern and the Observer pattern. Now you can really execute asynchronous algorithms and operations in your application that respond to events in your system.

The Observer pattern is commonly used in UI's. Android programming is filled with Observer patterns so that the Android SDK can delegate the actions to be performed by the programmers creating an app.

8
Introduction to Go's Concurrency

We have just finished with the *Gang Of Four* design patterns that are commonly used in object oriented programming languages. They have been used extensively for the last few decades (even before they were explicitly defined in a book).

In this chapter, we are going to see concurrency in the Go language. We will, learn that with multiple cores and multiple processes, applications can help us to achieve better performance and endless possibilities. We will look at how to use some of the already known patterns in concurrently safe ways.

A little bit of history and theory

When we talk about Go's concurrency, it's impossible not to talk about history. In the last decades, we saw an improvement in the speed of CPUs until we reached the hardware limits imposed by current hardware materials, design, and architectures. When we reached this point, we started to play with the first multicore computers, the first double CPU motherboards, and then single CPUs with more than one core in their heart.

Unfortunately, the languages we are using are still the ones created when we had single core CPUs, such as Java or C++. While being terrific systems languages, they lack a proper concurrency support by design. You can develop concurrent apps in both of the languages used in your project by using third party tools or by developing your own (not a very easy task).

Go's concurrency was designed with these caveats in mind. The creators wanted garbage collected and procedural language that is familiar for newcomers, but which, at the same time, can be used to write concurrent applications easily and without affecting the core of the language.

We have experienced this in the early chapters. We have developed more than 20 design patterns without a word about concurrency. This clearly shows that the concurrent features of the Go language are completely separated from the core language while being part of it, a perfect example of abstraction and encapsulation.

There are many concurrency models in computer science, the most famous being the actor model present in languages such as **Erlang** or **Scala**. Go, on the other side, uses **Communicating Sequential Processes** (**CSP**), which has a different approach to concurrency.

Concurrency versus parallelism

Many people have misunderstood the differences between both, even thinking that they are the same. There is a popular speech by Rob Pike, one of the creators of Go, *Concurrency is not parallelism*, which I really agree with. As a quick summary of the talk, we can extract the following:

- Concurrency is about dealing with many things at once
- Parallelism is about doing many things at the same time

Concurrency enables parallelism by designing a correct structure of concurrency work.

For example, we can think of the mechanism of a bike. When we pedal, we usually push down the pedal to produce force (and this push, raises our opposite leg on the opposite pedal). We cannot push with both legs at the same time because the cranks don't allow us to do it. But this design allows the construction of a parallel bike, commonly called a **tandem bike**. A tandem bike is a bike that two people can ride at the same time; they both pedal and apply force to the bike.

In the bike example, concurrency is the design of a bike that, with two legs (Goroutines), you can produce power to move the bike by yourself. The design is concurrent and correct. If we use a tandem bike and two people (two cores), the solution is concurrent, correct, and parallel. But the key thing is that with a concurrent design, we don't have to worry about parallelism; we can think about it as an extra feature if our concurrent design is correct. In fact, we can use the tandem bike with only one person, but the concurrent design of the legs, pedals, chain, wheels of a bike is still correct.

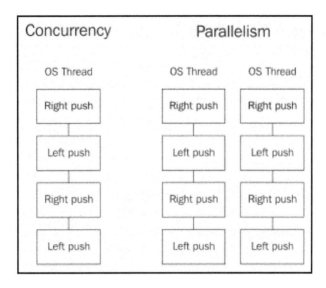

With concurrency, on the left side, we have a design and a structure that is executed sequentially by the same CPU core. Once we have this design and structure, parallelism can be achieved by simply repeating this structure on a different thread.

This is how Go eases the reasoning about concurrent and parallel programs by simply not worrying too much about parallel execution and focusing much more on concurrent design and structure. Breaking a big task into smaller tasks that can be run concurrently usually provides much better performance in a single-core computer, but, if this design can also be run in parallel, we could achieve an even higher throughput (or not, depending on the design).

In fact, we can set the number of cores in use in a Go app by setting the environment variable GOMAXPROCS to the number of cores we want. This is not only useful when using schedulers, such as **Apache Mesos**, but it gives us more control about how a Go app works and performs.

So, to recap, it is very important to keep in mind that concurrency is about structure and parallelism is about execution. We must think about making our programs concurrent in a better way, by breaking them down into smaller pieces of work, and Go's scheduler will try to make them parallel if it's possible and allowed.

CSP versus actor-based concurrency

The most common and, perhaps, intuitive way to think about concurrency is close to the way the actor model works.

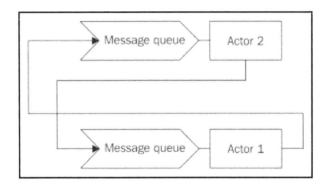

In the actor model, if **Actor 1** wants to communicate with **Actor 2**, then **Actor 1** must know **Actor 2** first; for example, it must have its process ID, maybe from the creation step, and put a message on its inbox queue. After placing the message, **Actor 1** can continue its tasks without getting blocked if **Actor 2** cannot process the message immediately.

CSP, on the other side, introduces a new entity into the equation-channels. Channels are the way to communicate between processes because they are completely anonymous (unlike actors, where we need to know their process IDs). In the case of CSP, we don't have a process ID to use to communicate. Instead, we have to create a channel to the processes to allow incoming and outgoing communication. In this case, what we know that the receiver is the channel it uses to receive data:

In this diagram, we can see that the processes are anonymous, but we have a channel with ID 1, that is, **Channel 1**, which connects them together. This abstraction does not tell us how many processes are on each side of the channel; it simply connects them and allows communication between processes by using the channel.

The key here is that channels isolate both extremes so that process A can send data through a channel that will be handled by potentially one or more processes that' are transparent to A. It also works the same in reverse; process B can receive data from many channels one at a time.

Goroutines

In Go, we achieve concurrency by working with Goroutines. They are like processes that run applications in a computer concurrently; in fact, the main loop of Go could be considered a Goroutine, too. Goroutines are used in places where we would use actors. They execute some logic and die (or keep looping if necessary).

But Goroutines are not threads. We can launch thousands of concurrent Goroutines, even millions. They are incredibly cheap, with a small growth stack. We will use Goroutines to execute code that we want to work concurrently. For example, three calls to three services to compose a response can be designed concurrently with three Goroutines to do the service calls potentially in parallel and a fourth Goroutine to receive them and compose the response. What's the point here? That if we have a computer with four cores, we could potentially run this service call in parallel, but if we use a one-core computer, the design will still be correct and the calls will be executed concurrently in only one core. By designing concurrent applications, we don't need to worry about parallel execution.

Returning to the bike analogy, we were pushing the pedals of the bike with our two legs. That's two Goroutines concurrently pushing the pedals. When we use the tandem, we had a total of four Goroutines, possibly working in parallel. But we also have two hands to handle the front and rear brakes. That's a total of eight Goroutines for our two threads bike. Actually, we don't pedal when we brake and we don't brake when we pedal; that's a correct concurrent design. Our nervous system transports the information about when to stop pedaling and when to start braking. In Go, our nervous system is composed of channels; we will see them after playing a bit with Goroutines first.

Our first Goroutine

Enough of the explanations now. Let's get our hands dirty. For our first Goroutine, we will print the message Hello World! in a Goroutine. Let's start with what we've been doing up until now:

```
package main

func main() {
  helloWorld()
}

func helloWorld(){
  println("Hello World!")
}
```

Running this small snippet of code will simply output `Hello World!` in the console:

```
$ go run main.go
Hello World!
```

Not impressive at all. To run it in a new Goroutine, we just need to add the keyword `go` at the beginning of the call to the function:

```
package main

func main() {
  go helloWorld()
}

func helloWorld(){
  println("Hello World!")
}
```

With this simple word, we are telling Go to start a new Goroutine running the contents of the `helloWorld` function.

So, let's run it:

```
$ go run main.go
$
```

What? It printed nothing! Why is that? Things get complicated when you start to deal with concurrent applications. The problem is that the `main` function finishes before the `helloWorld` function gets executed. Let's analyse it step by step. The `main` function starts and schedules a new Goroutine that will execute the `helloWorld` function, but the function isn't executed when the function finishes—it is still in the scheduling process.

So, our `main` problem is that the `main` function has to wait for the Goroutine to be executed before finishing. So let's pause for a second to give some room to the Goroutine:

```
package main
import "time"

func main() {
  go helloWorld()

  time.Sleep(time.Second)
}

func helloWorld(){
  println("Hello World!")
}
```

The `time.Sleep` function effectively sleeps the main Goroutine for one second before continuing (and exiting). If we run this now, we must get the message:

```
$ go run main.go
Hello World!
```

I suppose you must have noticed by now the small gap of time where the program is freezing before finishing. This is the function for sleeping. If you are doing a lot of tasks, you might want to raise the waiting time to whatever you want. Just remember that in any application the `main` function cannot finish before the rest of the Goroutines.

Anonymous functions launched as new Goroutines

We have defined the `helloWorld` function so that it can be launched with a different Goroutine. This is not strictly necessary because you can launch snippets of code directly in the function's scope:

```
package main
import "time"

func main() {
  go func() {
    println("Hello World")
  }()
  time.Sleep(time.Second)
}
```

This is also valid. We have used an anonymous function and we have launched it in a new Goroutine using the `go` keyword. Take a closer look at the closing braces of the function-they are followed by opening and closing parenthesis, indicating the execution of the function.

We can also pass data to anonymous functions:

```
package main
import "time"

func main() {
  go func(msg string) {
    println(msg)
  }("Hello World")
  time.Sleep(time.Second)
}
```

This is also valid. We had defined an anonymous function that received a string, which then printed the received string. When we called the function in a different Goroutine, we passed the message we wanted to print. In this sense, the following example would also be valid:

```
package main
import "time"

func main() {
  messagePrinter := func(msg string) {
    println(msg)
  }

  go messagePrinter("Hello World")
  go messagePrinter("Hello goroutine")
  time.Sleep(time.Second)
}
```

In this case, we have defined a function within the scope of our `main` function and stored it in a variable called `messagePrinter`. Now we can concurrently print as many messages as we want by using the `messagePrinter(string)` signature:

```
$ go run main.go
Hello World
Hello goroutine
```

We have just scratched the surface of concurrent programming in Go, but we can already see that it can be quite powerful. But we definitely have to do something with that sleeping period. WaitGroups can help us with this problem.

WaitGroups

WaitGroup comes in the synchronization package (the `sync` package) to help us synchronize many concurrent Goroutines. It works very easily–every time we have to wait for one Goroutine to finish, we add `1` to the group, and once all of them are added, we ask the group to wait. When the Goroutine finishes, it says `Done` and the WaitGroup will take one from the group:

```
package main

import (
  "sync"
  "fmt"
)

func main() {
```

```
    var wait sync.WaitGroup
    wait.Add(1)

    go func(){
        fmt.Println("Hello World!")
        wait.Done()
    }()
    wait.Wait()
}
```

This is the simplest possible example of a WaitGroup. First, we created a variable to hold it called the `wait` variable. Next, before launching the new Goroutine, we say to the WaitGroup `hey, you'll have to wait for one thing to finish` by using the `wait.Add(1)` method. Now we can launch the 1 that the WaitGroup has to wait for, which in this case is the previous Goroutine that prints `Hello World` and says `Done` (by using the `wait.Done()` method) at the end of the Goroutine. Finally, we indicate to the WaitGroup to wait. We have to remember that the function `wait.Wait()` was probably executed before the Goroutine.

Let's run the code again:

```
$ go run main.go
Hello World!
```

Now it just waits the necessary time and not one millisecond more before exiting the application. Remember that when we use the `Add(value)` method, we add entities to the WaitGroup, and when we use the `Done()` method, we subtract one.

Actually, the `Add` function takes a delta value, so the following code is equivalent to the previous:

```
package main

import (
    "sync"
    "fmt"
)

func main() {
    var wait sync.WaitGroup
    wait.Add(1)

    go func(){
        fmt.Println("Hello World!")
        wait.Add(-1)
    }()
```

```
    wait.Wait()
}
```

In this case, we added 1 before launching the Goroutine and we added −1 (subtracted 1) at the end of it. If we know in advance how many Goroutines we are going to launch, we can also call the Add method just once:

```
package main
import (
  "fmt"
  "sync"
)

func main() {
  var wait sync.WaitGroup

  goRoutines := 5
  wait.Add(goRoutines)

  for i := 0; i < goRoutines; i++ {
    go func(goRoutineID int) {
      fmt.Printf("ID:%d: Hello goroutines!\n", goRoutineID)
      wait.Done()
    }(i)
  }
  wait.Wait()
}
```

In this example, we are going to create five Goroutines (as stated in the goroutines variable). We know it in advance, so we simply add them all to the WaitGroup. We are then going to launch the same amount of goroutine variables by using a for loop. Every time one Goroutine finishes, it calls the Done() method of the WaitGroup that is effectively waiting at the end of the main loop.

Again, in this case, the code reaches the end of the main function before all Goroutines are launched (if any), and the WaitGroup makes the execution of the main flow wait until all Done messages are called. Let's run this small program:

```
$ go run main.go

ID:4: Hello goroutines!
ID:0: Hello goroutines!
ID:1: Hello goroutines!
ID:2: Hello goroutines!
ID:3: Hello goroutines!
```

We haven't mentioned it before, but we have passed the iteration index to each Goroutine as the parameter `GoroutineID` to print it with the message `Hello goroutines!` You might also have noticed that the Goroutines aren't executed in order. Of course! We are dealing with a scheduler that doesn't guarantee the order of execution of the Goroutines. This is something to keep in mind when programming concurrent applications. In fact, if we execute it again, we won't necessarily get the same order of output:

```
$ go run main.go
ID:4: Hello goroutines!
ID:2: Hello goroutines!
ID:1: Hello goroutines!
ID:3: Hello goroutines!
ID:0: Hello goroutines!
```

Callbacks

Now that we know how to use WaitGroups, we can also introduce the concept of callbacks. If you have ever worked with languages like JavaScript that use them extensively, this section will be familiar to you. A callback is an anonymous function that will be executed within the context of a different function.

For example, we want to write a function to convert a string to uppercase, as well as making it asynchronous. How do we write this function so that we can work with callbacks? There's a little trick-we can have have a function that takes a string and returns a string:

```
func toUpperSync(word string) string {
    //Code will go here
}
```

So take the returning type of this function (a string) and put it as the second parameter in an anonymous function, as shown here:

```
func toUpperSync(word string, f func(string)) {
    //Code will go here
}
```

Now, the `toUpperSync` function returns nothing, but also takes a function that, by coincidence, also takes a string. We can execute this function with the result we will usually return.

```
func toUpperSync(word string, f func(string)) {
    f(strings.ToUpper(word))
}
```

We execute the `f` function with the result of calling the `strings.ToUpper` method with the provided word (which returns the word `parameter` in uppercase). Let's write the `main` function too:

```go
package main

import (
  "fmt"
  "strings"
)

func main() {
  toUpperSync("Hello Callbacks!", func(v string) {
    fmt.Printf("Callback: %s\n", v) })
}

func toUpperSync(word string, f func(string)) {
  f(strings.ToUpper(word))
}
```

In our main code, we have defined our callback. As you can see, we passed the test `Hello Callbacks!` to convert it to uppercase. Next we pass the callback to be executed with the result of passing our string to uppercase. In this case, we simply print the text in the console with the text `Callback` in front of it. When we execute this code, we get the following result:

```
$ go run main.go
Callback: HELLO CALLBACKS!
```

Strictly speaking, this is a synchronous callback. To make it asynchronous we have to introduce some concurrent handling:

```go
package main
import (
  "fmt"
  "strings"
  "sync"
)

var wait sync.WaitGroup

func main() {
  wait.Add(1)

  toUpperAsync("Hello Callbacks!", func(v string) {
    fmt.Printf("Callback: %s\n", v)
    wait.Done()
```

```
    })

    println("Waiting async response...")
    wait.Wait()
}

func toUpperAsync(word string, f func(string)) {
    go func(){
        f(strings.ToUpper(word))
    }()
}
```

This is the same code executed asynchronously. We use WaitGroups to handle concurrency (we will see later that channels can also be used for this). Now, our function `toUpperAsync` is, as its name implies, asynchronous. We launched the callback in a different Goroutine by using the keyword `go` when calling the callback. We write a small message to show the ordering nature of the concurrent execution more precisely. We wait until the callback signals that it's finished and we can exit the program safely. When we execute this, we get the following result:

```
$ go run main.go

Waiting async response...
Callback: HELLO CALLBACKS!
```

As you can see, the program reaches the end of the `main` function before executing the callback in the `toUpperAsync` function. This pattern brings many possibilities, but leaves us open to one big problem called callback hell.

Callback hell

The term **callback hell** is commonly used to refer to when many callbacks have been stacked within each other. This makes them difficult to reason with and handle when they grow too much. For example, using the same code as before, we could stack another asynchronous call with the contents that we previously printed to the console:

```
func main() {
    wait.Add(1)

    toUpperAsync("Hello Callbacks!", func(v string) {
        toUpperAsync(fmt.Sprintf("Callback: %s\n", v), func(v string) {
            fmt.Printf("Callback within %s", v)
            wait.Done()
        })
    })
```

```
    println("Waiting async response...")
    wait.Wait()
}
```

(We have omitted imports, the package name, and the `toUpperAsync` function as they have not changed.) Now we have the `toUpperAsync` function within a `toUpperAsync` function, and we could embed many more if we want. In this case, we again pass the text that we previously printed on the console to use it in the following callback. The inner callback finally prints it on the console, giving the following output:

```
$ go run main.go
Waiting async response...
Callback within CALLBACK: HELLO CALLBACKS!
```

In this case, we can assume that the outer callback will be executed before the inner one. That's why we don't need to add one more to the WaitGroup.

The point here is that we must be careful when using callbacks. In very complex systems, too many callbacks are hard to reason with and hard to deal with. But with care and rationality, they are powerful tools.

Mutexes

If you are working with concurrent applications, you have to deal with more than one resource potentially accessing some memory location. This is usually called **race condition**.

In simpler terms, a race condition is similar to that moment where two people try to get the last piece of pizza at exactly the same time–their hands collide. Replace the pizza with a variable and their hands with Goroutines and we'll have a perfect analogy.

There is one character at the dinner table to solve this issues–a father or mother. They have kept the pizza on a different table and we have to ask for permission to stand up before getting our slice of pizza. It doesn't matter if all the kids ask at the same time–they will only allow one kid to stand.

Well, a mutex is like our parents. They'll control who can access the pizza–I mean, a variable–and they won't allow anyone else to access it.

To use a mutex, we have to actively lock it; if it's already locked (another Goroutine is using it), we'll have to wait until it's unlocked again. Once we get access to the mutex, we can lock it again, do whatever modifications are needed, and unlock it again. We'll look at this using an example.

An example with mutexes – concurrent counter

Mutexes are widely used in concurrent programming. Maybe not so much in Go because it has a more idiomatic way of concurrent programming in its use of channels, but it's worth seeing how they work for the situations where channels simply don't fit so well.

For our example, we are going to develop a small concurrent counter. This counter will add one to an integer field in a Counter type. This should be done in a concurrent-safe way.

Our Counter structure is defined like this:

```
type Counter struct {
    sync.Mutex
    value int
}
```

The Counter structure has a field of int type that stores the current value of the count. It also embeds the Mutex type from the sync package. Embedding this field will allow us to lock and unlock the entire structure without actively calling a specific field.

Our main function launches 10 Goroutines that try to add one to the field value of Counter structure. All of this is done concurrently:

```
package main

import (
    "sync"
    "time"
)

func main() {
    counter := Counter{}

    for i := 0; i < 10; i++ {
        go func(i int) {
            counter.Lock()
            counter.value++
            defer counter.Unlock()
        }(i)
    }
    time.Sleep(time.Second)

    counter.Lock()
    defer counter.Unlock()

    println(counter.value)
}
```

We have created a type called `Counter`. Using a `for` loop, we have launched a total of 10 Goroutines, as we saw in the *Anonymous functions launched as new Goroutines* section. But inside every Goroutine, we are locking the counter so that no more Goroutines can access it, adding one to the field value, and unlocking it again so others can access it.

Finally, we'll print the value held by the counter. It must be 10 because we have launched 10 Goroutines.

But how can we know that this program is thread safe? Well, Go comes with a very handy built-in feature called the "race detector".

Presenting the race detector

We already know what a race condition is. To recap, it is used when two processes try to access the same resource at the same time with one or more writing operations (both processes writing or one process writing while the other reads) involved at that precise moment.

Go has a very handy tool to help diagnose race conditions, that you can run in your tests or your main application directly. So let's reuse the example we just wrote for the *mutexes* section and run it with the race detector. This is as simple as adding the `-race` command-line flag to the command execution of our program:

```
$ go run -race main.go
10
```

Well, not very impressive is it? But in fact it is telling us that it has not detected a potential race condition in the code of this program. Let's make the detector of `-race` flag warn us of a possible race condition by not locking `counter` before we modify it:

```
for i := 0; i < 10; i++ {
    go func(i int) {
        //counter.Lock()
        counter.value++
        //counter.Unlock()
    }(i)
}
```

Inside the `for` loop, comment the `Lock` and `Unlock` calls before and after adding `1` to the field value. This will introduce a race condition. Let's run the same program again with the race flag activated:

```
$ go run -race main.go
==================
```

```
WARNING: DATA RACE
Read at 0x00c42007a068 by goroutine 6:
  main.main.func1()
      [some_path]/concurrency/locks/main.go:19 +0x44
Previous write at 0x00c42007a068 by goroutine 5:
  main.main.func1()
      [some_path]/concurrency/locks/main.go:19 +0x60
Goroutine 6 (running) created at:
  main.main()
      [some_path]/concurrency/locks/main.go:21 +0xb6
Goroutine 5 (finished) created at:
  main.main()
      [some_path]/concurrency/locks/main.go:21 +0xb6
==================
10
Found 1 data race(s)
exit status 66
```

I have reduced the output a bit to see things more clearly. We can see a big, uppercase message reading `WARNING: DATA RACE`. But this output is very easy to reason with. First, it is telling us that some memory position represented by *line 19* on our `main.go` file is reading some variable. But there is also a write operation in *line 19* of the same file!

This is because a "++" operation requires a read of the current value and a write to add one to it. That's why the race condition is in the same line, because every time it's executed it reads and writes the field in the `Counter` structure.

But let's keep in mind that the race detector works at runtime. It doesn't analyze our code statically! What does it mean? It means that we can have a potential race condition in our design that the race detector will not detect. For example:

```go
package main

import "sync"

type Counter struct {
  sync.Mutex
  value int
}

func main() {
  counter := Counter{}

  for i := 0; i < 1; i++ {
    go func(i int) {
      counter.value++
    }(i)
```

```
    }
  }
```

We will leave the code as shown in the preceding example. We will take all locks and unlocks from the code and launch a single Goroutine to update the `value` field:

```
$ go run -race main.go
$
```

No warnings, so the code is correct. Well, we know, by design, it's not. We can raise the number of Goroutines executed to two and see what happens:

```
for i := 0; i < 2; i++ {
  go func(i int) {
    counter.value++
  }(i)
}
```

Let's execute the program again:

```
$ go run -race main.go
WARNING: DATA RACE
Read at 0x00c42007a008 by goroutine 6:
  main.main.func1()
    [some_path]concurrency/race_detector/main.go:15 +0x44
Previous write at 0x00c42007a008 by goroutine 5:
  main.main.func1()
    [some_path]/concurrency/race_detector/main.go:15 +0x60
Goroutine 6 (running) created at:
  main.main()
    [some_path]/concurrency/race_detector/main.go:16 +0xad
Goroutine 5 (finished) created at:
  main.main()
    [some_path]/concurrency/race_detector/main.go:16 +0xad
==================
Found 1 data race(s)
exit status 66
```

Now yes, the race condition is detected. But what if we reduce the number of processors in use to just one? Will we have a race condition too?

```
$ GOMAXPROCS=1 go run -race main.go
$
```

It seems that no race condition has been detected. This is because the scheduler executed one Goroutine first and then the other, so, finally, the race condition didn't occur. But with a higher number of Goroutines it will also warn us about a race condition, even using only one core.

So, the race detector can help us to detect race conditions that are happening in our code, but it won't protect us from a bad design that is not immediately executing race conditions. A very useful feature that can save us from lots of headaches.

Channels

Channels are the second primitive in the language that allows us to write concurrent applications. We have talked a bit about channels in the *Communicating sequential processes* section.

Channels are the way we communicate between processes. We could be sharing a memory location and using mutexes to control the processes' access. But channels provide us with a more natural way to handle concurrent applications that also produces better concurrent designs in our programs.

Our first channel

Working with many Goroutines seems pretty difficult if we can't create some synchronization between them. The order of execution could be irrelevant as soon as they are synchronized. Channels are the second key feature to write concurrent applications in Go.

A TV channel in real life is something that connects an emission (from a studio) to millions of TVs (the receivers). Channels in Go work in a similar fashion. One or more Goroutines can work as emitters, and one or more Goroutine can act as receivers.

One more thing channels, by default, block the execution of Goroutines until something is received. It is as if our favourite TV show delays the emission until we turn the TV on so we don't miss anything.

How is this done in Go?

```
package main

import "fmt"

func main() {
  channel := make(chan string)
  go func() {
    channel <- "Hello World!"
  }()
```

```
    message := <-channel
    fmt.Println(message)
}
```

To create channels in Go, we use the same syntax that we use to create slices. The `make` keyword is used to create a channel, and we have to pass the keyword `chan` and the type that the channel will transport, in this case, strings. With this, we have a blocking channel with the name `channel`. Next, we launch a Goroutines that sends the message `Hello World!` to the channel. This is indicated by the intuitive arrow that shows the flow–the `Hello World!` text going to (`<-`) a channel. This works like an assignment in a variable, so we can only pass something to a channel by first writing the channel, then the arrow, and finally the value to pass. We cannot write `"Hello World!" -> channel`.

As we mentioned earlier, this channel is blocking the execution of Gorountines until a message is received. In this case, the execution of the `main` function is stopped until the message from the launched Gorountines reaches the other end of the channel in the line `message := <-channel`. In this case, the arrow points in the same direction, but it's placed before the channel, indicating that the data is being extracted from the channel and assigned to a new variable called `message` (using the new assignment ":=" operator).

In this case, we don't need to use a WaitGroup to synchronize the `main` function with the created Goroutines, as the default nature of channels is to block until data is received. But does it work the other way around? If there is no receiver when the Goroutine sends the message, does it continue? Let's edit this example to see this:

```
package main

import (
  "fmt"
  "time"
)

func main() {
  channel := make(chan string)

  var waitGroup sync.WaitGroup

  waitGroup.Add(1)
  go func() {
    channel <- "Hello World!"
    println("Finishing goroutine")
    waitGroup.Done()
  }()

  time.Sleep(time.Second)
```

```
message := <-channel
fmt.Println(message)
waitGroup.Wait()
}
```

We are going to use the `Sleep` function again. In this case, we print a message when the Goroutine is finished. The big difference is in the `main` function. Now we wait one second before we listen to the channel for data:

```
$ go run main.go

Finishing goroutine
Hello World!
```

The output can differ because, again, there are no guarantees in the order of execution, but now we can see that no message is printed until one second has passed. After the initial delay, we start listening to the channel, take the data, and print it. So the emitter also has to wait for a cue from the other side of the channel to continue its execution.

To recap, channels are ways to communicate between Goroutines by sending data through one end and receiving it at the other (like a pipe). In their default state, an emitter Goroutine will block its execution until a receiver Goroutine takes the data. The same goes for a receiver Goroutine, which will block until some emitter sends data through the channel. So you can have passive listeners (waiting for data) or passive emitters (waiting for listeners).

Buffered channels

A buffered channel works in a similar way to default unbuffered channels. You also pass and take values from them by using the arrows, but, unlike unbuffered channels, senders don't need to wait until some Goroutine picks the data that they are sending:

```
package main

import (
  "fmt"
  "time"
)

func main() {
  channel := make(chan string, 1)

  go func() {
    channel <- "Hello World!"
    println("Finishing goroutine")
  }()
```

```
        time.Sleep(time.Second)

        message := <-channel
        fmt.Println(message)
    }
```

This example is like the first example we used for channels, but now we have set the capacity of the channel to one in the `make` statement. With this, we tell the compiler that this channel has a capacity of one string before getting blocked. So the first string doesn't block the emitter, but the second would. Let's run this example:

```
$ go run main.go

Finishing goroutine
Hello World!
```

Now we can run this small program as many times as we want–the output will always be in the same order. This time, we have launched the concurrent function and waited for one second. Previously, the anonymous function wouldn't continue until the second has passed and someone can pick the sent data. In this case, with a buffered channel, the data is held in the channel and frees the Goroutine to continue its execution. In this case, the Goroutine is always finishing before the wait time passes.

This new channel has a size of one, so a second message would block the Goroutine execution:

```
package main

import (
    "fmt"
    "time"
)

func main() {
    channel := make(chan string, 1)

    go func() {
        channel <- "Hello World! 1"
        channel <- "Hello World! 2"
        println("Finishing goroutine")
    }()

    time.Sleep(time.Second)

    message := <-channel
    fmt.Println(message)
}
```

Here, we add a second `Hello world! 2` message, and we provide it with an index. In this case, the output of this program could be like the following:

```
$ go run main.go

Hello World! 1
```

Indicating that we have just taken one message from the channel buffer, we have printed it, and the `main` function finished before the launched Goroutine could finish. The Goroutine got blocked when sending the second message and couldn't continue until the other end took the first message. Then it prints it so quickly that it doesn't have time to print the message to show the ending of the Goroutine. If you keep executing the program on the console, sooner or later the scheduler will finish the Goroutine execution before the main thread.

Directional channels

One cool feature about Go channels is that, when we use them as parameters, we can restrict their directionality so that they can be used only to send or to receive. The compiler will complain if a channel is used in the restricted direction. This feature applies a new level of static typing to Go apps and makes code more understandable and more readable.

We'll take a simple example with channels:

```
package main

import (
  "fmt"
  "time"
)

func main() {
  channel := make(chan string, 1)

  go func(ch chan<- string) {
    ch <- "Hello World!"
    println("Finishing goroutine")
  }(channel)

  time.Sleep(time.Second)

  message := <-channel
  fmt.Println(message)
}
```

The line where we launch the new Goroutine `go func(ch chan<- string)` states that the channel passed to this function can only be used as an input channel, and you can't listen to it.

We can also pass a channel that will be used as a receiver channel only:

```
func receivingCh(ch <-chan string) {
  msg := <-ch
  println(msg)
}
```

As you can see, the arrow is on the opposite side of the keyword `chan`, indicating an extracting operation from the channel. Keep in mind that the channel arrow always points left, to indicate a receiving channel, it must go on the left, and to indicate an inserting channel, it must go on the right.

If we try to send a value through this *receive only* channel, the compiler will complain about it:

```
func receivingCh(ch <-chan string) {
  msg := <-ch
  println(msg)
  ch <- "hello"
}
```

This function has a receive only channel that we will try to use to send the message `hello` through. Let's see what the compiler says:

```
$ go run main.go

./main.go:20: invalid operation: ch <- "hello2" (send to receive-only type
<-chan string)
```

It doesn't like it and asks us to correct it. Now the code is even more readable and safe, and we have just placed an arrow in front or behind the `chan` argument.

The select statement

The select statement is also a key feature in Go. It is used to handle more than one channel input within a Goroutine. In fact, it opens lots of possibilities, and we will use it extensively in the following chapters.

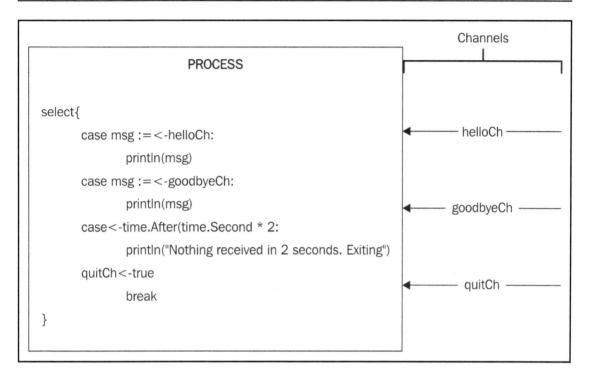

In the `select` structure, we ask the program to choose between one or more channels to receive their data. We can save this data in a variable and make something with it before finishing the select. The `select` structure is just executed once; it doesn't matter if it is listening to more channels, it will be executed only once and the code will continue executing. If we want it to handle the same channels more than once, we have to put it in a `for` loop.

We will make a small app that will send the message `hello` and the message `goodbye` to the same Goroutine, which will print them and exit if it doesn't receive anything else in five seconds.

First, we will make a generic function that sends a string over a channel:

```
func sendString(ch chan<- string, s string) {
  ch <- s
}
```

Now we can send a string over a channel by simply calling the `sendString` method. It's time for the receiver. The receiver will take messages from both channels–the one that sends `hello` messages and the one that sends `goodbye` messages. You can also see this in the previous diagram:

```
func receiver(helloCh, goodbyeCh <-chan string, quitCh chan<- bool) {
  for {
    select {
    case msg := <-helloCh:
      println(msg)
    case msg := <-goodbyeCh:
      println(msg)
    case <-time.After(time.Second * 2):
      println("Nothing received in 2 seconds. Exiting")
      quitCh <- true
      break
    }
  }
}
```

Let's start with the arguments. This function takes three channels–two receiving channels and one to send something through it. Then, it starts an infinite loop with the `for` keyword. This way we can keep listening to both channels forever.

Inside the scope of `select` block, we have to use a case for each channel we want to handle (have you realized how similar it is to the `switch` statement?). Let's see the three cases step by step:

- The first case takes the incoming data from the `helloCh` argument and saves it in a variable called `msg`. Then it prints the contents of this variable.
- The second case takes the incoming data from the `goodbyeCh` argument and saves it in a variable called `msg` too. Then it also prints the content of this variable.
- The third case is quite interesting. It calls the `time` function. After that, if we check its signature, it accepts a time and duration value and returns a receiving channel. This receiving channel will receive a time, the value of `time` after the specified duration has passed. In our example, we use the channel it returns as a timeout. Because the select is restarted after each handle, the timer is restarted too. This is a very simple way to set a timer to a Goroutine waiting for the response of one or many channels.

Everything is ready for the `main` function:

```
package main
```

```
import "time"

func main() {
    helloCh := make(chan string, 1)
    goodbyeCh := make(chan string, 1)
    quitCh := make(chan bool)
    go receiver(helloCh, goodbyeCh, quitCh)

    go sendString(helloCh, "hello!")

    time.Sleep(time.Second)

    go sendString(goodbyeCh, "goodbye!")
    <-quitCh
}
```

Again, step by step, we created the three channels that we'll need in this exercise. Then, we launched our `receiver` function in a different Goroutine. This Goroutine is handled by Go's scheduler and our program continues. We launched a new Goroutine to send the message `hello` to the `helloCh` arguments. Again, this is going to occur eventually when the Go's scheduler decides.

Our program continues again and waits for a second. In this break, Go's scheduler will have time to execute the receiver and the first message (if it hasn't done so yet), so the `hello!` message will appear on the console during the break.

A new message is sent over the `goodbye` channel with the `goodbye!` text in a new Goroutine, and our program continues again to a line where we wait for an incoming message in the `quitCh` argument.

We have launched three Goroutines already—the receiver that it is still running, the first message that had finished when the message was handled by the `select` statement, and the second message was been printed almost immediately and had finished too. So just the receiver is running at this moment, and if it doesn't receive any other message in the following two seconds, it will handle the incoming message from the `time` structure. After `channel` type, print a message to say that it is quitting, send a `true` to the `quitCh`, and break the infinite loop where it was looping.

Let's run this small app:

```
$ go run main.go

hello!
goodbye!
Nothing received in 2 seconds. Exiting
```

The result may not be very impressive, but the concept is clear. We can handle many incoming channels in the same Goroutine by using the select statement.

Ranging over channels too!

The last feature about channels that we will see is ranging over channels. We are talking about the range keyword. We have used it extensively to range over lists, and we can use it to range over a channel too:

```go
package main

import "time"

func main() {
    ch := make(chan int)

    go func() {
        ch <- 1
        time.Sleep(time.Second)

        ch <- 2

        close(ch)
    }()
    for v := range ch {
        println(v)
    }
}
```

In this case, we have created an unbuffered channel, but it would work with a buffered one too. We launched a function in a new Goroutine that sends the number "1" over a channel, waits a second, sends the number "2", and closes the channel.

The last step is to range over the channel. The syntax is quite similar to a list range. We store the incoming data from the channel in the variable v and we print this variable to the console. The range keeps iterating until the channel is closed, taking data from the channel.

Can you guess the output of this little program?

```
$ go run main.go

1
2
```

Again, not very impressive. It prints the number "1", then waits a second, prints the number "2", and exits the application.

According to the design of this concurrent app, the range was iterates over possible incoming data from the

channel

until the concurrent Goroutine closes this channel. At that moment, the range finishes and the app can exit.

Range is very useful in taking data from a channel, and it's commonly used in fan-in patterns where many different Goroutines send data to the same channel.

Using it all – concurrent singleton

Now that we know how to create Goroutines and channels, we'll put all our knowledge in a single package. Think back to the first few chapter, when we explained the singleton pattern-it was some structure or variable that could only exist once in our code. All access to this structure should be done using the pattern described, but, in fact, it wasn't concurrent safe.

Now we will write with concurrency in mind. We will write a concurrent counter, like the one we wrote in the *mutexes* section, but this time we will solve it with channels.

Unit test

To restrict concurrent access to the `singleton` instance, just one Goroutine will be able to access it. We'll access it using channels–the first one to add one, the second one to get the current count, and the third one to stop the Goroutine.

We will add one 10,000 times using 10,000 different Goroutines launched from two different `singleton` instances. Then, we'll introduce a loop to check the count of the `singleton` until it is 5,000, but we'll write how much the count is before starting the loop.

Once the count has reached 5,000, the loop will exit and quit the running Goroutine-the test code looks like this:

```
package channel_singleton
import (
  "testing"
```

```
    "time"
    "fmt"
)

func TestStartInstance(t *testing.T) {
   singleton := GetInstance()
   singleton2 := GetInstance()

   n := 5000

   for i := 0; i < n; i++ {
      go singleton.AddOne()
      go singleton2.AddOne()
   }

   fmt.Printf("Before loop, current count is %d\n", singleton.GetCount())

   var val int
   for val != n*2 {
      val = singleton.GetCount()
      time.Sleep(10 * time.Millisecond)
   }
   singleton.Stop()
}
```

Here, we can see the full test we'll use. After creating two instances of the `singleton`, we have created a `for` loop that launches the `AddOne` method 5,000 times from each instance. This is not happening yet; they are being scheduled and will be executed eventually. We are printing the count of the `singleton` instance to clearly see this eventuality; depending on the computer, it will print some number greater than 0 and lower than 10,000.

The last step before stopping the Goroutine that is holding the count is to enter a loop that checks the value of the count and waits 10 milliseconds if the value is not the expected value (10,000). Once it reaches this value, the loop will exit and we can stop the `singleton` instance.

We'll jump directly to the implementation as the requirement is quite simple.

Implementation

First of all, we'll create the Goroutine that will hold the count:

```
var addCh chan bool = make(chan bool)
var getCountCh chan chan int = make(chan chan int)
var quitCh chan bool = make(chan bool)
```

```
func init() {
  var count int

  go func(addCh <-chan bool, getCountCh <-chan chan int, quitCh <-chan
bool) {
    for {
      select {
      case <-addCh:
        count++
      case ch := <-getCountCh:
        ch <- count
      case <-quitCh:
        return
      }
    }
  }(addCh, getCountCh, quitCh)
}
```

We created three channels, as we mentioned earlier:

- The addCh channel is used to communicate with the action of adding one to the count, and receives a bool type just to signal "add one" (we don't need to send the number, although we could).
- The getCountCh channel will return a channel that will receive the current value of the count. Take a moment to reason about the getCountCh channel-it's a channel that receives a channel that receives integer types. It sounds a bit complicated, but it will make more sense when we finish the example, don't worry.
- The quitCh channel will communicate to the Goroutine that it should end its infinite loop and finish itself too.

Now we have the channels that we need to perform the actions we want. Next, we launch the Goroutine passing the channels as arguments. As you can see, we are restricting the direction of the channels to provide more type safety. Inside this Goroutine, we create an infinite for loop. This loop won't stop until a break is executed within it.

Finally, the select statement, if you remember, was a way to receive data from different channels at the same time. We have three cases, so we listen to the three incoming channels that entered as arguments:

- The addCh case will add one to the count. Remember that only one case can be executed on each iteration so that no Goroutine could be accessing the current count until we finish adding one.

- The getCountCh channel receives a channel that receives an integer, so we capture this new channel and send the current value through it to the other end.
- The quitCh channel breaks the for loop, so the Goroutine ends.

One last thing. The init() function in any package will get executed on program execution, so we don't need to worry about executing this function specifically from our code.

Now, we'll create the type that the tests are expecting. We will see that all the magic and logic is hidden from the end user in this type (as we have seen in the code of the test):

```
type singleton struct {}

var instance singleton
func GetInstance() *singleton {
  return &instance
}
```

The singleton type works similar to the way it worked in Chapter 2, *Creational Patterns – Singleton, Builder, Factory, Prototype, and Abstract Factory*, but this time it won't hold the count value. We created a local value for it called instance, and we return the pointer to this instance when we call the GetInstance() method. It is not strictly necessary to do it this way, but we don't need to allocate a new instance of the singleton type every time we want to access the count variable.

First, the AddOne() method will have to add one to the current count. How? By sending true to the addCh channel. That's simple:

```
func (s *singleton) AddOne() {
  addCh <- true
}
```

This small snippet will trigger the addCh case in our Goroutine in turn. The addCh case simply executes count++ and finishes, letting select channel control flow that is executed on init function above to execute the next instruction:

```
func (s *singleton) GetCount() int {
  resCh := make(chan int)
  defer close(resCh)
  getCountCh <- resCh
  return <-resCh
}
```

The GetCount method creates a channel every time it's called and defers the action of closing it at the end of the function. This channel is unbuffered as we have seen previously in this chapter. An unbuffered channel blocks the execution until it receives some data. So we send this channel to getCountCh which is a channel too and, effectively, expects a chan int type to send the current count value back through it. The GetCount() method will not return until the value of count variable arrives to the resCh channel.

You might be thinking, why aren't we using the same channel in both directions to receive the value of the count? This way we will avoid an allocation. Well, if we use the same channel inside the GetCount() method, we will have two listeners in this channel–one in select statement, at the beginning of the file on the init function, and one there, so it could resolve to any of them when sending the value back:

```
func (s *singleton) Stop() {
    quitCh <- true
    close(addCh)
    close(getCountCh)
    close(quitCh)
}
```

Finally, we have to stop the Goroutine at some moment. The Stop method sends the value to the singleton type Goroutine so that the quitCh case is triggered and the for loop is broken. The next step is to close all channels so that no more data can be sent through them. This is very convenient when you know that you won't be using some of your channels anymore.

Time to execute the tests and take a look:

```
$ go test -v .

=== RUN    TestStartInstance
Before loop, current count is 4911
--- PASS: TestStartInstance (0.03s)
PASS
ok
```

Very little code output, but everything has worked as expected. In the test, we printed the value of the count before entering the loop that iterates until it reaches the value 10,000. As we saw previously, the Go scheduler will try to run the content of the Goroutines using as many OS threads as you configured by using the GOMAXPROCS configuration. In my computer, it is set to 4 because my computer has four cores. But the point is that we can see that a lot of things can happen after launching a Goroutine (or 10,000) and the next execution line.

But what about its use of mutexes?

```go
type singleton struct {
  count int
  sync.RWMutex
}

var instance singleton

func GetInstance() *singleton {
  return &instance
}

func (s *singleton) AddOne() {
  s.Lock()
  defer s.Unlock()
  s.count++
}

func (s *singleton) GetCount()int {
  s.RLock()
  defer s.RUnlock()
  return s.count
}
```

In this case, the code is much leaner. As we saw previously, we can embed the mutex within the `singleton` structure. The count is also held in the `count` field and the `AddOne()` and `GetCount()` methods lock and unlock the value to be concurrently safe.

One more thing. In this `singleton` instance, we are using the `RWMutex` type instead of the already known `sync.Mutex` type. The main difference here is that the `RWMutex` type has two types of locks–a read lock and a write lock. The read lock, executed by calling the `RLock` method, only waits if a write lock is currently active. At the same time, it only blocks a write lock, so that many read actions can be done in parallel. It makes a lot of sense; we don't want to block a Goroutine that wants to read a value just because another Goroutine is also reading the value-it won't change. The `sync.RWMutex` type helps us to achieve this logic in our code.

Summary

We have seen how to write a concurrent Singleton using mutexes and channels. While the channels example was more complex, it also shows the core power of Go's concurrency, as you can achieve complex levels of event-driven architectures by simply using channels.

Just keep in mind that, if you haven't written concurrent code in the past, it can take some time to start thinking concurrently in a comfortable way. But it's nothing that practice cannot solve.

We have seen the importance of designing concurrent apps to achieve parallelism in our programs. We have dealt with most of Go's primitives to write concurrent applications, and now we can write common concurrent design patterns.

9
Concurrency Patterns - Barrier, Future, and Pipeline Design Patterns

Now that we are familiar with the concepts of concurrency and parallelism, and we have understood how to achieve them by using Go's concurrency primitives, we can see some patterns regarding concurrent work and parallel execution. In this chapter we'll see the following patterns:

- Barrier is a very common pattern, especially when we have to wait for more than one response from different Goroutines before letting the program continue
- Future pattern allows us to write an algorithm that will be executed eventually in time (or not) by the same Goroutine or a different one
- Pipeline is a powerful pattern to build complex synchronous flows of Goroutines that are connected with each other according to some logic

Take a quick look at the description of the three patterns. They all describe some sort of logic to synchronize execution in time. It's very important to keep in mind that we are now developing concurrent structures with all the tools and patterns we have seen in the previous chapters. With Creational patterns we were dealing with creating objects. With the Structural patterns we were learning how to build idiomatic structures and in Behavioral patterns we were managing mostly with algorithms. Now, with Concurrency patterns, we will mostly manage the timing execution and order execution of applications that has more than one *flow*.

Barrier concurrency pattern

We are going to start with the Barrier pattern. Its purpose is simple–put up a barrier so that nobody passes until we have all the results we need, something quite common in concurrent applications.

Description

Imagine the situation where we have a microservices application where one service needs to compose its response by merging the responses of another three microservices. This is where the Barrier pattern can help us.

Our Barrier pattern could be a service that will block its response until it has been composed with the results returned by one or more different Goroutines (or services). And what kind of primitive do we have that has a blocking nature? Well, we can use a lock, but it's more idiomatic in Go to use an unbuffered channel.

Objectives

As its name implies, the Barrier pattern tries to stop an execution so it doesn't finish before it's ready to finish. The Barrier pattern's objectives are as follows:

- Compose the value of a type with the data coming from one or more Goroutines.
- Control the correctness of any of those incoming data pipes so that no inconsistent data is returned. We don't want a partially filled result because one of the pipes has returned an error.

An HTTP GET aggregator

For our example, we are going to write a very typical situation in a microservices application-an app that performs two HTTP GET calls and joins them in a single response that will be printed on the console.

Our small app must perform each request in a different Goroutine and print the result on the console if both responses are correct. If any of them returns an error, then we print just the error.

The design must be concurrent, allowing us to take advantage of our multicore CPUs to make the calls in parallel:

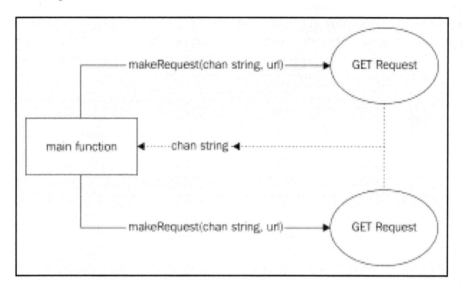

In the preceding diagram, the solid lines represent calls and the dashed lines represent channels. The balloons are Goroutines, so we have two Goroutines launched by the main function (which could also be considered a Goroutine). These two functions will communicate back to the main function by using a **common channel** that they received when they were created on the makeRequest calls.

Acceptance criteria

Our main objective in this app is to get a merged response of two different calls, so we can describe our acceptance criteria like this:

- Print on the console the merged result of the two calls to http://httpbin.org/headers and http://httpbin.org/User-Agent URLs. These are a couple of public endpoints that respond with data from the incoming connections. They are very popular for testing purposes. You will need an internet connection to do this exercise.
- If any of the calls fails, it must not print any result-just the error message (or error messages if both calls failed).
- The output must be printed as a composed result when both calls have finished. It means that we cannot print the result of one call and then the other.

Unit test – integration

To write unit or integration tests for concurrent designs can sometimes be tricky, but this won't stop us from writing our awesome unit tests. We will have a single `barrier` method that accepts a set of endpoints defined as a `string` type. The barrier will make a `GET` request to each endpoint and compose the result before printing it out. In this case, we will write three integration tests to simplify our code so we don't need to generate mock responses:

```
package barrier

import (
    "bytes"
    "io"
    "os"
    "strings"
    "testing"
)

func TestBarrier(t *testing.T) {
  t.Run("Correct endpoints", func(t *testing.T) {
    endpoints := []string{"http://httpbin.org/headers",
"http://httpbin.org/User-Agent"
    }
  })

  t.Run("One endpoint incorrect", func(t *testing.T) {
    endpoints := []string{"http://malformed-url",
"http://httpbin.org/User-Agent"}
  })

  t.Run("Very short timeout", func(t *testing.T) {
    endpoints := []string{"http://httpbin.org/headers",
"http://httpbin.org/User-Agent"}
  })
}
```

We have a single test that will execute three subtests:

- The first test makes two calls to the correct endpoints
- The second test will have an incorrect endpoint, so it must return an error
- The last test will return the maximum timeout time so that we can force a timeout error

We will have a function called `barrier` that will accept an undetermined number of endpoints in the form of strings. Its signature could be like this:

```
func barrier(endpoints ...string) {}
```

As you can see, the `barrier` function doesn't return any value because its result will be printed on the console. Previously, we have written an implementation of an `io.Writer` interface to emulate the writing on the operating system's `stdout` library. Just to change things a bit, we will capture the `stdout` library instead of emulating one. The process to capture the `stdout` library isn't difficult once you understand concurrency primitives in Go:

```
func captureBarrierOutput(endpoints ...string) string {
    reader, writer, _ := os.Pipe()

    os.Stdout = writer
    out := make(chan string)
    go func() {
      var buf bytes.Buffer
      io.Copy(&buf, reader)
      out <- buf.String()
    }()

    barrier(endpoints...)

    writer.Close()
    temp := <-out

    return temp
}
```

Don't feel daunted by this code; it's really simple. First we created a pipe; we have done this before in `Chapter 3`, *Structural Patterns – Adapter, Bridge, and Composite Design Patterns,* when we talked about the Adapter design pattern. To recall, a pipe allows us to connect an `io.Writer` interface to an `io.Reader` interface so that the reader input is the `Writer` output. We define the `os.Stdout` as the writer. Then, to capture `stdout` output, we will need a different Goroutine that listens while we write to the console. As you know, if we write, we don't capture, and if we capture, we are not writing. The keyword here is `while`; it is a good rule of thumb that if you find this word in some definition, you'll probably need a concurrent structure. So we use the `go` keyword to launch a different Goroutine that copies reader input to a bytes buffer before sending the contents of the buffer through a channel (that we should have previously created).

At this point, we have a listening Goroutine, but we haven't printed anything yet, so we call our (not yet written) function `barrier` with the provided endpoints. Next, we have to close the writer to signal the Goroutine that no more input is going to come to it. Our channel called out blocks execution until some value is received (the one sent by our launched Goroutine). The last step is to return the contents captured from the console.

OK, so we have a function called `captureBarrierOutput` that will capture the outputs in `stdout` and return them as a string. We can write our tests now:

```
t.Run("Correct endpoints", func(t *testing.T) {
    endpoints := []string{"http://httpbin.org/headers",
"http://httpbin.org/User-Agent"
    }

    result := captureBarrierOutput(endpoints...)
    if !strings.Contains(result, "Accept-Encoding") || strings.Contains
(result, "User-Agent")
  {
    t.Fail()
  }
  t.Log(result)
})
```

All the tests are very easy to implement. All in all, it is the `captureBarrierOutput` function that calls the `barrier` function. So we pass the endpoints and check the returned result. Our composed response directed to `http://httpbin.org` must contain the text *Accept-Encoding* and *User-Agent* in the responses of each endpoint. If we don't find those texts, the test will fail. For debugging purposes, we log the response in case we want to check it with the -v flag on the go test:

```
t.Run("One endpoint incorrect", func(t *testing.T) {
  endpoints := []string
  {
    "http://malformed-url", "http://httpbin.org/User-Agent"}

    result := captureBarrierOutput(endpoints...)
    if !strings.Contains(result, "ERROR") {
        t.Fail()
    }
    t.Log(result)
})
```

This time we used an incorrect endpoint URL, so the response must return the error prefixed with the word *ERROR* that we will write ourselves in the `barrier` function.

The last function will reduce the timeout of the HTTP GET client to a minimum of 1 ms, so we force a timeout:

```
t.Run("Very short timeout", func(t *testing.T) {
  endpoints := []string
  {
    "http://httpbin.org/headers", "http://httpbin.org/User-Agent"}
    timeoutMilliseconds = 1
    result := captureBarrierOutput(endpoints...)
    if !strings.Contains(result, "Timeout") {
      t.Fail()
    }
    t.Log(result)
})
```

The timeoutMilliseconds variable will be a package variable that we will have to define later during implementation.

Implementation

We needed to define a package variable called timeoutMilliseconds. Let's start from there:

```
package barrier

import (
    "fmt"
    "io/ioutil"
    "net/http"
    "time"
)

var timeoutMilliseconds int = 5000
```

The initial timeout delay is 5 seconds (5,000 milliseconds) and we will need those packages in our code.

OK, so we need a function that launches a Goroutine for each endpoint URL. Do you remember how we achieve the communication between Goroutines? Exactly–channels! So we will need a channel to handle responses and a channel to handle errors.

But we can simplify it a bit more. We will receive two correct responses, two errors, or a response and an error; in any case, there are always two responses, so we can join errors and responses in a merged type:

```
type barrierResp struct {
    Err  error
    Resp string
}
```

So, each Goroutine will send back a value of the `barrierResp` type. This value will have a value for `Err` or a value for the `Resp` field.

The procedure is simple: we create a channel of size 2, the one that will receive responses of the `barrierResp` type, we launch both requests and wait for two responses, and then check to see if there is any error:

```
func barrier(endpoints ...string) {
    requestNumber := len(endpoints)

    in := make(chan barrierResp, requestNumber)
    defer close(in)

    responses := make([]barrierResp, requestNumber)

    for _, endpoint := range endpoints {
        go makeRequest(in, endpoint)
    }

    var hasError bool
    for i := 0; i < requestNumber; i++ {
        resp := <-in
        if resp.Err != nil {
            fmt.Println("ERROR: ", resp.Err)
            hasError = true
        }
        responses[i] = resp
    }

    if !hasError {
        for _, resp := range responses {
            fmt.Println(resp.Resp)
        }
    }
}
```

Following the previous description, we created a buffered channel called `in`, making it the size of the incoming endpoints, and we deferred channel closing. Then, we launched a function called `makeRequest` with each endpoint and the response channel.

Now we will loop twice, once for each endpoint. In the loop, we block the execution waiting for data from the `in` channel. If we find an error, we print it prefixed with the word *ERROR* as we expect in our tests, and set `hasError`var to true. After two responses, if we don't find any error (`hasError== false`) we print every response and the channel will be closed.

We still lack the `makeRequest` function:

```
func makeRequest(out chan<- barrierResp, url string) {
    res := barrierResp{}
    client := http.Client{
        Timeout: time.Duration(time.Duration(timeoutMilliseconds) *
time.Millisecond),
    }

    resp, err := client.Get(url)
    if err != nil {
        res.Err = err
        out <- res
        return
    }

    byt, err := ioutil.ReadAll(resp.Body)
    if err != nil {
        res.Err = err
        out <- res
        return
    }

    res.Resp = string(byt)
    out <- res
}
```

The `makeRequest` function is a very straightforward functions that accepts a channel to output `barrierResp` values to and a URL to request. We create an `http.Client` and set its timeout field to the value of the `timeoutMilliseconds` package variable. This is how we can change the timeout delay before the `in` function tests. Then, we simply make the GET call, take the response, parse it to a byte slice, and send it through the `out` channel.

We do all this by filling a variable called `res` of the `barrierResp` type. If we find an error while performing a `GET` request or parsing the body of the result, we fill the `res.Err` field, send it to the `out` channel (which has the opposite side connected to the original Goroutine), and exit the function (so we don't send two values through the `out` channel by mistake).

Time to run the tests. Remember that you need an Internet connection, or the first two tests will fail. We will first try the test that has two endpoints that are correct:

```
go test -run=TestBarrier/Correct_endpoints -v .
=== RUN    TestBarrier
=== RUN    TestBarrier/Correct_endpoints
--- PASS: TestBarrier (0.54s)
    --- PASS: TestBarrier/Correct_endpoints (0.54s)
        barrier_test.go:20: {
          "headers": {
            "Accept-Encoding": "gzip", "Host": "httpbin.org","User-
Agent": "Go-http-client/1.1"
                }
        }
        {
            "User-Agent": "Go-http-client/1.1"
        }
    ok
```

Perfect. We have a JSON response with a key, `headers`, and another JSON response with a key `User-Agent`. In our integration tests, we were looking for the strings, `User-Agent` and `Accept-Encoding`, which are present, so the test has passed successfully.

Now we will run the test that has an incorrect endpoint:

```
go test -run=TestBarrier/One_endpoint_incorrect -v .
=== RUN    TestBarrier
=== RUN    TestBarrier/One_endpoint_incorrect
--- PASS: TestBarrier (0.27s)
    --- PASS: TestBarrier/One_endpoint_incorrect (0.27s)
        barrier_test.go:31: ERROR:  Get http://malformed-url: dial tcp:
lookup malformed-url: no such host
    ok
```

We can see that we have had an error where `http://malformed-url` has returned a *no such host* error. A request to this URL must return a text with the word `ERROR:` prefixed, as we stated during the acceptance criteria, that's why this test is correct (we don't have a false positive).

In testing, it's very important to understand the concepts of "false positive" and "false negative" tests. A false positive test is roughly described as a test that passes a condition when it shouldn't (result: all passed) while the false negative is just the reverse (result: test failed). For example, we could be testing that a string is returned when doing the requests but, the returned string could be completely empty! This will lead to a false negative, a test that doesn't fail even when we are checking a behavior that is incorrect on purpose (a request to `http://malformed-url`).

The last test reduced the timeout time to 1 ms:

```
go test -run=TestBarrier/Very_short_timeout -v .
=== RUN    TestBarrier
=== RUN    TestBarrier/Very_short_timeout
--- PASS: TestBarrier (0.00s)
    --- PASS: TestBarrier/Very_short_timeout (0.00s)
        barrier_test.go:43: ERROR:  Get http://httpbin.org/User-Agent:
net/http: request canceled while waiting for connection (Client.Timeout
exceeded while awaiting headers)
        ERROR:  Get http://httpbin.org/headers: net/http: request canceled
while waiting for connection (Client.Timeout exceeded while awaiting
headers)
ok
```

Again, the test passed successfully and we have got two timeout errors. The URLs were correct, but we didn't have a response in less than one millisecond, so the client has returned a timeout error.

Waiting for responses with the Barrier design pattern

The Barrier pattern opens the door of microservices programming with its composable nature. It could be considered a Structural pattern, as you can imagine.

The Barrier pattern is not only useful to make network requests; we could also use it to split some task into multiple Goroutines. For example, an expensive operation could be split into a few smaller operations distributed in different Goroutines to maximize parallelism and achieve better performance.

Future design pattern

The Future design pattern (also called **Promise**) is a quick and easy way to achieve concurrent structures for asynchronous programming. We will take advantage of first class functions in Go to develop *Futures*.

Description

In short, we will define each possible behavior of an action before executing them in different Goroutines. Node.js uses this approach, providing event-driven programming by default. The idea here is to achieve a *fire-and-forget* that handles all possible results in an action.

To understand it better, we can talk about a type that has embedded the behavior in case an execution goes well or in case it fails.

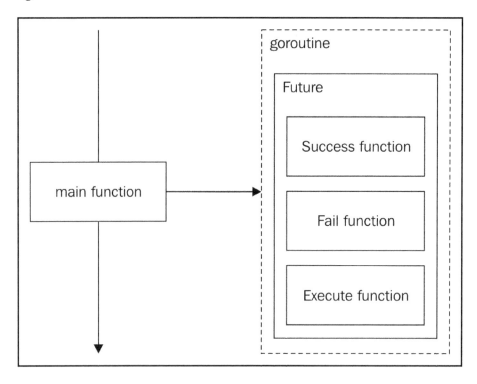

In the preceding diagram, the `main` function launches a **Future** within a new Goroutine. It won't wait for anything, nor will it receive any progress of the Future. It really fires and forgets it.

The interesting thing here is that we can launch a new Future within a Future and embed as many Futures as we want in the same Goroutine (or new ones). The idea is to take advantage of the result of one Future to launch the next. For example:

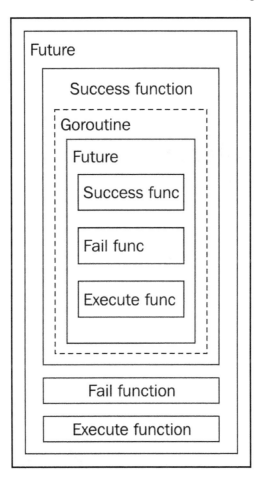

Here, we have the same Future. In this case, if the `Execute` function returned a correct result, the `Success` function is executed, and only in this case we execute a new Goroutine with another Future inside (or even without a Goroutine).

This is a kind of lazy programming, where a Future could be calling to itself indefinitely or just until some rule is satisfied. The idea is to define the behavior in advance and let the future resolve the possible solutions.

Objectives

With the Future pattern, we can launch many new Goroutines, each with an action and its own handlers. This enables us to do the following:

- Delegate the action handler to a different Goroutine
- Stack many asynchronous calls between them (an asynchronous call that calls another asynchronous call in its results)

A simple asynchronous requester

We are going to develop a very simple example to try to understand how a Future works. In this example, we will have a method that returns a string or an error, but we want to execute it concurrently. We have learned ways to do this already. Using a channel, we can launch a new Goroutine and handle the incoming result from the channel.

But in this case, we will have to handle the result (string or error), and we don't want this. Instead, we will define what to do in case of success and what to do in case of error and fire-and-forget the Goroutine.

Acceptance criteria

We don't have functional requirements for this task. Instead, we will have technical requirements for it:

- Delegate the function execution to a different Goroutine
- The function will return a string (maybe) or an error
- The handlers must be already defined before executing the function
- The design must be reusable

Unit tests

So, as we mentioned, we will use first class functions to achieve this behavior, and we will need three specific types of function:

- `type SuccessFunc func(string)`: The `SuccessFunc` function will be executed if everything went well. Its string argument will be the result of the operation, so this function will be called by our Goroutine.
- `type FailFunc func(error)`: The `FailFunc` function handles the opposite result, that is, when something goes wrong, and, as you can see, it will return an error.
- `type ExecuteStringFunc func() (string, error)`: Finally, the `ExecuteStringFunc` function is a type that defines the operation we want to perform. Maybe it will return a string or an error. Don't worry if this all seems confusing; it will be clearer later.

So, we create the `future` object, we define a success behavior, we define a fail behavior, and we pass an `ExecuteStringFunc` type to be executed. In the implementation file, we'll need a new type:

```
type MaybeString struct {}
```

We will also create two tests in the `_test.go` file:

```
package future

import (
  "errors"
  "testing"
  "sync"
)

func TestStringOrError_Execute(t *testing.T) {
  future := &MaybeString{}
  t.Run("Success result", func(t *testing.T) {
    ...
  })
  t.Run("Error result", func(t *testing.T) {
    ...
  })
}
```

We will define functions by chaining them, as you would usually see in Node.js. Code like this is compact and not particularly difficult to follow:

```
t.Run("Success result", func(t *testing.T) {
    future.Success(func(s string) {
        t.Log(s)
    }).Fail(func(e error) {
        t.Fail()
    })
    future.Execute(func() (string, error) {
        return "Hello World!", nil
    })
})
```

The `future.Success` function must be defined in the `MaybeString` structure to accept a `SuccessFunc` function that will be executed if everything goes correctly and return the same pointer to the `future` object (so we can keep chaining). The `Fail` function must also be defined in the `MaybeString` structure and must accept a `FailFunc` function to later return the pointer. We return the pointer in both cases so we can define the `Fail` and the `Success` or vice versa.

Finally, we use the `Execute` method to pass an `ExecuteStringFunc` type (a function that accepts nothing and returns a string or an error). In this case, we return a string and nil, so we expect that the `SuccessFunc` function will be executed and we log the result to the console. In case that fail function is executed, the test has failed because the `FailFunc` function shouldn't be executed for a returned nil error.

But we still lack something here. We said that the function must be executed asynchronously in a different Goroutine, so we have to synchronize this test somehow so that it doesn't finish too soon. Again, we can use a channel or a `sync.WaitGroup`:

```
t.Run("Success result", func(t *testing.T) {
    var wg sync.WaitGroup     wg.Add(1)
    future.Success(func(s string) {
        t.Log(s)

        wg.Done()
    }).Fail(func(e error) {
        t.Fail()
        wg.Done()
    })

    future.Execute(func() (string, error) {
        return "Hello World!", nil
    })
    wg.Wait()
```

```
    })
```

We have seen WaitGroups before in the previous channel. This WaitGroup is configured to wait for one signal (wg.Add(1)). The Success and Fail methods will trigger the Done() method of the WaitGroup to allow execution to continue and finish testing (that is why the Wait() method is at the end). Remember that each Done() method will subtract one from the WaitGroup, and we have added only one, so our Wait() method will only block until one Done() method is executed.

Using what we know of making a Success result unit test, it's easy to make a Failed result unit test by swapping the t.Fail() method call from the error to success so that the test fails if a call to success is done:

```
t.Run("Failed result", func(t *testing.T) {
    var wg sync.WaitGroup
    wg.Add(1)
    future.Success(func(s string) {
        t.Fail()
        wg.Done()
    }).Fail(func(e error) {
        t.Log(e.Error())
        wg.Done()
    })
    future.Execute(func() (string, error) {
        return "", errors.New("Error ocurred")
    })
    wg.Wait()
})
```

If you are using an IDE like me, your Success, Fail, and Execute method calls must be in red. This is because we lack our method's declaration in the implementation file:

```
package future

type SuccessFunc func(string)
type FailFunc func(error)
type ExecuteStringFunc func() (string, error)

type MaybeString struct {
    ...
}

func (s *MaybeString) Success(f SuccessFunc) *MaybeString {
  return nil
}

func (s *MaybeString) Fail(f FailFunc) *MaybeString {
```

```
    return nil
}

func (s *MaybeString) Execute(f ExecuteStringFunc) {
    ...
}
```

Our test seems ready to execute. Let's try it out:

```
go test -v .
=== RUN   TestStringOrError_Execute
=== RUN   TestStringOrError_Execute/Success_result
fatal error: all goroutines are asleep - deadlock!
goroutine 1 [chan receive]:
testing.(*T).Run(0xc4200780c0, 0x5122e9, 0x19, 0x51d750, 0xc420041d30)
        /usr/lib/go/src/testing/testing.go:647 +0x316
testing.RunTests.func1(0xc4200780c0)
        /usr/lib/go/src/testing/testing.go:793 +0x6d
testing.tRunner(0xc4200780c0, 0xc420041e20)
        /usr/lib/go/src/testing/testing.go:610 +0x81
testing.RunTests(0x51d758, 0x5931e0, 0x1, 0x1, 0x50feb4)
        /usr/lib/go/src/testing/testing.go:799 +0x2f5
testing.(*M).Run(0xc420041ee8, 0xc420014550)
        /usr/lib/go/src/testing/testing.go:743 +0x85
main.main()
        go-design-patterns/future/_test/_testmain.go:54 +0xc6
...continue
```

Well... the tests have failed, yes... but not in a controllable way. Why is this? We don't have any implementation yet, so no `Success` or `Fail` functions are being executed either. Our WaitGroup is waiting forever for a call to the `Done()` method that will never arrive, so it can't continue and finish the test. That's the meaning of *All Goroutines are asleep – deadlock!*. In our specific example, it would mean *Nobody is going to call Done(), so we are dead!*.

Thanks to the Go compiler and the runtime executor, we can detect deadlocks easily. Imagine if Go runtime couldn't detect deadlocks–we would be effectively stuck in a blank screen without knowing what was wrong.

So how can we solve this? Well, an easy way would be with a timeout that calls the `Done()` method after waiting a while for completion. For this code, it's safe to wait for 1 second because it's not doing long-running operations.

We will declare a `timeout` function within our `test` file that waits for a second, then prints a message, sets the test as failed, and lets the WaitGroup continue by calling its `Done()` method:

```
func timeout(t *testing.T, wg *sync.WaitGroup) {
  time.Sleep(time.Second)
  t.Log("Timeout!")

  t.Fail()
  wg.Done()
}
```

The final look of each subtest is similar to our previous example of the `"Success result"`:

```
t.Run("Success result", func(t *testing.T) {
  var wg sync.WaitGroup
  wg.Add(1)

  //Timeout!
  go timeout(t, wg)
  // ...
})
```

Let's see what happens when we execute our tests again:

```
go test -v .
=== RUN    TestStringOrError_Execute
=== RUN    TestStringOrError_Execute/Success_result
=== RUN    TestStringOrError_Execute/Failed_result
--- FAIL: TestStringOrError_Execute (2.00s)
    --- FAIL: TestStringOrError_Execute/Success_result (1.00s)
        future_test.go:64: Timeout!
    --- FAIL: TestStringOrError_Execute/Failed_result (1.00s)
        future_test.go:64: Timeout!
FAIL
exit status 1
FAIL
```

Our tests failed, but in a controlled way. Look at the end of the FAIL lines–notice how the elapsed time is 1 second because it has been triggered by the timeout, as we can see in the logging messages.

It's time to pass to the implementation.

Implementation

According to our tests, the implementation must take a `SuccessFunc`, a `FailFunc`, and an `ExecuteStringFunc` function in a chained fashion within the `MaybeString` type and launches the `ExecuteStringFunc` function asynchronously to call `SuccessFunc` or `FailFunc` functions according to the returned result of the `ExecuteStringFunc` function.

The chain is implemented by storing the functions within the type and returning the pointer to the type. We are talking about our previously declared type methods, of course:

```
type MaybeString struct {
  successFunc SuccessFunc
  failFunc    FailFunc
}

func (s *MaybeString) Success(f SuccessFunc) *MaybeString {
  s.successFunc = f
  return s
}

func (s *MaybeString) Fail(f FailFunc) *MaybeString {
  s.failFunc = f
  return s
}
```

We needed two fields to store the `SuccessFunc` and `FailFunc` functions, which are named the `successFunc` and `failFunc` fields respectively. This way, calls to the `Success` and `Fail` methods simply store their incoming functions to our new fields. They are simply setters that also return the pointer to the specific `MaybeString` value. These type methods take a pointer to the `MaybeString` structure, so don't forget to put "*" on `MaybeString` after the `func` declaration.

Execute takes the `ExecuteStringFunc` method and executes it asynchronously. This seems quite simple with a Goroutine, right?

```
func (s *MaybeString) Execute(f ExecuteStringFunc) {
  go func(s *MaybeString) {
    str, err := f()
    if err != nil {
      s.failFunc(err)
    } else {
      s.successFunc(str)
    }
  }(s)
```

```
}
```

Looks quite simple because it is simple! We launch the Goroutine that executes the `f`
method (an `ExecuteStringFunc`) and takes its result–maybe a string and maybe an error.
If an error is present, we call the field `failFunc` in our `MaybeString` structure. If no error
is present, we call the `successFunc` field. We use a Goroutine to delegate a function
execution and error handling so our Goroutine doesn't have to do it.

Let's run unit tests now:

```
go test -v .
=== RUN   TestStringOrError_Execute
=== RUN   TestStringOrError_Execute/Success_result
=== RUN   TestStringOrError_Execute/Failed_result
--- PASS: TestStringOrError_Execute (0.00s)
    --- PASS: TestStringOrError_Execute/Success_result (0.00s)
        future_test.go:21: Hello World!
    --- PASS: TestStringOrError_Execute/Failed_result (0.00s)
        future_test.go:49: Error ocurred
PASS
ok
```

Great! Look how the execution time is now nearly zero, so our timeouts have not been
executed (actually, they were executed, but the tests already finished and their result was
already stated).

What's more, now we can use our `MaybeString` type to asynchronously execute any type
of function that accepts nothing and returns a string or an error. A function that accepts
nothing seems a bit useless, right? But we can use closures to introduce a context into this
type of function.

Let's write a `setContext` function that takes a string as an argument and returns
an `ExecuteStringFunc` method that returns the previous argument with the suffix
`Closure!`:

```
func setContext(msg string) ExecuteStringFunc {
  msg = fmt.Sprintf("%d Closure!\n", msg)
  return func() (string, error){
    return msg, nil
  }
}
```

So, we can write a new test that uses this closure:

```
t.Run("Closure Success result", func(t *testing.T) {
    var wg sync.WaitGroup
```

```
wg.Add(1)
//Timeout!
go timeout(t, &wg)

future.Success(func(s string) {
  t.Log(s)
  wg.Done()
}).Fail(func(e error) {
  t.Fail()
  wg.Done()
})
future.Execute(setContext("Hello"))
wg.Wait()
})
```

The `setContext` function returns an `ExecuteStringFunc` method it can pass directly to the `Execute` function. We call the `setContext` function with an arbitrary text that we know will be returned.

Let's execute our tests again. Now everything has to go well!

```
go test -v .
=== RUN    TestStringOrError_Execute
=== RUN    TestStringOrError_Execute/Success_result
=== RUN    TestStringOrError_Execute/Failed_result
=== RUN    TestStringOrError_Execute/Closure_Success_result
--- PASS: TestStringOrError_Execute (0.00s)
    --- PASS: TestStringOrError_Execute/Success_result (0.00s)
        future_test.go:21: Hello World!
    --- PASS: TestStringOrError_Execute/Failed_result (0.00s)
        future_test.go:49: Error ocurred
    --- PASS: TestStringOrError_Execute/Closure_Success_result (0.00s)
        future_test.go:69: Hello Closure!
PASS
ok
```

It gave us an OK too. Closure test shows the behavior that we explained before. By taking a message `"Hello"` and appending it with something else (`"Closure!"`), we can change the context of the text we want to return. Now scale this to a HTTP GET call, a call to a database, or anything you can imagine. It will just need to end by returning a string or an error. Remember, however, that everything within the `setContext` function but outside of the anonymous function that we are returning is not concurrent, and will be executed asynchronously before calling execute, so we must try to put as much logic as possible within the anonymous function.

Putting the Future together

We have seen a good way to achieve asynchronous programming by using a function type system. However, we could have done it without functions by setting an interface with `Success`, `Fail`, and `Execute` methods and the types that satisfy them, and using the Template pattern to execute them asynchronously, as we have previously seen in this chapter. It is up to you!

Pipeline design pattern

The third and final pattern we will see in this chapter is the Pipeline pattern. You will use this pattern heavily in your concurrent structures, and we can consider it one of the most useful too.

Description

We already know what a pipeline is. Every time that we write any function that performs some logic, we are writing a pipeline: If *this* then *that*, or else *something else*. Pipelines pattern can be made more complex by using a few functions that call to each other. They can even get looped in their out execution.

The Pipeline pattern in Go works in a similar fashion, but each step in the Pipeline will be in a different Goroutine and communication, and synchronizing will be done using channels.

Objectives

When creating a Pipeline, we are mainly looking for the following benefits:

* We can create a concurrent structure of a multistep algorithm
* We can exploit the parallelism of multicore machines by decomposing an algorithm in different Goroutines

However, just because we decompose an algorithm in different Goroutines doesn't necessarily mean that it will execute the fastest. We are constantly talking about CPUs, so ideally the algorithm must be CPU-intensive to take advantage of a concurrent structure. The overhead of creating Goroutines and channels could make an algorithm smaller.

A concurrent multi-operation

We are going to do some math for our example. We are going to generate a list of numbers starting with 1 and ending at some arbitrary number N. Then we will take each number, power it to 2, and sum the resulting numbers to a unique result. So, if *N=3*, our list will be [1,2,3]. After powering them to 2, our list becomes [1,4,9]. If we sum the resulting list, the resulting value is 14.

Acceptance criteria

Functionally speaking, our Pipeline pattern needs to raise to the power of 2 every number and then sum them all. It will be divided into a number generator and two operations, so:

1. Generate a list from 1 to N where N can be any integer number.
2. Take each number of this generated list and raise it to the power of 2.
3. Sum each resulting number into a final result and return it.

Beginning with tests

We will create only one function that will manage everything. We will call this function `LaunchPipeline` to simplify things. It will take an integer as an argument, which will be our N number, the number of items in our list. The declaration in the implementation file looks like this:

```
package pipelines

func LaunchPipeline(amount int) int {
  return 0
}
```

In our test file, we will create a table of tests by using a slice of slices:

```
package pipelines

import "testing"

func TestLaunchPipeline(t *testing.T) {
  tableTest := [][]int{
    {3, 14},
    {5, 55},
  }
  // ...
}
```

Our table is a slice of slices of integer types. On each slice, the first integer represents the list size and the second position represents the item within the list. It is, effectively, a matrix. When passing 3, it must return 14. When passing 5, it must return 55. Then we have to iterate over the table and pass the first index of each array to the LaunchPipeline function:

```
  // ...

  var res int
  for _, test := range tableTest {
    res = LaunchPipeline(test[0])
    if res != test[1] {
      t.Fatal()
    }

    t.Logf("%d == %d\n", res, test[1])
  }
}
```

Using range, we get every row in the matrix . Each row is contained in a temporary variable called test. test[0] represents N and test[1] the expected result. We compare the expected result with the returning value of the LaunchPipeline function. If they aren't the same, the test fails:

```
go test -v .
=== RUN   TestLaunchPipeline
--- FAIL: TestLaunchPipeline (0.00s)
        pipeline_test.go:15:
FAIL
exit status 1
FAIL
```

Implementation

The key for our implementation is to separate every operation in a different Goroutine and connect them with channels. The `LaunchPipeline` function is the one that orchestrates them all, as shown in the following diagram:

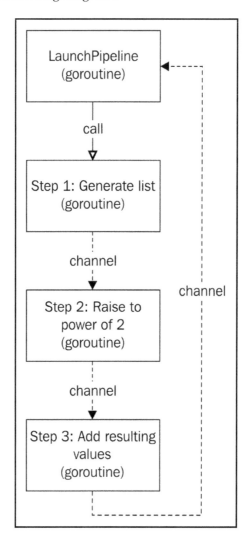

The operation consist of three steps: generate a list of numbers, raise them to the power of 2, and add the resulting numbers.

Each step in this Pipeline pattern will have the following structure:

```
func functionName(in <-chan int) (<-chan int){
   out := make(chan bool, 100)

   go func(){
      for v := range in {
         // Do something with v and send it to channel out
}

close(out)
   }()

   return out
}
```

This function represents a common step. Let's dissect it in the same order that the Go scheduler will probably take to execute it:

1. The `functionName` function will commonly receive a channel to take values from (`in <-chan int`). We call it the `in` function, as in the word incoming. We can't send values through it within the scope of this function; that's why the arrow points `out` of the keyword `chan`.
2. The `functionName` function returns a channel (`<-chan in`) that the function caller will only be allowed to take values from (again, represented by the arrow pointing `out` of the keyword `chan`). This also means that any value that goes through that channel must be generated within the scope of the function.
3. In the first line of the function, we create a channel called `out` that will be the return of the function (*point 2* in this list).
4. Then, we will launch a new Goroutine. Its scope will enter into play after returning this function, so let's continue.
5. We return the previously created `out` channel.
6. Eventually, after finishing the execution of the function and returning the channel `out`, the Goroutine executes. It will take values from the `in` channel until it's closed. So the caller of this function is responsible for closing this channel, otherwise the Goroutine will never end!
7. When the `in` channel is closed, the for loop finishes and we close the `out` channel. Any Goroutine making use of this channel will not receive any new values since the last that was sent.

The only step that doesn't completely fit this approach is the first step that receives a number, representing the upper threshold on the list instead of a channel of incoming values. So, if we code this operation for each step in our pipeline, the final diagram looks more like this:

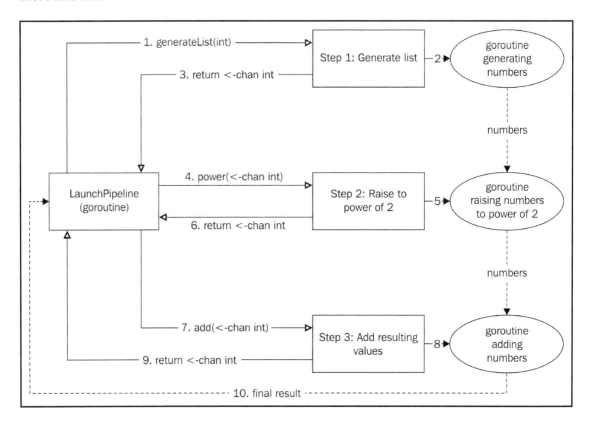

Although the idea is exactly the same, now we can see that it's the function LaunchPipeline that is the one that is going to be receiving channels and sending them back to the next step in the Pipeline. Using this diagram, we can clearly see the flow of the pipeline creation by following the numbers of the arrows. A solid arrow represents a function call and a dashed arrow a channel.

Let's look a little more closely at the code.

The list generator

The first step in the operation is list generation. The list starts at 1 and we will receive an integer representing the higher threshold. We have to pass each number in the list to the next step:

```
func generator(max int) <-chan int {
  outChInt := make(chan int, 100)

  go func() {
    for i := 1; i <= max; i++ {
      outChInt <- i
    }

    close(outChInt)
  }()
  return outChInt
}
```

As we mentioned earlier, this is the pattern that we will follow in each step: create a channel, launch the Goroutine that will send the data through the channel, and immediately return the channel. This Goroutine will iterate from 1 to the max argument, which is the higher threshold for our list, and send each number through the channel. After sending every number, the channel is closed so that no more data can be sent through it, but the data already buffered can be retrieved.

Raising numbers to the power of 2

The second step will take every incoming number from the first step's channel (that is taken from the arguments) and raise it to the power of 2. Every result must be sent to the third step using a new channel:

```
func power(in <-chan int) <-chan int {
  out := make(chan int, 100)

  go func() {
    for v := range in {
      out <- v * v
    }
    close(out)
  }()
  return out
}
```

We use the same pattern again: create a channel and launch the Goroutine while we return the created channel.

 The `for-range` loop keeps taking values from a channel indefinitely until the channel is closed.

Final reduce operation

The third and final step receives every number from the second step and keeps adding them to a local value until the connection channel is closed:

```go
func sum(in <-chan int) <-chan int {
  out := make(chan int, 100)
  go func() {
    var sum int

    for v := range in {
      sum += v
    }

    out <- sum
    close(out)
  }()

  return out
}
```

The function sum also takes a channel as an argument (the one returned from *step 2*). It also follows the same pattern of creating a channel, launching the Goroutine, and returning a channel. Goroutine keeps adding values to a variable called `sum` until the `in` channel is closed. When the `in` channel is closed, the value of sum is sent to the `out` channel, and it's immediately closed.

Launching the Pipeline pattern

Finally, we can implement the `LaunchPipeline` function:

```go
func LaunchPipeline(amount int) int {
  firstCh := generator(amount)
  secondCh := power(firstCh)
  thirdCh := sum(secondCh)
```

```
    result := <-thirdCh

    return result
}
```

The function `generator` first returns the channel that is passed to the power function. The `power` function returns the second channel that is passed to the `sum` function. The function `sum` finally returns the first channel that will receive a unique value, the result. Let's try to test this now:

```
go test -v .
=== RUN    TestLaunchPipeline
--- PASS: TestLaunchPipeline (0.00s)
        pipeline_test.go:18: 14 == 14
        pipeline_test.go:18: 55 == 55
PASS
ok
```

Awesome! It's worth mentioning that the `LaunchPipeline` function doesn't need to allocate every channel, and can be rewritten like this:

```
func LaunchPipeline(amount int) int {
    return <-sum(power(generator(amount)))
}
```

The result of the `generator` function is passed directly to the `power` function and the result of `power` to `sum` functions.

Final words on the Pipeline pattern

With the Pipeline pattern, we can create really complex concurrent workflows in a very easy way. In our case, we created a linear workflow, but it could also have conditionals, pools, and fan-in and fan-out behavior. We will see some of these in the following chapter.

Summary

Concurrency design patterns are a step forward in difficulty, and take some time to grasp. Our biggest mistake as concurrent programmers is thinking in terms of parallelism (How can I make this parallel? or How can I run this in a new thread?) instead of in terms of concurrent structures.

Pure functions (functions that will always produce the same output (given the same input) without affecting anything outside their scope) help in this design.

Concurrent programming requires practice and more practice. Go makes it easy once you understand the basic primitives. Diagrams can help you to understand the possible flow of data, but the best way of understanding it all is simply to practice.

In the following chapter, we will see how to use a pool of pipeline workers to do some work instead of having a unique pipeline. Also, we will learn how to create the publish/subscriber pattern in a concurrent structure and see how different the same pattern can be when we build by using concurrency.

10
Concurrency Patterns - Workers Pool and Publish/Subscriber Design Patterns

We have reached the final chapter of the book, where we will discuss a couple of patterns with concurrent structures. We will explain every step in detail so you can follow the examples carefully.

The idea is to learn about patterns to design concurrent applications in idiomatic Go. We are using channels and Goroutines heavily, instead of locks or sharing variables.

- We will look at one way to develop a pool of workers. This is useful to control the number of Goroutines in an execution.
- The second example is a rewrite of the Observer pattern, which we saw on Chapter 7, *Behavioral Patterns – Visitor, State, Mediator, and Observer Design Patterns*, written with a concurrent structure. With this example we'll dig a bit more into the concurrent structures and look at how they can differ from a common approach.

Workers pool

One problem we may face with some of the previous approaches to concurrency is their unbounded context. We cannot let an app create an unlimited amount of Goroutines.

Goroutines are light, but the work they perform could be very heavy. A workers pool helps us to solve this problem.

Description

With a pool of workers, we want to bound the amount of Goroutines available so that we have a deeper control of the pool of resources. This is easy to achieve by creating a channel for each worker and having workers with either an idle or busy status. The task can seem daunting, but it's not at all.

Objectives

Creating a Worker pool is all about resource control: CPU, RAM, time, connections, and so on. The workers pool design pattern helps us to do the following:

- Control access to shared resources using quotas
- Create a limited amount of Goroutines per app
- Provide more parallelism capabilities to other concurrent structures

A pool of pipelines

In the previous chapter, we saw how to work with a pipeline. Now we will launch a bounded number of them so that the Go scheduler can try to process requests in parallel. The idea here is to control the number of Goroutines, stop them gracefully when the app has finished, and maximize parallelism using a concurrent structure without race conditions.

The pipeline we will use is similar to the one we used in the previous chapter, where we were generating numbers, raising them to the power of 2, and summing the final results. In this case, we are going to pass strings to which we will append and prefix data.

Acceptance criteria

In business terms, we want something that tells us that, worker has processed a request, a predefined ending, and incoming data parsed to uppercase:

1. When making a request with a string value (any), it must be uppercase.

2. Once the string is uppercase, a predefined text must be appended to it. This text should not be uppercase.
3. With the previous result, the worker ID must be prefixed to the final string.
4. The resulting string must be passed to a predefined handler.

We haven't talked about how to do it technically, just what the business wants. With the entire description, we'll at least have workers, requests, and handlers.

Implementation

The very beginning is a request type. According to the description, it must hold the string that will enter the pipeline as well as the handler function:

```
// workers_pipeline.go file
type Request struct {
    Data    interface{}
    Handler RequestHandler
}
```

Where is the `string`? We have a `Data` field of type `interface{}` so we can use it to pass a string. By using an interface, we can reuse this type for a `string`, an `int`, or a `struct` data type. The receiver is the one who must know how to deal with the incoming interface.

The `Handler` field has the type `Request` handler, which we haven't defined yet:

```
type RequestHandler func(interface{})
```

A request handler is any function that accepts an interface as its first argument, and returns nothing. Again, we see the `interface{}`, where we would usually see a string. This is one of the receivers we mentioned previously, which we'll need to cast the incoming result.

So, when sending a request, we must fill it with some value in the `Data` field and implement a handler; for example:

```
func NewStringRequest(s string, id int, wg *sync.WaitGroup) Request {
    myRequest := Request{
        Data: "Hello", Handler: func(i interface{})
        {
            defer wg.Done()
            s, ok := i.(string)
                if !ok{
                    log.Fatal("Invalid casting to string")
                }
            fmt.Println(s)
```

```
            }
        }
    }
```

The handler is defined by using a closure. We again check the type if the interface (and we defer the call to the `Done()` method at the end). In case of an improper interface, we simply print its contents and return. If the casting is OK, we also print them, but here is where we will usually do something with the result of the operation; we have to use type casting to retrieve the contents of the `interface{}` (which is a string). This must be done in every step in the pipeline, although it will introduce a bit of overhead.

Now we need a type that can handle `Request` types. Possible implementations are virtually infinite, so it is better to define an interface first:

```
// worker.go file
 type WorkerLauncher interface {
     LaunchWorker(in chan Request)
 }
```

The `WorkerLauncher` interface must implement only the `LaunchWorker(chan Request)` method. Any type that implements this interface will have to receive a channel of `Request` type to satisfy it. This channel of the `Request` type is the single entrance point to the pipeline.

The dispatcher

Now, to launch workers in parallel and handle all the possible incoming channels, we'll need something like a dispatcher:

```
// dispatcher.go file
 type Dispatcher interface {
     LaunchWorker(w WorkerLauncher)
     MakeRequest(Request)
     Stop()
 }
```

A `Dispatcher` interface can launch an injected `WorkerLaunchers` type in its own `LaunchWorker` method. The `Dispatcher` interface must use the `LaunchWorker` method of any of the `WorkerLauncher` types to initialize a pipeline. This way we can reuse the `Dispatcher` interface to launch many types of `WorkerLaunchers`.

When using `MakeRequest(Request)`, the `Dispatcher` interface exposes a nice method to inject a new `Request` into the workers pool.

Finally, the user must call stop when all Goroutines must be finished. We must handle graceful shutdown in our apps, and we want to avoid Goroutine leaks.

We have enough interfaces, so let's start with the dispatcher which is a bit less complicated:

```
type dispatcher struct {
    inCh chan Request
}
```

Our `dispatcher` structure stores a channel of `Request` type in one of its fields. This is going to be the single point of entrance for requests in any pipeline. We said that it must implement three methods, as follows:

```
func (d *dispatcher) LaunchWorker(id int, w WorkerLauncher) {
    w.LaunchWorker(d.inCh)
}

func (d *dispatcher) Stop(){
    close(d.inCh)
}

func (d *dispatcher) MakeRequest(r Request) {
    d.inCh <- r
}
```

In this example, the `Dispatcher` interface doesn't need to do anything special to itself before launching a worker, so the `LaunchWorker` method on the `Dispatcher` simply executes the `LaunchWorker` method of the incoming `WorkerLauncher`, which also has a `LaunchWorker` method to initiate itself. We have previously defined that a `WorkerLauncher` type needs at least an ID and a channel for incoming requests, so that's what we are passing through.

It may seem unnecessary to implement the `LaunchWorker` method in the `Dispatcher` interface. In different scenarios, it could be interesting to save running worker IDs in the dispatcher to control which ones are up or down; the idea is to hide launching implementation details. In this case, the `Dispatcher` interface is merely acting as a Facade design pattern hiding some implementation details from the user.

The second method is `Stop`. It closes the incoming requests channel, provoking a chain reaction. We saw in the pipeline example that, when closing the incoming channel, each for-range loop within the Goroutines breaks and the Goroutine is also finished. In this case, when closing a shared channel, it will provoke the same reaction, but in every listening Goroutine, so all pipelines will be stopped. Cool, huh?

Request implementation is very simple; we just pass the request in the argument to the channel of incoming requests. The Goroutine will block there forever until the opposite end of the channel retrieves the request. Forever? That seems like a lot if something happens. We can introduce a timeout, as follows:

```
func (d *dispatcher) MakeRequest(r Request) {
    select {
    case d.inCh <- r:
    case <-time.After(time.Second * 5):
        return
    }
}
```

If you remember from previous chapters, we can use select to control which operation is performed over a channel. Like a `switch` case, just one operation can be executed. In this case, we have two different operations: sending and receiving.

The first case is a sending operation–try to send this, and it will block there until someone takes the value in the opposite side of the channel. Not a huge improvement, then. The second case is a receiving operation; it will be triggered after 5 seconds if the upper request can't be sent successfully, and the function will return. It would be very convenient to return an error here, but to make things simple, we will leave it empty

Finally, in the dispatcher, for convenience, we will define a `Dispatcher` creator:

```
func NewDispatcher(b int) Dispatcher {
    return &dispatcher{
        inCh:make(chan Request, b),
    }
}
```

By using this function instead of creating the dispatcher manually, we can simply avoid small mistakes, such as forgetting to initialize the channel field. As you can see, the b argument refers to the buffer size in the channel.

The pipeline

So, our dispatcher is done and we need to develop the pipeline described in the acceptance criteria. First, we need a type to implement the `WorkerLauncher` type:

```
// worker.go file
  type PreffixSuffixWorker struct {
      id int
      prefixS string
      suffixS string
```

```
      }

      func (w *PreffixSuffixWorker) LaunchWorker(i int, in chan Request) {}
```

The `PreffixSuffixWorker` variable stores an ID, a string to prefix, and another string to suffix the incoming data of the `Request` type. So, the values to prefix and append will be static in these fields, and we will take them from there.

We will implement the `LaunchWorker` method later and begin with each step in the pipeline. According to *first acceptance criteria*, the incoming string must be uppercase. So, the uppercase method will be the first step in our pipeline:

```
      func (w *PreffixSuffixWorker) uppercase(in <-chan Request) <-chan
   Request {
          out := make(chan Request)

          go func() {
              for msg := range in {
                  s, ok := msg.Data.(string)
                  if !ok {
                      msg.handler(nil)
                      continue
                  }
                  msg.Data = strings.ToUpper(s)
                  out <- msg
              }

              close(out)
          }()

          return out
      }
```

Good. As in the previous chapter, a step in the pipeline accepts a channel of incoming data and returns a channel of the same type. It has a very similar approach to the examples we developed in the previous chapter. This time, though, we aren't using package functions, and uppercase is part of the `PreffixSuffixWorker` type and the incoming data is a `struct` instead of an `int`.

The `msg` variable is a `Request` type and it will have a handler function and data in the form of an interface. The `Data` field should be a string, so we type cast it before using it. When type casting a value, we will receive the same value with the requested type and a `true` or `false` flag (represented by the `ok` variable). If the `ok` variable is `false`, the cast could not be done and we won't throw the value down the pipeline. We stop this `Request` here by sending a `nil` to the handler (which will also provoke a type-casting error).

Once we have a nice string in the `s` variable, we can uppercase it and store it again in the `Data` field to send down the pipeline to the next step. Be aware that the value will be sent as an interface again, so the next step will need to cast it again. This is the downside of using this approach.

With the first step done, let's continue with the second. According to the *second acceptance criteria* now, a predefined text must be appended. This text is the one stored in the `suffixS` field:

```
func (w *PreffixSuffixWorker) append(in <-chan Request) <-chan Request {
    out := make(chan Request)
    go func() {
        for msg := range in {
        uppercaseString, ok := msg.Data.(string)
        if !ok {
            msg.handler(nil)
            continue
            }
        msg.Data = fmt.Sprintf("%s%s", uppercaseString, w.suffixS)
        out <- msg
        }
        close(out)
    }()
    return out
}
```

The `append` function has the same structure as the `uppercase` function. It receives and returns a channel of incoming requests, and launches a new Goroutine that iterates over the incoming channel until it is closed. We need to type cast the incoming value, as mentioned previously.

In this step in the pipeline the incoming string is uppercase (after doing a type assertion). To append any text to it, we just need to use the `fmt.Sprintf()` function, as we have done many times before, which formats a new string with the provided data. In this case, we pass the value of the `suffixS` field as the second value, to append it to the end of the string.

Just the last step in the pipeline is missing, the prefix operation:

```
func (w *PreffixSuffixWorker) prefix(in <-chan Request) {
    go func() {
        for msg := range in {
            uppercasedStringWithSuffix, ok := msg.Data.(string)
            if !ok {
                msg.handler(nil)
                continue
            }
```

```
            msg.handler(fmt.Sprintf("%s%s", w.prefixS,
    uppercasedStringWithSuffix))
        }
    }()
}
```

What's calling your attention in this function? Yes, it doesn't return any channel now. We could have done this entire pipeline in two ways. I suppose you have realized that we have used a `Future` handler function to execute with the final result in the pipeline. A second approach would be to pass a channel to return the data back to its origin. In some cases, a Future would be enough, while in others it could be more convenient to pass a channel so that it can be connected to a different pipeline (for example).

In any case, the structure of a step in a pipeline must be very familiar to you already. We cast the value, check the result of the casting, and send nil to the handler if anything went wrong. But, in case everything was OK, the last thing to do is to format the text again to place the `prefixS` field at the beginning of the text, to send the resulting string back to the origin by calling the request's handler.

Now, with our worker almost finished, we can implement the `LaunchWorker` method:

```
func (w *PreffixSuffixWorker) LaunchWorker(in chan Request) {
    w.prefix(w.append(w.uppercase(in)))
}
```

That's all for workers! We simply pass the returning channels to the next steps in the Pipeline, as we did in the previous chapter. Remember that the pipeline is executed from inside to outside of the calls. So, what's the order of execution of any incoming data to the pipeline?

1. The data enters the pipeline through the Goroutine launched in the `uppercase` method.
2. Then, it goes to the Goroutine launched in `append`.
3. Finally, in enters the Goroutine launched in `prefix` method, which doesn't return anything but executes the handler after prefixing the incoming string with more data.

Now we have a full pipeline and a dispatcher of pipelines. The dispatcher will launch as many instances of the pipelines as we want to route the incoming requests to any available worker.

If none of the workers takes the request within 5 seconds, the request is lost.

Let's use this library in a small app.

An app using the workers pool

We will launch three workers of our defined pipeline. We use the `NewDispatcher` function to create the dispatcher and the channel that will receive all requests. This channel has a fixed buffer, which will be able to store up to 100 incoming messages before blocking:

```
// workers_pipeline.go
 func main() {
     bufferSize := 100
     var dispatcher Dispatcher = NewDispatcher(bufferSize)
```

Then, we will launch the workers by calling the `LaunchWorker` method in the `Dispatcher` interface three times with an already filled `WorkerLauncher` type:

```
workers := 3
for i := 0; i < workers; i++ {
    var w WorkerLauncher = &PreffixSuffixWorker{
        prefixS: fmt.Sprintf("WorkerID: %d -> ", i),
        suffixS: " World",
        id:i,
    }
    dispatcher.LaunchWorker(w)
}
```

Each `WorkerLauncher` type is an instance of `PreffixSuffixWorker`. The prefix will be a small text showing the worker ID and the suffix text `world`.

At this point, we have three workers with three Goroutines, each running concurrently and waiting for messages to arrive:

```
requests := 10

var wg sync.WaitGroup
wg.Add(requests)
```

We will make 10 requests. We also need a WaitGroup to properly synchronize the app so that it doesn't exit too early. You can find yourself using WaitGroups quite a lot when dealing with concurrent applications. For 10 requests, we'll need to wait for 10 calls to the `Done()` method, so we call the `Add()` method with a *delta* of 10. It's called delta because you can also pass a -5 later to leave it in five requests. In some situations, it can be useful:

```
for i := 0; i < requests; i++ {
    req := NewStringRequest("(Msg_id: %d) -> Hello", i, &wg)
    dispatcher.MakeRequest(req)
}
```

```
    dispatcher.Stop()

    wg.Wait()
}
```

To make requests, we will iterate a `for` loop. First, we create a `Request` using the function `NewStringRequest` that we wrote at the beginning of the Implementation section. In this value, the `Data` field will be the text we'll pass down the pipeline, and it will be the text that is "in the middle" of the appending and suffixing operation. In this case, we will send the message number and the word `hello`.

Once we have a request, we call the `MakeRequest` method with it. After all requests have been done, we stop the dispatcher that, as explained previously, will provoke a chain reaction that will stop all Goroutines in the pipeline.

Finally, we wait for the group so that all calls to the `Done()` method are received, which signals that all operations have been finished. It's time to try it out:

```
go run *
WorkerID: 1 -> (MSG_ID: 0) -> HELLO World
WorkerID: 0 -> (MSG_ID: 3) -> HELLO World
WorkerID: 0 -> (MSG_ID: 4) -> HELLO World
WorkerID: 0 -> (MSG_ID: 5) -> HELLO World
WorkerID: 2 -> (MSG_ID: 2) -> HELLO World
WorkerID: 1 -> (MSG_ID: 1) -> HELLO World
WorkerID: 0 -> (MSG_ID: 6) -> HELLO World
WorkerID: 2 -> (MSG_ID: 9) -> HELLO World
WorkerID: 0 -> (MSG_ID: 7) -> HELLO World
WorkerID: 0 -> (MSG_ID: 8) -> HELLO World
```

Let's analyze the first message:

1. This would be zero, so the message sent is `(Msg_id: 0) -> Hello`.
2. Then, the text is uppercased, so now we have `(MSG_ID: 0) -> HELLO`.
3. After uppercasing an append operation with the text `world` (note the space at the beginning of the text) is done. This will give us the text `(MSG_ID: 0) -> HELLO World`.
4. Finally, the text `WorkerID: 1` (in this case, the first worker took the task, but it could be any of them) is appended to the text from step 3 to give us the full returned message, `WorkerID: 1 -> (MSG_ID: 0) -> HELLO World`.

No tests?

Concurrent applications are difficult to test, especially if you are doing networking operations. It can be difficult, and code can change a lot just to test it. In any case, it is not justifiable to not perform tests. In this case, it is not especially difficult to test our small app. Create a test and copy/paste the contents of the `main` function there:

```
//workers_pipeline.go file
package main

import "testing"

func Test_Dispatcher(t *testing.T){
    //pasted code from main function
    bufferSize := 100
    var dispatcher Dispatcher = NewDispatcher(bufferSize)
    workers := 3
    for i := 0; i < workers; i++
    {
        var w WorkerLauncher = &PreffixSuffixWorker{
            prefixS: fmt.Sprintf("WorkerID: %d -> ", i), suffixS: " World",
id: i,}
        dispatcher.LaunchWorker(w)
    }
    //Simulate Requests
    requests := 10
    var wg
    sync.WaitGroup
    wg.Add(requests)
}
```

Now we have to rewrite our handler to test that the returned contents are the ones we are expecting. Go to the `for` loop to modify the function that we are passing as a handler on each `Request`:

```
for i := 0; i < requests; i++ {
    req := Request{
        Data: fmt.Sprintf("(Msg_id: %d) -> Hello", i),
        handler: func(i interface{})
        {
            s, ok := i.(string)
            defer wg.Done()
            if !ok
            {
                t.Fail()
            }
            ok, err := regexp.Match(`WorkerID\: \d* -\> \(MSG_ID: \d*\) ->
```

```
        [A-Z]*\sWorld`, []byte(s))
                if !ok || err != nil {
                    t.Fail()
                }
            },
        }
        dispatcher.MakeRequest(req)
    }
```

We are going to use regular expressions to test the business. If you are not familiar with regular expressions, they are a quite powerful feature that help you to match content within a string. If you remember in our exercises when we were using the `strings` package. `Contains` is the function to find a text inside a string. We can also do it with regular expressions.

The problem is that regular expressions are quite expensive and consume a lot of resources.

We are using the `Match` function of the `regexp` package to provide a template to match. Our template is `WorkerID\: \d* -> \(MSG_ID: \d\) -> [A-Z]*\sWorld` (without quotes). Specifically, it describes the following:

- A string that has the content `WorkerID: \d* -> (MSG_ID: \d*"`, here `"\d*` indicates any digit written zero or more times, so it will match `WorkerID: 10 -> (MSG_ID: 1"` and `"WorkerID: 1 -> (MSG_ID: 10`.
- `"\) -> [A-Z]*\sWorld"` (parentheses must be escaped using backslashes). "*" means any uppercase character written zero or more times, so `"\s"` is a white space and it must finish with the text `World`, so `) -> HELLO World"` will match, but `) -> Hello World"` won't, because `"Hello` must be all uppercase.

Running this test gives us the following output:

```
go test -v .
=== RUN   Test_Dispatcher
--- PASS: Test_Dispatcher (0.00s)
PASS
ok
```

Not bad, but we aren't testing that code is being executed concurrently, so this is more a business test than a unit test. Concurrency testing would force us to write the code in a completely different manner to check that it is creating the proper amount of Goroutines and the pipeline is following the expected workflow. This is not bad, but it's quite complex, and outside of the context of this book.

Wrapping up the Worker pool

With the workers pool, we have our first complex concurrent application that can be used in real-world production systems. It also has room to improve, but it is a very good design pattern to build concurrent bounded apps.

It is key that we always have the number of Goroutines that are being launched under control. While it's easy to launch thousands to achieve more parallelism in an app, we must be very careful that they don't have code that can hang them in an infinite loop, too.

With the workers pool, we can now fragment a simple operation in many parallel tasks. Think about it; this could achieve the same result with one simple call to `fmt.Printf`, but we have done a pipeline with it; then, we launched few instances of this pipeline and finally, distributed the workload between all those pipes.

Concurrent Publish/Subscriber design pattern

In this section, we will implement the Observer design pattern that we showed previously on Behavioral patterns, but with a concurrent structure and thread safety.

Description

If you remember from the previous explanation, the Observer pattern maintains a list of observers or subscribers that want to be notified of a particular event. In this case, each subscriber is going to run in a different Goroutine as well as the publisher. We will have new problems with building this structure:

- Now, the access to the list of subscribers must be serialized. If we are reading the list with one Goroutine, we cannot be removing a subscriber from it or we will have a race.
- When a subscriber is removed, the subscriber's Goroutine must be closed too, or it will keep iterating forever and we will run into Goroutine leaks.
- When stopping the publisher, all subscribers must stop their Goroutines, too.

Objectives

The objectives of this publish/subscriber are the same as the ones we wrote on the Observer pattern. The difference here is the way we will develop it. The idea is to make a concurrent structure to achieve the same functionality, which is as follows:

- Providing an event-driven architecture where one event can trigger one or more actions
- Uncoupling the actions that are performed from the event that triggers them
- Providing more than one source event that triggers the same action

The idea is to uncouple senders from receivers, hiding from the sender the identity of the receivers that will process its event, and hiding the receivers from the number of senders that can communicate with them.

In particular, if I develop a click in a button in some application, it could do something (such as log us in somewhere). Weeks later, we might decide to make it show a popup, too. If, every time we want to add some functionality to this button, we have to change the code where it handles the click action, that function will become huge and not very portable to other projects. If we use a publisher and one observer for every action, the click function only needs to publish one single event using a publisher, and we will just write subscribers to this event every time we want to improve the functionality. This is especially important in applications with user interfaces where many things to do in a single UI action can slow the responsiveness of an interface, completely destroying the user experience.

By using a concurrent structure to develop the Observer pattern, a UI cannot feel all the tasks that are being executed in the background if a concurrent structure is defined and the device allows us to execute parallel tasks.

Example – a concurrent notifier

We will develop a *notifier* similar to the one we developed in `Chapter 7`, *Behavioral Patterns – Visitor, State, Mediator, and Observer Design Patterns*. This is to focus on the concurrent nature of the structure instead of detailing too many things that have already been explained. We have developed an observer already, so we are familiar with the concept.

This particular notifier will work by passing around `interface{}` values, like in the workers pool example. This way, we can use it for more than a single type by introducing some overhead when casting on the receiver.

We will work with two interfaces now. First, a `Subscriber` interface:

```
type Subscriber interface {
    Notify(interface{}) error
    Close()
}
```

Like in the previous example, it must have a `Notify` method in the `Subscriber` interface of new events. This is the `Notify` method that accepts an `interface{}` value and returns an error. The `Close()` method, however, is new, and it must trigger whatever actions are needed to stop the Goroutine where the subscriber is listening for new events.

The second and final interface is the `Publisher` interface:

```
type Publisher interface {
    start()
    AddSubscriberCh() chan<- Subscriber
    RemoveSubscriberCh() chan<- Subscriber
    PublishingCh() chan<- interface{}
    Stop()
}
```

The `Publisher` interface has the same actions we already know for a publisher but to work with channels. The `AddSubscriberCh` and `RemoveSubscriberCh` methods accepts a `Subscriber` interface (any type that satisfies the `Subscriber` interface). It must have a method to publish messages and a `Stop` method to stop them all (publisher and subscriber Goroutines)

Acceptance criteria

Requirements between this example and the one in the `Chapter 7`, *Behavioral patterns – Visitor, State, Mediator, and Observer Design Patterns* must not change. The objective in both examples is the same so the requirements must also be the same. In this case, our requirements are technical, so we actually need to add some more acceptance criteria:

1. We must have a publisher with a `PublishingCh` method that returns a channel to send messages through and triggers a `Notify` method on every observer subscribed.
2. We must have a method to add new subscribers to the publisher.
3. We must have a method to remove new subscribers from the publisher.
4. We must have a method to stop a subscriber.

5. We must have a method to stop a `Publisher` interface that will also stop all subscribers.

6. All inter Goroutine communication must be synchronized so that no Goroutine is locked waiting for a response. In such cases, an error is returned after the specified timeout period has passed.

Well, these criteria seem quite daunting. We have left out some requirements that would add even more complexity, such as removing non-responding subscribers or checks to monitor that the publisher Goroutine is always on.

Unit test

We have mentioned previously that testing concurrent applications can be difficult. With the correct mechanism, it still can be done, so let's see how much we can test without big headaches.

Testing subscriber

Starting with subscribers, which seem to have a more encapsulated functionality, the first subscriber must print incoming messages from the publisher to an `io.Writer` interface. We have mentioned that the subscriber has an interface with two methods, `Notify(interface{}) error` and the `Close()` method:

```
// writer_sub.go file
package main

import "errors"

type writerSubscriber struct {
    id int
    Writer io.Writer
}

func (s *writerSubscriber) Notify(msg interface{}) error {
    return erorrs.NeW("Not implemented yet")
}
func (s *writerSubscriber) Close() {}
```

OK. This is going to be our `writer_sub.go` file. Create the corresponding test file, called the `writer_sub_test.go` file:

```
package main
```

```
func TestStdoutPrinter(t *testing.T) {
```

Now, the first problem we have is that the functionality prints to the `stdout`, so there's no return value to check. We can solve it in three ways:

- Capturing the `stdout` method.
- Injecting an `io.Writer` interface to print to it. This is the preferred solution, as it makes the code more manageable.
- Redirecting the `stdout` method to a different file.

We'll take the second approach. Redirection is also a possibility. The `os.Stdout` is a pointer to an `os.File` type, so it involves replacing this file with one we control, and reading from it:

```
func TestWriter(t *testing.T) {
    sub := NewWriterSubscriber(0, nil)
```

The `NewWriterSubscriber` subscriber isn't defined yet. It must help in the creation of this particular subscriber, returning a type that satisfies the `Subscriber` interface, so let's quickly declare it on the `writer_sub.go` file:

```
func NewWriterSubscriber(id int, out io.Writer) Subscriber {
    return &writerSubscriber{}
}
```

Ideally, it must accept an ID and an `io.Writer` interface as the destination for its writes. In this case, we need a custom `io.Writer` interface for our test, so we'll create a `mockWriter` on the `writer_sub_test.go` file for it:

```
type mockWriter struct {
    testingFunc func(string)
}

func (m *mockWriter) Write(p []byte) (n int, err error) {
    m.testingFunc(string(p))
    return len(p), nil
}
```

The `mockWriter` structure will accept a `testingFunc` as one of its fields. This `testingFunc` field accepts a string that represents the bytes written to the `mockWriter` structure. To implement an `io.Writer` interface, we need to define a `Write([]byte) (int, error)` method. In our definition, we pass the contents of `p` as a string (remember that we always need to return the bytes read and an error, or not, on every `Write` method). This approach delegates the definition of `testingFunc` to the scope of the test.

We are going to call the `Notify` method on the `Subcriber` interface, which must write on the `io.Writer` interface like the `mockWriter` structure. So, we'll define the `testingFunc` of a `mockWriter` structure before calling the `Notify` method:

```
// writer_sub_test.go file
func TestPublisher(t *testing.T) {
    msg := "Hello"

    var wg sync.WaitGroup
    wg.Add(1)

    stdoutPrinter := sub.(*writerSubscriber)
    stdoutPrinter.Writer = &mockWriter{
        testingFunc: func(res string) {
            if !strings.Contains(res, msg) {
                t.Fatal(fmt.Errorf("Incorrect string: %s", res))
            }
            wg.Done()
        },
    }
}
```

We will send the `Hello` message. This also means that whatever the `Subscriber` interface does, it must eventually print the `Hello` message on the provided `io.Writer` interface.

So if, eventually, we receive a string on the testing function, we'll need to synchronize with the `Subscriber` interface to avoid race conditions on tests. That's why we use so much `WaitGroup`. It's a very handy and easy-to-use type to handle this scenario. One `Notify` method call will need to wait for one call to the `Done()` method, so we call the `Add(1)` method (with one unit).

Ideally, the `NewWriterSubscriber` function must return an interface, so we need to type assert it to the type we are working with during the test, in this case, the `stdoutPrinter` method. I have omitted error checking when doing the casting on purpose, just to make things easier. Once we have a `writerSubscriber` type, we can access its `Write` field to replace it with the `mockWriter` structure. We could have directly passed an `io.Writer` interface on the `NewWriterSubscriber` function, but we wouldn't cover the scenario where a nil object is passed and it sets the `os.Stdout` instance to a default value.

So, the testing function will eventually receive a string containing what was written by the subscriber. We just need to check if the received string, the one that the `Subscriber` interface will receive, prints the word `Hello` at some point and nothing better that `strings.Contains` function for it. Everything is defined under the scope of the testing function, so we can use the value of the `t` object to also signal that the test has failed.

Once we have done the checking, we must call to the `Done()` method to signal that we have already tested the expected result:

```
err := sub.Notify(msg)
if err != nil {
    t.Fatal(err)
    }

    wg.Wait()
    sub.Close()
}
```

We must actually call the `Notify` and `Wait` methods for the call to the `Done` method to check that everything was correct.

Did you realize that we have defined the behavior on tests more or less in reverse? This is very common in concurrent apps. It can be confusing sometimes, as it becomes difficult to know what a function could be doing if we can't follow calls linearly, but you get used to it quite quickly. Instead of thinking "it does this, then this, then that," it's more like "this will be called when executing that." This is also because the order of execution in a concurrent application is unknown until some point, unless we use synchronization primitives (such as WaitGroups and channels) to pause execution at certain moments.

Let's execute the test for this type now:

```
go test -cover -v -run=TestWriter .
=== RUN   TestWriter
--- FAIL: TestWriter (0.00s)
        writer_sub_test.go:40: Not implemented yet
FAIL
coverage: 6.7% of statements
exit status 1
FAIL
```

It has exited fast but it has failed. Actually, the call to the `Done()` method has not been executed, so it would be nice to change the last part of our test to this instead:

```
err := sub.Notify(msg)
if err != nil {
    wg.Done()
    t.Error(err)
        }
        wg.Wait()
        sub.Close()
```

```
    }
```

Now, it doesn't stop execution because we are calling the `Error` function instead of the `Fatal` function, but we call the `Done()` method and the test ends where we prefer it to end, after the `Wait()` method is called. You can try to run the tests again, but the output will be the same.

Testing publisher

We have already seen a `Publisher` interface and the type that will satisfy which was the `publisher` type. The only thing we know for sure is that it will need some way to store subscribers, so it will at least have a `Subscribers` slice:

```go
// publisher.go type
type publisher struct {
    subscribers []Subscriber
}
```

To test the `publisher` type, we will also need a mock for the `Subscriber` interface:

```go
// publisher_test.go
type mockSubscriber struct {
    notifyTestingFunc func(msg interface{})
    closeTestingFunc func()
}

func (m *mockSubscriber) Close() {
    m.closeTestingFunc()
}

func (m *mockSubscriber) Notify(msg interface{}) error {
    m.notifyTestingFunc(msg)
    return nil
}
```

The `mockSubscriber` type must implement the `Subscriber` interface, so it must have a `Close()` and a `Notify(interface{}) error` method. We can embed an existing type that implements it, such as, the `writerSubscriber`, and override just the method that is interesting for us, but we will need to define both, so we won't embed anything.

So, we need to override the `Notify` and `Close` methods in this case to call the testing functions stored on the fields of the `mockSubscriber` type:

```go
func TestPublisher(t *testing.T) {
    msg := "Hello"
```

```
p := NewPublisher()
```

First of all, we will be sending messages through channels directly, this could lead to potential unwanted deadlocks so the first thing to define is a panic handler for cases such as, sending to close channels or no Goroutines listening on a channel. The message we will send to subscribers is `Hello`. So, each subscriber that has been received using the channel returned by the `AddSubscriberCh` method must receive this message. We will also use a *New* function to create Publishers, called `NewPublisher`. Change the `publisher.go` file now to write it:

```
// publisher.go file
 func NewPublisher() Publisher {
     return &publisher{}
 }
```

Now we'll define the `mockSubscriber` to add it to the publisher list of known subscribers. Back to the `publisher_test.go` file:

```
var wg sync.WaitGroup

sub := &mockSubscriber{
    notifyTestingFunc: func(msg interface{}) {
        defer wg.Done()

        s, ok := msg.(string)
        if !ok {
            t.Fatal(errors.New("Could not assert result"))
        }

        if s != msg {
            t.Fail()
        }
    },
    closeTestingFunc: func() {
        wg.Done()
    },
}
```

As usual, we start with a WaitGroup. First, testing the function in our subscriber defers a call to the `Done()` method at the end of its execution. Then it needs to type cast `msg` variable because it's coming as an interface. Remember that this way, we can use the `Publisher` interface with many types by introducing the overhead of the type assertion. This is done on line `s, ok := msg.(string)`.

Once we have type cast `msg` to a string, `s`, we just need to check if the value received in the subscriber is the same as the value we sent, or fail the test if not:

```
p.AddSubscriberCh() <- sub
wg.Add(1)

p.PublishingCh() <- msg
wg.Wait()
```

We add the `mockSubscriber` type using the `AddSubscriberCh` method. We publish our message just after getting ready, by adding one to the `WaitGroup`, and just before setting the `WaitGroup` to wait so that the test doesn't continue until the `mockSubscriber` type calls the `Done()` method.

Also, we need to check if the number of the `Subscriber` interface has grown after calling the `AddSubscriberCh` method, so we'll need to get the concrete instance of publisher on the test:

```
pubCon := p.(*publisher)
if len(pubCon.subscribers) != 1 {
    t.Error("Unexpected number of subscribers")
}
```

Type assertion is our friend today! Once we have the concrete type, we can access the underlying slice of subscribers for the `Publisher` interface. The number of subscribers must be 1 after calling the `AddSubscriberCh` method once, or the test will fail. The next step is to check just the opposite–when we remove a `Subscriber` interface, it must be taken from this list:

```
wg.Add(1)
p.RemoveSubscriberCh() <- sub
wg.Wait()

//Number of subscribers is restored to zero
if len(pubCon.subscribers) != 0 {
    t.Error("Expected no subscribers")
}

p.Stop()
}
```

The final step in our test is to stop the publisher so no more messages can be sent and all the Goroutines are stopped.

The test is finished, but we can't run tests until the `publisher` type has all the methods implemented; this must be the final result:

```
type publisher struct {
    subscribers []Subscriber
    addSubCh    chan Subscriber
    removeSubCh chan Subscriber
    in          chan interface{}
    stop        chan struct{}
}

func (p *publisher) AddSubscriberCh() chan<- Subscriber {
    return nil
}

func (p *publisher) RemoveSubscriberCh() chan<- Subscriber {
    return nil
}

func (p *publisher) PublishingCh() chan<- interface{} {
    return nil
}

func (p *publisher) Stop(){}
```

With this empty implementation, nothing good can happen when running the tests:

```
go test -cover -v -run=TestPublisher .
atal error: all goroutines are asleep - deadlock!
goroutine 1 [chan receive]:
    testing.(*T).Run(0xc0420780c0, 0x5244c6, 0xd, 0x5335a0, 0xc042037d20)
        /usr/local/go/src/testing/testing.go:647 +0x31d
    testing.RunTests.func1(0xc0420780c0)
        /usr/local/go/src/testing/testing.go:793 +0x74
    testing.tRunner(0xc0420780c0, 0xc042037e10)
        /usr/local/go/src/testing/testing.go:610 +0x88
    testing.RunTests(0x5335b8, 0x5ada40, 0x2, 0x2, 0x40d7e9)
        /usr/local/go/src/testing/testing.go:799 +0x2fc
    testing.(*M).Run(0xc042037ed8, 0xc04200a4f0)
        /usr/local/go/src/testing/testing.go:743 +0x8c
    main.main()
        go-design-patterns/concurrency_3/pubsub/_test/_testmain.go:56
+0xcd
goroutine 5 [chan send (nil chan)]:
    go-design-patterns/concurrency_3/pubsub.TestPublisher(0xc042078180)
        go-design-patterns/concurrency_3/pubsub/publisher_test.go:55
+0x372
    testing.tRunner(0xc042078180, 0x5335a0)
```

```
        /usr/local/go/src/testing/testing.go:610 +0x88
created by testing.(*T).Run
        /usr/local/go/src/testing/testing.go:646 +0x2f3
exit status 2
FAIL    go-design-patterns/concurrency_3/pubsub    1.587s
```

Yes it has failed but, it's not a controlled fail at all. This was done on purpose to show a couple of things to be careful of in Go. First of all, the error produced in this test is a **fatal** error, which usually points to a bug in the code. This is important because while a **panic** error can be recovered, you cannot do the same with a fatal error.

In this case, the error is telling us the problem: `goroutine 5 [chan send (nil chan)]`, a nil channel so it's actually a bug in our code. How can we solve this? Well, this is also interesting.

The fact that we have a `nil` channel is caused by the code we wrote to compile unit tests but this particular error won't be raised once the appropriate code is written (because we'll never return a nil channel in this case). We could return a channel that is never use we cause a fatal error with a deadlock, which wouldn't be any progress at all either.

An idiomatic way to solve it would be to return a channel and an error so that you can have an error package with a type implementing the `Error` interface that returns a specific error such as `NoGoroutinesListening` or `ChannelNotCreated`. We have already seen many of this implementations so we'll leave these as an exercise to the reader and we will move forward to maintain focus on the concurrent nature of the chapter.

Nothing surprising there, so we can move to the implementation phase.

Implementation

To recall, the `writerSubscriber` must receive messages that it will write on a type that satisfies the `io.Writer` interface.

So, where do we start? Well, each subscriber will run its own Goroutine, and we have seen that the best method to communicate with a Goroutine is a channel. So, we will need a field with a channel in the `Subscriber` type. We can use the same approach as in pipelines to end with the `NewWriterSubscriber` function and the `writerSubscriber` type:

```
type writerSubscriber struct {
    in      chan interface{}
    id      int
    Writer io.Writer
}
```

```
func NewWriterSubscriber(id int, out io.Writer) Subscriber {
    if out == nil {
        out = os.Stdout
    }

    s := &writerSubscriber{
        id:     id,
        in:     make(chan interface{}),
        Writer: out,
    }

    go func(){
        for msg := range s.in {
            fmt.Fprintf(s.Writer, "(W%d): %v\n", s.id, msg)
        }
    }()

    return s
}
```

In the first step, if no writer is specified (the out argument is nil), the default io.Writer interface is stdout. Then, we create a new pointer to the writerSubscriber type with the ID passed in the first argument, the value of out (os.Stdout, or whatever came in the argument if it wasn't nil), and a channel called in to maintain the same naming as in previous examples.

Then we launch a new Goroutine; this is the launching mechanism we mentioned. Like in the pipelines, the subscriber will iterate over the in channel every time a new message is received and it will format its contents to a string, which also contains the ID of the current subscriber.

As we learned previously, if the in channel is closed, the for range loop will stop and that particular Goroutine will finish, so the only thing we need to do in the Close method is to actually close the in channel:

```
func (s *writerSubscriber) Close() {
    close(s.in)
}
```

OK, only the Notify method is left; the Notify method is a convenient method to manage a particular behavior when communicating, and we will use a pattern that is common in many calls:

```
func (s *writerSubscriber) Notify(msg interface{}) (err error) {
    defer func(){
        if rec := recover(); rec != nil {
```

```
            err = fmt.Errorf("%#v", rec)
        }
    }()

    select {
    case s.in <- msg:
    case <-time.After(time.Second):
        err = fmt.Errorf("Timeout\n")
    }

    return
}
```

When communicating with a channel, there are two behavior that we must usually control: one is waiting time and the other is when the channel is closed. The deferred function actually works for any panicking error that can occur within the function. If the Goroutine panics, it will still execute the deferred function with the recover() method. The recover() method returns an interface of whatever the error was, so in our case, we set the returning variable error to the formatted value returned by recover (which is an interface). The "%#v" parameter gives us most of the information about any type when formatted to a string. The returned error will be ugly, but it will contain most of the information we can extract about the error. For a closed channel, for example, it will return "send on a closed channel". Well, this seems clear enough.

The second rule is about waiting time. When we send a value over a channel, we will be blocked until another Goroutine takes the value from it (it will happen the same with a filled buffered channel). We don't want to get blocked forever, so we set a timeout period of one second by using a select handler. In short, with select we are saying: either you take the value in less than 1 second or I will discard it and return an error.

We have the Close, Notify, and NewWriterSubscriber methods, so we can try our test again:

```
go test -run=TestWriter -v .
=== RUN   TestWriter
--- PASS: TestWriter (0.00s)
PASS
ok
```

Much better now. The `Writer` has taken the mock writer we wrote on the test and has written to it the value we pass to the Notify method. At the same time, close has probably closed the channel effectively, because the `Notify` method is returning an error after calling the `Close` method. One thing to mention is that we can't check if a channel is closed or not without interacting with it; that's why we had to defer the execution of a closure that will check the contents of the `recover()` function in the `Notify` method.

Implementing the publisher

OK, the publisher will need also a launching mechanism, but the main problems to deal with are race conditions accessing the subscriber list. We can solve this issue with a Mutex object from the `sync` package but we have already seen how to use this so we will use channels instead.

When using channels, we will need a channel for each action that can be considered dangerous–add a subscriber, remove a subscriber, retrieve the list of subscribers to `Notify` method them of a message, and a channel to stop all the subscribers. We also need a channel for incoming messages:

```
type publisher struct {
    subscribers []Subscriber
    addSubCh    chan Subscriber
    removeSubCh chan Subscriber
    in          chan interface{}
    stop        chan struct{}
}
```

Names are self-descriptive but, in short, subscribers maintain the list of subscribers; this is the slice that needs multiplexed access. The `addSubCh` instance is the channel to communicate with when you want to add a new subscriber; that's why it's a channel of subscribers. The same explanation applies to the `removeSubCh` channel, but this channel is to remove the subscriber. The `in` channel will handle incoming messages that must be broadcast to all subscribers. Finally, the stop channel must be called when we want to kill all Goroutines.

OK, let's start with the `AddSubscriberCh`, `RemoveSubscriber` and `PublishingCh` methods, which must return the channel to add and remove subscribers and the channel to send messages to all of them:

```
func (p *publisher) AddSubscriber() {
    return p.addSubCh
}
```

```
    func (p *publisher) RemoveSubscriberCh() {
        return p.removeSubCh
    }

    func (p *publisher) PublishMessage(){
        return p.in
    }
```

The `Stop()` function the `stop` channel by closing it. This will effectively spread the signal to every listening Goroutine:

```
func (p *publisher) Stop(){
  close(p.stop)
}
```

The `Stop` method, the function to stop the publisher and the subscribers, also pushes to its respective channel, called stop.

You may be wondering why we don't simply leave the channels available so that users push directly to this channel instead of using the proxying function. Well, the idea is that the user that integrates the library in their app doesn't have to deal with the complexity of the concurrent structure associated with the library, so they can focus on their business while maximizing performance as much as possible.

Handling channels without race conditions

Until now, we have forwarded data to the channels on the publisher but we haven't actually handled any of that data. The launcher mechanism that is going to launch a different Goroutine will handle them all.

We will create a launch method that we will execute by using the `go` keyword instead of embedding the whole function inside the `NewPublisher` function:

```
func (p *publisher) start() {
  for {
    select {
    case msg := <-p.in:
      for _, ch := range p.subscribers {
        sub.Notify(msg)
    }
```

`Launch` is a private method and we haven't tested it. Remember that private methods are usually called from public methods (the ones we have tested). Generally, if a private method is not called from a public method, it can't be called at all!

The first thing we notice with this method is that it is an infinite for loop that will repeat a select operation between many channels but only one of them can be executed each time. The first of these operations is the one that receives a new message to publish to subscribers. The `case msg := <- p.in:` code handles this incoming operation.

In this case, we are iterating over all subscribers and executing their `Notify` method. You may be wondering why we don't add the `go` keyword in front so that the `Notify` method is executed as a different Goroutine and therefore iterates much faster. Well, this because we aren't demultiplexing the actions of receiving a message and of closing the message. So, if we launch the subscriber in a new Goroutine and it is closed while the message is processed in the `Notify` method, we'll have a race condition where a message will try to be sent within the `Notify` method to a closed channel. In fact, we are considering this scenario when we develop the `Notify` method but, still, we won't control the number of Goroutines launched if we call the `Notify` method in a new Goroutine each time. For simplicity, we just call the `Notify` method, but it is a nice exercise to control the number of Goroutines waiting for a return in a `Notify` method execution. By buffering the `in` channel in each subscriber, we can also achieve a good solution:

```
case sub := <-p.addSubCh:
p.subscribers = append(p.subscribers, sub)
```

The next operation is what to do when a value arrives to the channel to add subscribers. In this case it's simple: we update it, appending the new value to it. While this case is executed, not other calls can be executed in this selection:

```
case sub := <-p.removeSubCh:
for i, candidate := range p.subscribers {
    if candidate == sub {
        p.subscribers = append(p.subscribers[:i],
p.subscribers[i+1:]...)
        candidate.Close()
        break
    }
}
```

When a value arrives at the remove channel, the operation is a bit more complex because we have to search for the subscriber in the slice. We use a *O(N)* approach for it, iterating from the beginning until we find it, but the search algorithm could be greatly improved. Once we find the corresponding `Subscriber` interface, we remove it from the subscribers slice and stop it. One thing to mention is that on tests, we are accessing the length of the subscribers slice directly without demultiplexing the operation. This is clearly a race condition, but generally, it isn't reflected when running the race detector.

The solution will be to develop a method just to multiplex calls to get the length of the slice, but it won't belong to the public interface. Again, for simplicity, we'll leave it like this, or this example may become too complex to handle:

```
case <-p.stop:
for _, sub := range p.subscribers {
    sub.Close()
        }

    close(p.addSubCh)
    close(p.in)
    close(p.removeSubCh)

    return
    }
}
}
```

The last operation to demultiplex is the `stop` operation, which must stop all Goroutines in the publisher and subscribers. Then we have to iterate through every Subscriber stored in the subscribers field to execute their `Close()` method, so their Goroutines are closed, too. Finally, if we return this Goroutine, it will finish, too.

OK, time to execute all tests and see how is it going:

```
go test -race .
ok
```

Not so bad. All tests have passed successfully and we have our Observer pattern ready. While the example can still be improved, it is a great example of how we must handle an Observer pattern using channels in Go. As an exercise, we encourage you to try the same example using mutexes instead of channels to control access. It's a bit easier, and will also give you an insight of how to work with mutexes.

A few words on the concurrent Observer pattern

This example has demonstrated how to take advantage of multi-core CPUs to build a concurrent message publisher by implementing the Observer pattern. While the example was long, we have tried to show a common pattern when developing concurrent apps in Go.

Summary

We have seen few approaches to develop concurrent structures that can be run in parallel. We have tried to show a few ways to solve the same problem, one without concurrency primitives and one with them. We have seen how different the publish/subscriber example written with a concurrent structure can be compared to the classic one.

We have also seen how to build a concurrent operation using a pipeline and we have parallelize it by using a worker pool, a very common Go pattern to maximize parallelism.

Both examples were simple enough to grasp, while digging as much as possible in to the nature of the Go language instead of in the problem itself.

Index